TERROR FROM THE SKY

TERROR FROM THE SKY
The Bombing of German Cities in World War II

Edited by
Igor Primoratz

berghahn
NEW YORK · OXFORD
www.berghahnbooks.com

First published in 2010 by
Berghahn Books
www.berghahnbooks.com

©2010, 2014 Igor Primoratz
First paperback edition published in 2014

All rights reserved. Except for the quotation of short passages
for the purposes of criticism and review, no part of this book
may be reproduced in any form or by any means, electronic or
mechanical, including photocopying, recording, or any information
storage and retrieval system now known or to be invented,
without written permission of the publisher.

Library of Congress Cataloging-in-Publication Data

Terror from the sky : the bombing of German cities in World War II / edited by Igor Primoratz.
  p. cm.
Includes bibliographical references and index.
ISBN 978-1-84545-687-0 (hardback : acid-free paper) – ISBN 978-1-78238-671-1 (paperback) – ISBN 978-1-84545-844-7 (ebook)
 1. World War, 1939–1945—Aerial operations. 2. Bombing, Aerial—Germany—History—20th century. 3. World War, 1939–1945—Campaigns—Germany. 4. World War, 1939–1945—Moral and ethical aspects. 5. Germany—History—1933–1945. 6. Terrorism—History—20th century. I. Primoratz, Igor.
  D785.T47 2010
  940.54'4941—dc22

2009042384

British Library Cataloguing in Publication Data

A catalogue record for this book is available from the British Library

Printed on acid-free paper.

ISBN: 978-1-84545-687-0 hardback
ISBN: 978-1-78238-671-1 paperback
ISBN: 978-1-84545-844-7 ebook

To the memory of the victims

Contents

Introduction / *Igor Primoratz*   1

Part I: The Bombing

1. The Bombing Campaign: the RAF / *Stephen A. Garrett*   19
2. The Bombing Campaign: the USAAF / *Douglas P. Lackey*   39
3. Under the Bombs / *Earl R. Beck*   60
4. Firestorm / *Martin Middlebrook*   85

Part II: The Moral Issues

5. Can the Bombing Be Morally Justified? / *Igor Primoratz*   113
6. Four Types of Mass Murderer: Stalin, Hitler, Churchill, Truman / *Douglas P. Lackey*   134
7. Was It Genocidal? / *Eric Markusen and David Kopf*   158

Part III: The Debates

8. The British Debate / *Mark Connelly*   181
9. The German Debate / *Lothar Kettenacker*   203

Contributors   223

Bibliography   225

Index   235

Introduction

Igor Primoratz

In World War II, the Allies bombed Germany's cities and towns in an attempt to undermine the morale of its civilian population and force its government to halt the war and accept unconditional surrender. More than sixty years later, the bombing campaign remains one of the most controversial issues of the war. One strand of the debate approaches the subject in purely strategic terms. Some cling to the view of those who planned and carried out the bombing, according to which the campaign made a major contribution to the victory over Germany. Others argue that it was unsuccessful on its own terms and a waste of limited resources that could have been put to better use.

Another strand of the debate focuses on the morality of the bombing. Here, too, the bombing campaign has both its defenders and its critics. But the moral issue has been approached in different ways by those who won and those who lost the war. At the time the bombing campaign was devised and carried out, the former—the government, the political and military establishment as a whole, the press—gave the bombing very strong support. There were critical voices as well, but they were few and their objections were ignored. Immediately after the war, the victors preferred not to look very closely into what their air forces had visited upon German civilians over more than three years and ponder its moral, political, and cultural significance. They had killed about 600,000 civilians, some 100,000 of them children. Some had been killed quickly, by being blown to pieces or crushed by the walls of their homes. Others had died slowly: asphyxiated, or burned alive, or buried alive under the ruins. Another 800,000 civilians had been seriously injured. Some thirteen million had been made homeless.[1] Many cities and towns across the country had been devastated. Untold cultural treasures had been destroyed. As the official history of the RAF put it, by early 1945, "the destruction in Germany was … on a scale which might have appalled Attila or Genghis Khan."[2]

Later on, the initial unease receded. Neither statesmen, nor Royal Air Force or United States Army Air Force commanders, nor members of the air crews who had been involved in this destruction have tended to express in public any serious misgivings about the morality of it. The fate of Arthur Harris, chief of Bomber Command—the RAF branch that carried out the bombing—is emblematic in this respect. Immediately after the war, he was the sole commander of a major branch of the British military not to be honored with a peerage. But in 1992, a larger-than-life statue of "Bomber Harris" was unveiled in the heart of London by the Queen Mother, restoring him to the heroic status he had enjoyed throughout the war years.

In Germany, discussing German victims of World War II was not considered politically correct for almost half a century. The assumption was that such discussion would somehow detract from the enormity of Nazi crimes. This assumption was generally accepted, but not examined—neither for its exact meaning, nor for validity. Yet it is not clear just how the general acknowledgment, in Germany and elsewhere, of the nature and scale of the crimes of Nazi leaders and their henchmen would be undermined if the victimization of common citizens of Germany at the hands of the Allies were to be acknowledged as well. Nor is it clear how acknowledging both would entail, or suggest, their moral equivalence.

This changed only at the outset of the twenty-first century. Günter Grass' novel *Im Krebsgang* (2002) was the first major literary work to bring up the subject of the ethnic cleansing of Germany's eastern provinces annexed to Poland and the Soviet Union and of members of German minority throughout East Europe in the wake of the war. *Der Brand. Deutschland im Bombenkrieg 1940–1945* (2002) by Jörg Friedrich, an historian with impeccable professional *and* political credentials, put the issues to do with the bombing of German cities firmly on the agenda of the mainstream, nationwide debate.[3] There is now a vigorous public discussion in Germany about the ways German civilians were victimized during the war and in its aftermath, by the Nazi regime and by the Allies. The discussion opens up a new perspective on the central issue of German historical consciousness, that of *Vergangenheitsbewältigung*—the working through and coming to terms with the past.

The Fate of Civilians in War

The bombing of German cities and towns in World War II constitutes an important chapter in the evolution of warfare in the last hundred years or so because it was not directed at military targets; those killed, maimed, or made homeless were civilians. It was in breach of a fundamental principle of civilized warfare, that of civilian (or non-combatant) immunity.

The idea that all is *not* fair in war, that civilized values and moral rules have a claim on our choices and actions relating to war, has roots in ancient philosophy and religion. In the Middle Ages, it evolved into a major tradition in philosophy and moral theology and was then developed in an ever more systematic and comprehensive way by philosophers and legal thinkers of the modern age. The ethics of war lays down a number of requirements for morally justified warfare under two headings: *jus ad bellum,* justice (or morality) *of* war, and *jus in bello,* justice (or morality) *in* war. The former tells us when it is morally justified to go to war, the latter what we may and may not do in the course of fighting. The two parts of the ethics of war are independent in that each is binding in its own right. Our decision to go to war may be morally justified, but that does not absolve us from the obligation to fight in accordance with the rules of war. On the other hand, if we go to war without a compelling moral justification for doing so, we will compound our wrongdoing if we also fight in ways prohibited by the rules of war. If a war waged by a country or a coalition of countries is to be morally justified, those fighting it must live up to the requirements of both *jus ad bellum* and *jus in bello.*

A central principle of *jus in bello* is that of civilian immunity. It enjoins discrimination between soldiers and civilians and, more generally, military and civilian targets, determines that only the former may be attacked, and prohibits military attacks on the latter. By the eighteenth century, major European powers had adopted this principle as a central tenet of their military practice. Civilian immunity was then included in the Hague conventions of 1899 and 1907, and thus became part of international law. As British historian Eric Hobsbawm points out, it came to be acknowledged even by revolutionaries:

> The programme of the Russian Narodnaya Volya, the group which killed Tsar Alexander II, stated explicitly "that individuals and groups standing outside its fight against the government would be treated as neutrals, their person and property were to be inviolate." At about the same time Frederick Engels condemned the Irish Fenians (with whom all his sympathies lay) for placing a bomb in Westminster Hall, thus risking the lives of innocent bystanders. War, he felt as an old revolutionary with experience of armed conflict, should be waged against combatants and not against civilians.[4]

This development was considered one of the great achievements of moral progress. But World War I brought about a reversal; it was the beginning of what Hobsbawm calls "the descent into barbarism" that marked much of the twentieth century and, apparently, may yet mark the twenty-first as well. At the outset of the twentieth century, the number of civilian casualties in war was low relative to that of military casualties: one civilian for every eight soldiers killed. By its end, this ratio was reversed: now eight *civilians* are killed for every soldier that falls in battle.[5]

The Great War was deadlier by far than any conflict that had preceded it, and this affected political attitudes: "the limitless sacrifices which governments imposed on their own men as they drove them into the holocausts of Verdun and Ypres set a sinister precedent, if only for imposing even more unlimited massacres on the enemy."[6] As the war dragged on, the economy and society at large became ever more extensively involved in it. This spawned the idea of "total war": war in which the resources mobilized, the ends sought, and the means employed were no longer to be limited, but rather ever more comprehensive and, ideally, "total." "Total war," of course, recognizes no immunity.

The first major blow to civilian immunity was the naval blockade Britain imposed on Germany in the second year of World War I. It contributed to Germany's defeat by starving its civilian population and was then continued for eight months after the armistice in order to force Germany to ratify the Versailles peace treaty. The next main stage in the process of involving civilians in warfare was the bombing of German cities and towns in World War II, described and discussed in this book. The decision to embark on this campaign crossed another important moral line: while the blockade had killed civilians indirectly, by denying them food and medicines, the bombing killed them directly. Yet both strategies are based on the same principle: war aims no longer are to be achieved (solely) by fighting enemy soldiers on the battlefield, but (also) by large-scale killing of enemy civilians in the rear. Defenders of the bombing tend to point out this continuity. Thus, Arthur Harris wrote in his memoirs:

> ... Bombing proved a comparatively humane method. For one thing, it saved the flower of the youth of this country and of our allies from being mown down by the military in the field, as it was in Flanders in the war of 1914–1918. But the point is often made that bombing is especially wicked because it causes casualties among civilians. This is true, but then all wars have caused casualties among civilians. For instance, after the last war the British Government issued a White Paper in which it was estimated that our blockade of Germany had caused nearly 800,000 deaths ... [7]

While the bombing of German cities and towns was in full swing, the same strategy was adopted in the Pacific theater of war: Japanese cities were subjected to the same kind of bombing, first by conventional, and then by nuclear bombs. The "descent into barbarism" did not stop with the end of World War II. During much of the Cold War, peace was maintained by the threat that in the event of war, the nuclear powers would attack each other's civilian population centers with nuclear missiles. In the same period, many wars of national liberation involved large-scale civilian casualties, inflicted both by guerrillas and by colonial powers trying to suppress them. By the turn of the century, the term "new wars" was coined to help distinguish ethnic wars of the 1990s from more familiar "old wars" between states. These wars aim not only at conquering territory, but also at ethnically cleansing it; accordingly, *most* violence targets civilians, rather than enemy armed forces. In two recent cases of military intervention, in Kosova and (at least at first) in Afghanistan, Western powers sought to achieve their objectives by means of air power alone. They had their aircraft fly at very high altitudes to make sure they remain beyond reach of anti-aircraft fire. This led to a very high amount of "collateral damage"—the killing of civilians that was neither intended nor (necessarily) predicted, but was certainly predictable. By now, some observers are wondering, only half in jest, whether the principle of civilian immunity has been replaced by that of Western *combatant* immunity.

The intervention in Afghanistan has been part of the global "war on terrorism." The bombing of German cities and towns also needs to be seen in the context of the history of terrorism: as a major and historically highly important campaign of state terrorism. The term "state terrorism" may be thought odd. In everyday discourse, the media, and government officials' usage, terrorism is usually understood as violence perpetrated by insurgents; this implies that "state terrorism" is a contradiction in terms. But this usage is informed by a double standard. For it describes, and condemns, a certain type of violence as terrorism, when employed by rebels and revolutionaries, while withholding this description from, and thereby in effect exonerating, the same type of violence when employed by the state and its military:

> Throwing a bomb is bad,
> Dropping a bomb is good;
> Terror, no need to add,
> Depends on who's wearing the hood.[8]

If what we seek is historical understanding and discerning moral and political judgment, we should resist any usage that indicates a double standard. What, then, *is* terrorism? The use of the term has always reflected strong moral feelings and political passions, and its application has almost always been contested—never more so, perhaps, than at the present time. Still, this does not mean that we cannot define it in a reasonably clear and helpful way, at least in certain contexts. If we focus on a string of paradigmatic cases of terrorism over the last hundred years or so, we can define it as the deliberate use of violence, or threat of its use, against innocent people, with the aim of intimidating some other people into a course of action they otherwise would not take.⁹ In peacetime or in a violent conflict falling short of war, those innocent in the relevant sense will be common citizens; in wartime, they will be civilians (non-combatants).

Defining terrorism in an agent-neutral way has several advantages. There are also historical grounds for adopting a definition that allows for state terrorism. When it first entered political discourse, "terrorism" referred to the reign of terror imposed in France by the Jacobins—a case of state terrorism. Students of both Nazi and communist totalitarianism have emphasized the state's use of terrorism against its own population as one of the salient traits of totalitarian rule. Total political control of society, which is the paramount yet elusive aim of totalitarianism, could not be pursued by less radical methods. Moreover, terrorism is not the preserve of totalitarian regimes. Non-totalitarian states, including some liberal democracies, have resorted to it in wartime. The bombing campaign that is the subject of this book is a case in point. Its explicit aim was the destruction of German cities and towns and the killing of their inhabitants. Civilians were not killed accidentally, as an unintended, unforeseen, and unforeseeable side-effect of attacks on military targets. They were not killed incidentally, as a foreseen, but unintended side-effect of attacks on military targets. They were the direct, intended target of those attacks. Killing them was meant to undermine the morale of the German civilian population at large, to intimidate the German government, and to force it to capitulate.¹⁰ The four components of the bombing campaign—*violence* against the *innocent* with the aim of *intimidation* and *coercion*—are the four defining traits of terrorism. Indeed, those who devised the bombing campaign and directed its course themselves called it "terror bombing"—not in public, to be sure, only in internal communications.

The bombing of German cities and towns has a special place in the history of state terrorism, which, in wartime, is for the most part "terror from the sky." It was the longest such campaign. It killed the highest number of civilians. Several colonial powers previously had engaged in terror bombing to pacify the natives. Germany, France, and Britain occasionally had engaged in such bombing in World War I; so did Japan in its war on China in the 1930s. But the Allies' bombing of Germany in World War II was the first to kill hundreds of thousands of civilians, make millions homeless, devastate scores of cities across an entire country, and destroy untold cultural treasures. It introduced a new era in the history of both warfare and terrorism—an era we still live in. As Douglas Lackey says in an essay on "The Evolution of the Modern Terrorist State":

> There is a continuous line of historical development from Churchill's decision to commence area bombing, to the bombing of Dresden, Tokyo, Hiroshima, and Nagasaki, to Curtis LeMay and SAC [Strategic Air Command] plans for nuclear attacks on Russia, and finally to the American SIOPs [Single Integrated Operational Plans] for nuclear war. … The British policy of area bombing inaugurated a new era of warfare: a kind of state terrorism, now routinely added to the repertoire of policy options of powerful nations.[11]

The Bombing

The essays brought together in this book fall into three parts. Part I reviews the bombing campaign itself. Part II addresses the moral issues raised by the bombing. Part III looks into the debates relating to the bombing campaign conducted at the time and more recently. Of course, this division of labor does not commit the authors of the chapters comprising parts I and III to try to describe or explain historical events and processes in a language that is utterly morally neutral; that would be a misguided and hopeless project.

The decision to embark on a campaign of terror bombing of German cities and towns was made by British political and military leaders and largely carried out by the RAF. The book accordingly starts with a chapter on the RAF role in the campaign. Stephen A. Garrett first sets out a typology of bombing. He explains the difference between tactical and strategic bombing and between two varieties of the latter, precision and area bombing. He then distinguishes two types of area bombing in terms of their aim. Such bombing may aim either at forcing the enemy to divert important resources from the battlefield to the rear, or at terrorizing enemy civilians, undermining their morale, and getting them to force their leaders to sue for peace.

In the period between the two world wars, a number of air power strategists became convinced that it was air power, in particular when used for terror bombing, that held out the prospect of winning future wars quickly and with incomparably lower casualties than the traditional, "cannon-fodder" wars. Garrett shows how this view of the role of air force exerted great influence on the RAF, which began a slide toward terror bombing as soon as it was instructed, in May 1940, to engage in strategic bombing beyond the Rhine. By February 1942, the RAF Bomber Command was ordered *not* to go for military or industrial targets, but rather to focus on destroying German cities and breaking the morale of the civilian population. That is what the Bomber Command largely did until the last days of the war. It succeeded in devastating scores of cities and towns and killing hundreds of thousands of their inhabitants, but failed to attain its aim of breaking the morale of those who survived. Garrett describes the main stages of the bombing and explains what it did and did not achieve and why, summing up the entire campaign with a sarcastic aphorism: "It was worse than a crime, it was a blunder."

In chapter 2, Douglas Lackey looks into the US role in the bombing. According to the received view, although both the RAF and the USAAF bombed Germany's cities and towns, most of the time they had different tasks within their joint enterprise. The British took to area bombing early on and before long focused on terror bombing, persisting in it until the end of the war. The US, on the other hand, was initially committed to precision bombing, and joined the British in terror bombing only at a late stage and under their ally's pressure. Thus, the moral record of the two air forces is significantly different. The picture that emerges from Lackey's analysis is different. Lackey looks into the USAAF plan for the bombing of Germany that was prepared six months before the United States entered the war and that informed the decisions made in the course of the war. The plan provided for both precision and terror bombing. The USAAF was to set out to destroy the social and economic structure of Germany by strategic precision bombing. That was expected to affect the morale of the civilian population. When the morale began to crack, the bombing was to proceed to the second stage, that of direct attacks on concentrations of civilian population, that is, to terror bombing. The plan points out that if such attacks are weak and sporadic, they actually may stiffen the resolve of civilians; but if they are heavy and sustained enough, they should crush civilian morale once and for all. When the proper psychological conditions obtain, the entire bombing effort is to be geared to this aim. Contrary to the traditional view, then, the moral record of the two Allied air forces is not so different. The US plan delayed USAAF terror bombing by almost two years. But, by 1944, the conditions for terror bombing set in the plan were thought to have been met and the US joined the British in such bombing. Moreover, the US plan legitimized terror bombing in advance and thus prepared the ground for such bombing of Japanese cities in 1945.

While the first two chapters examine the decisions that led to the bombing campaign, its rationale, and main stages, the next two give us some idea of how it was to be on the receiving end. Coming to appreciate that, at least in some small measure, is indispensable if we are to understand the bombing campaign historically and to pass a well-grounded moral judgment on it. Chapter 3 is excerpted from the late Earl R. Beck's book *Under the Bombs: The German Home Front, 1942–1945* (1986). Early in 1946, Beck traversed Germany by train, from Bavaria in the south to Bremerhaven in the north, wondering how the Germans had survived the devastation and how they were coping with life in the ruins. Four decades later, he wrote a book on the subject. Most of the text selected for inclusion here deals with the events of 1943, a crucial year for several reasons. It brought the phenomenon of almost total devastation of a city by bombing. It also introduced the firestorm—caused by human action, deliberately, and on a scale that can encompass a large part of a modern city and kill tens of thousands of people in a single raid. The book draws on a variety of sources, including the (relatively few) accessible wartime diaries of civilians and a rich fund of reports of the SS Security Service informants who were monitoring the conduct and mood of the population throughout the war years. Beck seeks to tell a story, not proffer an analysis, yet he certainly helps us understand a number of things—not least why the terror bombing of German cities and towns failed to achieve its ultimate aim. The civilian population carried on because there was nothing to do but carry on and hope to survive. "*Überleben* (survival) became the motif of life—not to be burned up in a firestorm, killed on the battle front, or executed by a dying regime." There was evidence of panic, of apathy, of resignation—but none of widespread disorder, of rioting, or of rebellion. Basic discipline was generally upheld.

Beck's chapter describes the way German authorities and civilian population as a whole sought to cope with the onslaught of the Allied air forces over several months in mid-1943. Martin Middlebrook's contribution (chapter 4) concerns one single raid—the RAF raid on Hamburg in the night of 27/28 July of that year, known as the firestorm raid. Middlebrook interviewed many survivors and witnesses of that raid as well as RAF and USAAF air crew, and is thus in a position to convey to us some of the experiences of the individual at the time of the bombing raid and immediately afterwards—to help us understand some of the thoughts, feelings, choices, and actions of common citizens of various ages and walks of life, trapped in an immense firestorm induced with the aim of killing them and destroying their city. The Hamburg firestorm was the first; it was also the deadliest, killing about 40,000 civilians. Yet, as Middlebrook points out, "what happened in Hamburg may have been an extreme example of Allied success but the results obtained were the results that were hoped for every time the Allied heavy-bomber forces set out for Germany. ... What happened at Hamburg was what happened when Bomber Command 'got everything right'."[12]

The Moral Issues

In Stephen A. Garrett's contribution (chapter 1), the bombing campaign is assessed as a blunder. But Garrett points out that this was not a blunder caused by honest miscalculation and therefore something to be deplored but also excused; it was, rather, a blunder of the sort that "demands an extensive moral query." The authors of chapters making up part II undertake such a query.

The first question is whether the bombing can be justified. This is the subject of my own contribution (chapter 5). In response to a demand for moral justification of the bombing, one might grant that a decision to go to war is in need of such justification, but argue that, once war breaks out, morality has no bearing on the way it is fought. This view is sometimes called the "war is hell" doctrine. A similar, but somewhat less radical line is to argue that there may be some moral constraints *in* war as well, but that civilian immunity is not one of them, perhaps because, at least in modern wars, civilians too are involved. A basically different approach is to accept civilian immunity as a binding moral principle, but try to show that in the particular case of German civilians in World War II, there were good moral reasons for overriding it. Some arguments along these lines portray the bombing as retaliation or reprisal for what the German air force did to British cities and towns. Another argument defends the bombing as permitted and indeed enjoined by the "supreme emergency" created by the prospect of imminent German victory and the enslavement of most of Europe under the Nazis. Still another judges the bombing in purely consequentialist terms, as a means justified by the end it was meant to achieve. I examine these defenses and try to show that none succeeds. If my argument is sound, the bombing campaign was an unmitigated moral atrocity that seriously compromised the just cause for which the Allies were fighting.

Who was responsible for this atrocity? The crew of the bomber aircraft that carried out the bombing; those in the chain of command (and of responsibility) involved in the bombing; finally, those who designed the campaign, took the decision to carry it out, and oversaw its course. If any one person is to be singled out as ultimately responsible for the campaign as a whole, that is Winston Churchill, British Prime Minister from 1940 to 1945. If the bombing lacked moral justification, it did not simply kill, but rather murdered its victims. It was a case of mass murder, and those who took part in it were mass murderers. It is often said that the twentieth century was a century of mass murder, and one in which some mass murderers played prominent, if not defining, roles. This class of mass murderers, in its unity and variety, is the subject of Douglas Lackey's second contribution to this book (chapter 6), which adds a comparative perspective to the narrowly focused discussions in other chapters. Lackey looks into four cases of mass murder in the twentieth century: the Ukrainian famine, the Jewish genocide, Dresden, and Hiroshima. He concentrates on Dresden, rather than the entire bombing campaign against German cities, because "whatever arguments, limited, inadequate, morally shallow, could be produced for area bombing in 1943, they had completely evaporated by February 1945." In discussing the rationale for the terror bombing of Dresden, Lackey highlights Churchill's vindictiveness combined with a crude, premodern type of thinking about human affairs in which the individual's choices and actions do not matter—only collectivities do.[13] Lackey does not seek to equate the four cases of mass murder and does not claim that the four national leaders involved were equally evil. Nor does he construct a scale of atrocity. What he does is display different types of mass murder and different types of mass murderers, and a small but diverse set of rationales the latter invoke to justify mass murder. "Stalin and Hitler and Churchill and Truman were all evil," he writes, "but they were evil in different ways."

If the bombing of Dresden and the entire terror bombing campaign against German cities and towns was a case of mass murder, was it also genocidal? Works on the history and sociology of genocide usually say nothing about the bombing.[14] One might think this odd, in view of the definition of genocide in the United Nations Convention on Genocide. The definition lists such acts as killing members of a national, ethnic, racial, or religious group, causing them serious bodily or mental harm, and deliberately inflicting on the group conditions of life calculated to bring about its physical destruction in whole or in part. When committed with the intent to destroy the group as such in whole or in part, these acts qualify as acts of genocide.[15] The definition is neutral as to why the complete or partial destruction of a national, ethnic, racial, or religious group is sought. This allows both for cases where the perpetrators consider the destruction of a group desirable in itself, and cases where the perpetrators seek the complete or partial destruction of a group as a means to a further end. The killing of some 600,000 German civilians by terror bombing as a means to an end would seem to fit the bill; yet most genocide researchers apparently do not think so.

In 1995, Eric Markusen and David Kopf published a book titled *The Holocaust and Strategic Bombing: Genocide and Total War in the Twentieth Century*, arguing that the bombing of both German and Japanese cities in World War II *was* genocidal. The penultimate chapter of that book, in which they summarize their argument and state their conclusions, is reprinted as chapter 7 of this volume. The discussion proceeds in two stages:

Markusen and Kopf examine the similarities and differences between the two types of mass killing, and inquire whether the bombing campaigns satisfy the criteria of genocide derived from the UN definition of the crime. Their position is that terror bombing is indeed genocidal. One advantage of this way of understanding genocide is that it helps us see that "the capacity for genocidal killing is not limited to obvious monsters like Joseph Stalin, Adolf Hitler, Idi Amin, and Pol Pot but is widely shared," and that "not only totalitarian regimes but also democracies have been willing to directly engage in genocidal killing."

The Debates

When a democracy at war resorts to a morally and legally dubious strategy, one would expect the decision to be challenged in public debate, and the campaign itself to be continuously scrutinized and criticized by the public. When the RAF was sent to destroy German cities and towns and while it was at it, there was some public debate in Britain, mostly in the media and occasionally in Parliament as well; but the debate was rather limited in both scope and depth. The British debate is the subject of Mark Connelly's contribution (chapter 8). The limitations of the debate were due to a sort of heightened patriotism, indeed jingoism, that is virtually inevitable in any country in wartime. But they were also due to the systematic obfuscation of the issues and occasional downright deception about the nature of the bombing on the part of the government. The media readily joined in this obfuscation and deception. Forceful public challenge of the bombing was rare, and those challenging it tended to present their case in practical, rather than moral terms. In either case, they were not taken very seriously. The vast majority of those taking part in the debate offered strong support to the campaign; some demanded shortening the war and saving British lives by any means, others invoked crude notions of collective responsibility and called for retaliation. Connelly shows how the media presented the British public with a range of interpretations of the bombing and "fed it a diet of truths, half-truths and outright lies." So did the government. When the war ended, that made it possible for both the public and politicians to claim they did not know the true character of the bombing and the full extent of destruction it had wreaked. Nevertheless, Connelly submits, "the British people had a shrewd idea of the implications of the policy pursued in their name but shied away from them, taking comfort in the ambiguities of the reportage."

Once it was over, the Germans, too, preferred not to remember—at least not publicly and collectively—but for very different reasons. In her study of German historical consciousness in the second half of the twentieth century, Dagmar Barnouw deplores "the still pervasive unreflected ignorance and suspicion of German war experience," brought about by "the enduring perception of German evil [that] has caused the memory of [World War II] to be uncommonly abstract and incomplete, and its history uncommonly selective."[16] After all,

> the war had hit different regions and populations differently, but many millions of Germans had gone through terrible experiences. They were asked to forget them so that they could feel true remorse for the evil deeds of their criminal regime and remember forever its victims: as if there was and would be no space in memory to accommodate all the painful experiences of warfare.[17]

The same view of history and memory as a zero-sum game is at work in the strange worry that Jörg Friedrich's book, which undermined this taboo as far as the bombing campaign is concerned, might encourage the notion that "the name of true evil is 'Bomber Harris' and not Adolf Hitler."[18] This worry has been voiced in the German debate about Friedrich's book that still goes on. The debate is reviewed and analyzed by Lothar Kettenacker in chapter 9. Kettenacker also looks into the political and psychological reasons for the failure of German collective memory, historiography, and literature over half a century to address properly the ways in which German civilians were victimized by the Allies during the war and in its aftermath.[19] None of the reasons apply today. After half a century of *Vergangenheitsbewältigung* that relegated those events and experiences beyond the pale, German scholars and the general public need no longer be hindered, whether by their own inhibitions or by pressure from other quarters, from taking a close look at them and trying to understand better their human, moral, and political significance.

The British and US public, too, have reason to take a fresh look at the bombing campaign against German civilians; for the view on the subject that has prevailed since the end of the war can be sustained only by willful ignorance and abdication of moral judgment. In his *History of Bombing*, Swedish author Sven Lindqvist relates:

> During the summer of 1948 I lived with a working-class family in St. Albans, outside London. ... Somehow my thoughts flew to the burned-out cities of Germany, and I told them how on my trip across the country the train had struggled, hour after hour, to make its way through the blackened ruins of what were once the homes of human beings.
>
> "We were bombing the military transports on the railways," my host family said. If some houses by the side of the railway were damaged it was unfortunate but unavoidable. "It was war, you know."

"This is not a question of 'a few houses,'" I said. "Hamburg was razed by British bombs. This was the third time I've traveled through the city, and I have seen nothing but ruins."

"That must have been the Americans," said my host. "The British bombers never attacked civilians."

"I am sorry to contradict you, but it was the other way around. The Americans bombed the industries by day, and the British the residential areas by night. That was the general pattern, I'm afraid."

"I am not going to listen to any more German war propaganda in my house," my host said, cutting me short. "The British bombers attacked military targets, period."[20]

Later in the book, Lindqvist adds: "Even today there is no hint in any British [military] museum of the systematic attacks on German civilians in their homes."[21] Apparently, the same is true of US World War II museums. There is, then, room for *Vergangenheitsbewältigung* on the part of the victors in that war as well

Notes

1. See Hans Rumpf, *The Bombing of Germany*, trans. Edward Fitzgerald (London: Frederick Muller Ltd., 1963), ch. 9: The Casualties of Air Warfare.
2. Denis Richards and Hilary St. George Saunders, *Royal Air Force, 1939–1945*, vol. 3 (London: HMSO, 1954), 271.
3. Both books are now available in English: Günter Grass, *Crabwalk*, trans. Krishna Winston (London: Faber and Faber, 2002); Jörg Friedrich, *The Fire: The Bombing of Germany 1940–1945*, trans. Allison Brown (New York: Columbia University Press, 2006).
4. Eric Hobsbawm, "Barbarism: A User's Guide," *On History* (London: Weidenfeld & Nicolson, 1997), 255–256.
5. Mary Kaldor, *New and Old Wars: Organized Violence in a Global Era* (Cambridge: Polity Press, 1999), 8.
6. Hobsbawm, "Barbarism," 256.
7. Sir Arthur Harris, *Bomber Offensive* (London: Collins, 1947), 176.
8. Roger Woddis, "Ethics for Everyman," quoted in C.A.J. Coady, *Morality and Political Violence* (Cambridge: Cambridge University Press, 2008), 154.
9. See my "What Is Terrorism?" in Igor Primoratz, ed., *Terrorism: The Philosophical Issues* (Basingstoke and New York: Palgrave Macmillan, 2004).
10. Sir Charles Webster and Noble Frankland, *The Strategic Air Offensive against Germany 1939–1945*, vol. 1 (London: HMSO, 1961), 323–324.
11. Douglas Lackey, "The Evolution of the Modern Terrorist State: Area Bombing and Nuclear Deterrence," in Primoratz, ed., *Terrorism*, 136.
12. Martin Middlebrook, *The Battle of Hamburg: Allied Bomber Forces against a German City in 1943* (London: Cassell & Co., 2000), 11–12. Having devastated Ham-

burg, the Allied air forces went on to induce firestorms in fifteen other German cities, in some cases killing only a few hundred civilians, and in others killing thousands, or even tens of thousands.
13. In chapter 1, Garrett, too, refers to retaliation in this connection. But rather than emphasizing Churchill's personal vengefulness, Garrett sees him as holding that the British public wanted revenge and that this wish had to be expressed and satisfied, if British morale was to be sustained.
14. For a recent example, see Ben Kiernan, *Blood and Soil: A World History of Genocide and Extermination from Sparta to Darfour* (New Haven: Yale University Press, 2007).
15. "Convention on the Prevention and Punishment of the Crime of Genocide," Art. II, in Frank Chalk and Kurt Jonassohn, *The History and Sociology of Genocide: Analyses and Case Studies* (New Haven: Yale University Press, 1990), 44.
16. Dagmar Barnouw, *The War in the Empty Air: Victims, Perpetrators, and Postwar Germans* (Bloomington: Indiana University Press, 2005), 142.
17. Ibid., 152.
18. Ralf Giordano, "Ein Volk von Opfern?" in *Ein Volk von Opfern? Die neue Debatte um den Bombenkrieg 1940–45*, ed. Lothar Kettenacker (Berlin: Rowohlt, 2003), 168.
19. Throughout that period, no such taboo applied outside Germany. Earl R. Beck's book *Under the Bombs: The German Home Front, 1942–45* (Lexington: The University Press of Kentucky, 1986), excerpted in this volume, gives a sympathetic and vivid account. Alfred M. de Zayas' *Nemesis at Potsdam: Anglo-Americans and the Expulsion of the Germans* (London: Routledge & Kegan Paul, 1977), is a pioneering study of the ethnic cleansing of Germany's eastern provinces annexed to Poland and the Soviet Union and of the German minority from East European countries. General studies of ethnic cleansing now as a matter of course deal in detail with the German case; see Norman M. Naimark, *Fires of Hatred: Ethnic Cleansing in Twentieth-Century Europe* (Cambridge, MA: Harvard University Press, 2001), ch. 4, or Benjamin Lieberman, *Terrible Fate: Ethnic Cleansing in the Making of Modern Europe* (Chicago: Ivan R. Dee, 2006), ch. 6. For the first postwar years, see Giles MacDonogh, *After the Reich: The Brutal History of the Allied Occupation* (New York: Basic Books, 2007). However, these writings do not seem to have affected appreciably the way the general public in Britain and the United States thinks (and feels) about these matters.
20. Sven Lindqvist, *A History of Bombing*, trans. Linda Haverty Rugg (London: Granta Books, 2001), sec. 11.
21. Ibid., sec. 200; see also ibid., sec. 391.

PART I
THE BOMBING

 CHAPTER 1

The Bombing Campaign
the RAF
Stephen A. Garrett

In June 1938, British Prime Minister Neville Chamberlain issued the following instructions to British Bomber Command in the event of an outbreak of war with Germany:

> 1. It is against international law to bomb civilians as such and to make deliberate attacks on the civilian population.
>
> 2. Targets which are aimed at from the air must be legitimate military objectives and must be capable of identification.
>
> 3. Reasonable care must be taken in attacking those military objectives so that by carelessness a civilian population in the neighbourhood is not bombed.[1]

The Prime Minister reiterated his position on this matter even after war had broken out. "Whatever be the lengths to which others may go, his Majesty's government will never resort to the deliberate attack on women and children, and other civilians for purposes of mere terrorism."[2]

It is instructive to consider British policy on air warfare as enunciated by Chamberlain in relation to the events of 13 February 1945. On this occasion, the British air force attacked the German city of Dresden in two waves totaling almost 800 heavy bombers. Some 2,700 tons of bombs were dropped, about 75 percent of which were incendiaries. The results were such that Dresden was converted into a household word symbolizing the terror that could be inflicted on a city by a modern bombing force. The worst effects of the bombing came shortly after the initial British assault, when a tremendous firestorm of the sort only seen previously at Hamburg developed. About 1,600 acres were engulfed by the flames, which was practically the whole of the older part of Dresden. Estimates on casualties vary widely, from a minimal guess of about 25,000 dead to the most drastic estimate of over 200,000. Whatever the final accounting, there was no question but that Dresden had suffered a catastrophic blow. In order to prevent the spread of disease, the authorities cordoned off the center of the city and constructed 25-foot-long grills where thousands of the victims were cremated.[3]

How does one account for the drastic change in British bombing policy that developed from Chamberlain's initial stance to the attack on Dresden that took place around seven years later? The discussion here focuses on the interwar debate over the character and promise of a major air campaign in a future conflict between the major powers. It then analyzes the factors that led Britain to abandon its original policy of avoiding deliberate attacks on civilians. Finally, it assesses the impact of British bombing on the capacity of Germany to successfully wage war.

The Past as Prologue

Amongst the many profound effects of World War I on the future conduct of military operations, none was perhaps to weigh as heavily as the introduction of attacks on enemy's cities by the then-limited airpower resources of the combatants. Leading the way in this regard were German assaults on the British homeland, first by the use of airships (Zeppelins) and later by fixed-wing bombers. Overall, there were a total of 208 airship and 435 airplane sorties undertaken against England by the German air force. About 300 tons of bombs were dropped, killing around 1,400 people and wounding another 3,400.[4]

Compared to the figures that were to be produced by the next great war, these may have been relatively modest results, but they established an ominous precedent. Certainly, many informed analysts at the time were concerned about the implication of these raids. The notion that civilians could be a legitimate, and even important, target of air strikes seemed to have acquired at least a tentative acceptance. One authority on the use of airpower in World War I thus wrote that "demoralization of the enemy by means of aerial bombardment was accepted as part of the functions of the bombardment groups [of all major powers]."[5]

As a consequence of the city attacks by airpower in World War I (the British and French also undertook some relatively minor steps in this direction), a considerable debate developed in the interwar year as to what this new use of military technology portended for the conduct of a future war. There were certain basic alternatives that presented themselves. Emphasis could be placed on the use of airpower in an essentially *tactical* role, that is, in support of ground operations by field armies and potentially in naval engagements as well. In this sense, airpower could be seen largely in terms of its capacity to influence direct battlefield outcomes. A second approach to the use of aircraft was to emphasize air defense, and in particular the development of substantial fighter squadrons that hopefully would blunt the enemy's capability for air attacks against one's homeland.

Each of these emphases in the use of airpower was to have its advocates in Great Britain and elsewhere in the interwar period. For present purposes, however, it was the promise (or threat) of airpower being used in a *strategic* mode that is of principal interest. In the generic sense, the strategic application of airpower simply meant the use of aircraft for direct assaults on the enemy's homeland and his fundamental capacity to make war. Approached in this fashion, the prospective use of airpower indeed represented something quite novel in the conduct of war: a strategy for overcoming the enemy not (or not *only*) through direct defeat of his land or naval forces, but through an assault on the nation itself quite aside from battlefield operations.

In analyzing the concept of the strategic air offensive, it is important to note that even those generally supportive of such a strategy could and did differ a great deal on what might be called the targeting philosophy to be followed in carrying out such an effort. Broadly speaking, the targets of an air offensive could be defined in terms of what came to be called either *precision* or *area* bombing. The theory of precision bombing held that the objects to be attacked should be more or less traditional military objectives, such as airfields, defense industries (e.g., steel and chemicals), the communications network, petroleum installations, and other sites that had a reasonably direct connection to the enemy's war effort, that is, were in direct support of that effort.

The idea of area bombing, sometimes referred to as "indiscriminate bombing" (although, not surprisingly, rarely so by advocates of area bombing), basically rejected the notion that air strikes should be limited to precision targets such as arms factories. This is not to say that there was no interest in destroying these factories. Instead, the controlling theory of area bombing was that to concentrate *only* on the destruction of such a military objective was a far too narrow approach to the potential of the strategic air offensive. In plain terms, area bombing meant that the arms factory along with *much else* (and *legitimately* much else) should or could be equally the objective of the air campaign. This "much else" basically involved the entire social, economic, and even political infrastructure of the enemy—in particular, for an urbanized country such as Germany, the infrastructure of its cities. In even plainer terms, then, area bombing meant a generalized assault on civilians and the very life of the population.

To what purpose? Several rationales were offered for such an air campaign. In the first place, the dislocations caused by the bombing of cities would divert resources from the war effort. The enemy would have to put enormous effort into feeding, clothing, and housing the affected civilian population as well as restoring a minimal level of public services. Secondly (and here there was some agreement with the adherents of precision bombing), the enemy would have to expend considerable effort on air defenses such as fighter aircraft and anti-aircraft installations, which in turn would mean that these resources could not be used for offensive operations. Finally, there was the matter of morale, or the enemy society's will to continue the war effort. Area bombing advocates felt that civilian morale was inherently fragile, the Achilles' heel, as it were, of the enemy's military position. A steady barrage of attacks on civilian life would, it was argued, cause civilian morale to crack fairly rapidly, and this in turn would lead to irresistible pressure on the government to end the war.

Two observations are necessary concerning the interwar debate over precision versus area bombing in the strategic air offensive. In the first place, certain technical questions played a prominent role in shaping attitudes toward either form of air attack, in particular the matter of whether aircraft could actually attain the bombing accuracies necessary to hit precise targets and, a related issue, whether bomber forces could attack such targets in daytime (which seemed critical to accuracy) without overwhelming losses from the enemy's air defenses. If the answer was no to either or both of these questions, then it did not matter much if one *in theory* held that precision bombing was the better system. The question became whether there was to be a strategic air offensive at all, whether bombers were in fact to be used against the enemy's homeland. If the decision was to do so, area bombing was, *faute de meilleur,* the strategy that seemed to present itself.

The acceptance of area bombing as part of a strategic air offensive, as it was discussed prior to 1939, is especially associated with the Italian theorist General Giulio Douhet. His essential proposition was that a massive air offensive by a fully developed strategic bomber force at the outbreak of hostilities—"undertaken with the greatest possible intensity"—would prove decisive to the outcome of the war. One of the purposes of such an effort would be to attain "command of the air, [being] in a position to prevent the enemy from flying while retaining the ability to fly oneself."[6] Phrased in this way, the concept of "preemption" was inherent to Douhet's thinking. He was convinced, as were others, that there was no effective defense against the modern bomber, and that the country that struck first would therefore achieve a preponderance in the air after destroying the enemy's own bomber forces.

Assuming command of the air was achieved, the more fundamental purpose of the bombing offensive would unfold and once again the stress was on the factor of morale and the enemy society's will to continue the war. Douhet's comments on this matter differed from those of other strategic airpower advocates in their certitude and notably florid presentation, rather than content:

> A complete breakdown of the social structure cannot but take place in a country subjected to this kind of merciless pounding from the air. The time would soon come when, to put an end to horror and suffering, the people themselves, driven by the instinct of self-preservation, would rise up and demand an end to the war—this before their army and navy had time to mobilize at all![7]

Douhet can also be distinguished from other writers by his frank willingness to lay to rest the notion that non-combatants would enjoy any privileged position in the coming conflict.

> No longer can areas exist in which life can be lived in safety and tranquility, nor can the battlefield be limited to actual combatants. ... All of [a country's] citizens will become combatants since all of them will be exposed to the aerial offensives of the enemy. There will be no distinction any longer between soldiers and civilians.[8]

In Britain itself, the debate over the use of airpower can perhaps best be summarized by reference to an exchange amongst the chiefs of the various branches of the British armed services in May 1928. The Chief of the Air Staff, Sir Hugh Trenchard, initiated the exchange with a note setting forth the claims of the Royal Air Force (RAF) for a major share of defense funding and of a continuing independent role.[9] He was convinced that the proper application of a strategic bombing offensive against a potential enemy could well prove vital in any future conflict, even though he conceded that the RAF could not be expected by itself to win the victory. Rather than devoting the bulk of the resources of the RAF to close air support of ground operations, to assaults on opposing army and naval targets, or even to air defense of the homeland, Trenchard proposed concentrating on developing a capacity for striking directly at the enemy's sources of power. As he put it, "it is not necessary for an air force, in order to defeat the enemy nation, to defeat its armed forces first. Air power can dispense with that intermediate step ... and attack directly the centres of production, transportation and communication from which the enemy war effort is maintained." Trenchard envisioned his bombing campaign as having two fundamental purposes: to destroy the enemy's technical *capacity* for continuing the war effort and to undermine his *will* for doing so. On the latter point, he put the "moral" effects of bombing as more important than the physical effects by a factor of 20 to 1.

What is especially interesting about the Trenchard memorandum is how it attempted to blur the distinction between precision and area bombing and in fact to defuse the debate over the appropriateness of each. In effect, Trenchard seemed to say that he was proposing a precision bombing offensive, but that it could on occasion take on some of the characteristics of an area offensive. In addressing the possible moral objections to his outlined strategy, he stressed that the air offensive would be directed not at civilians as such, but rather at defined military objectives, among which would be "the enemy's great centres of production of every kind of war materials, from battleships to boots, his essential munition factories, the centres of all his systems of communications and transportation, his docks and shipyards, railway workshops, wireless stations, and postal and telegraph systems." In a comment that is rather striking (and ironic) in view of subsequent activity by Bomber Command, he accepted that "the indiscriminate bombing of a city for the sole purpose of terrorising the civilian population" was "contrary to the dictates of humanity." On the other hand, claimed Trenchard, it was "an entirely different matter" to terrorize munitions workers into ceasing working or stevedores to stop loading arms onto ships. "Moral effect is created by the bombing in such circumstances but it is the inevitable result of a lawful operation of war—the bombing of a military objective." Put in this way, many later critics of British bombing policy in World War II would have been forced to nod assent. The question was, however, how the concept of a "military objective" was subject to elaboration and expansion as the air offensive evolved.

The response of the Army and Navy chiefs to Trenchard's memorandum was itself a curious blend of practical and moral objections. On the matter of practicality, the Chief of the Imperial General Staff, General G.F. Milne, argued that Britain would be at a clear disadvantage in any environment of unrestricted air warfare. The major issue was geography: British cities would be far more vulnerable to attack than the more remote urban centers of an enemy on the Continent, particularly if the enemy should acquire air bases in the Low Countries or in France. An additional argument was that unrestricted air warfare would inevitably spill over into unrestricted submarine warfare at sea, which would threaten Britain's naval lifelines (the experience of World War I was a sobering precedent in this regard).

Other practical objections to Trenchard's views on the strategic air offensive were voiced as well. Thus, the Chief of the Naval Staff argued that there was little evidence to support the notion that enemy civilian morale would crack under aerial bombardment. In fact, such attacks might even serve to stiffen it. Also in serious doubt was the claim that enemy war production could be seriously disrupted by air power, particularly if there were any sort of effective air defense against such attacks (the rebuttal to Trenchard was far more pessimistic about the ability of bomber squadrons to penetrate unscathed to their targets). Moreover, committing large resources to a potentially ineffective air offensive risked dispersal of the nation's military assets, with a concomitant lessening of the overall effectiveness of the war effort. The recommendation from the Army and Navy, then, was that Britain should never initiate unlimited air combat, but only hold such a possibility open in response to an enemy's introduction of such tactics.

The response to Trenchard also addressed the moral issue, and in a language of some asperity. "As regards the ethical aspects of his [Trenchard's] proposals, it is for His Majesty's Government to accept or to refuse a doctrine which, put into plain English, amounts to one which advocates unrestricted warfare against the civilian population of one's enemy." There was a barely concealed impatience with Trenchard's references to striking "military objectives" in an air offensive. In effect, the charge was that Trenchard was actually proposing an area bombing strategy thinly disguised as an exercise in precision bombing. Even if the effort might be directed, say, at destroying a factory making boots for the army,

> the actual target would be the town in which the factory happened to be located. ... It is ridiculous to contend that the dropping of bombs would hit only the so-called military targets. ... The impression produced by the acceptance and publication of such a doctrine will indubitably be that we are advocating what might be termed the indiscriminate bombing of undefended towns and of their unarmed inhabitants.[10]

The Decision to Bomb Cities

Despite the often heated debate in prewar Britain about the use of airpower in a future conflict, during the period stretching from the British declaration of war on Germany on 3 September 1939 to about the middle of May 1940, the idea of a "strategic bombing offensive" against Germany was little more than a gleam in the eye of its British advocates. Bomber Command divided its time between dropping leaflets over the German Reich inviting its surrender and occasional "precise" attacks on naval and other military targets. One problem was the relative paucity of resources: at the outbreak of war, Britain had only about 272 aircraft at its disposal and a number were not operational. There was also a continuing concern about avoiding any unnecessary harm to enemy civilians. For example, in November 1939, the War Cabinet secretly considered a plan for bombing targets in the Ruhr in response to a German invasion of Belgium, but there was great reluctance to do so because of the expected effect on the civilian population.[11] This sensitivity was reinforced by the position adopted by the United States, potentially a key partner in the war on the Axis. On 1 September 1939, President Franklin Roosevelt had addressed an appeal to all the belligerent powers, calling for a restriction of aerial warfare to specifically military targets, and at this point the British government felt they could hardly ignore such an admonition, a position reinforced by fears of a drastic German retaliation against British cities should the informal prohibition against attacks on urban areas be broken.

What may be regarded as a period of innocence for Bomber Command during the first eight months of the war came to a close on 15 May 1940, when in a directive signed by Winston Churchill, who had replaced Neville Chamberlain as Prime Minister a few days earlier, the RAF was now authorized to attack land targets east of the Rhine. The spur to this decision was evidently a reduced concern about the possibilities of German retaliation on British cities as well as the fact that at least some strategic bombing of the enemy seemed at this point to be one of the few ways in which the British could carry the war to the enemy, a consideration that acquired particular currency after the evacuation at Dunkirk.

For approximately the next two years, Bomber Command undertook a steadily widening series of strikes against the German homeland. At the official level, the stated emphasis was on precision or selective attacks against carefully defined military and industrial objectives (the German oil industry, communications, and aircraft plants, for example). There were further references to the necessity of sparing civilians as much as possible. An instruction from the War Cabinet to the Air Ministry in early June 1940, for example, stressed that air attacks "must be made with reasonable care to avoid undue loss of civil life in the vicinity of the target."[12] At the same time, what would come to be called "area bombing," or generalized assaults on urban targets, was, like Banquo's ghost, never very far from the proceedings. As early as October 1940, the Air Staff issued a new directive that oil targets should be attacked on clear nights, but that whole cities could at least be considered as alternative targets in less favorable weather. In December 1940, what is generally considered the first open British effort at area bombing came with an attack on the city of Mannheim, a raid specifically described as retaliation for the earlier German assault on Coventry.

The Government's wavering between an ostensible program of precision bombing and an increasing tendency toward area bombing was resolved finally in a policy statement of 14 February 1942. The bomber offensive, according to Directive No. 22 issued to Bomber Command, was now to be "focussed on the morale of the enemy civil population and in particular of the industrial workers." In case there was any doubt at Bomber Command headquarters about what was now intended, the Chief of the Air Staff sent a follow-on communication the next day: "Ref the new bombing directive: I suppose it is clear that the aiming points are to be the built-up areas, *not*, for instance, the dockyards or aircraft factories. ... This must be made quite clear if it is not already understood."[13] Sir Arthur Harris, who was to become head of Bomber Command on February 23, indicated that he at least had no misunderstanding on this point.

The decision by the British to adopt a straightforward strategy of area or indiscriminate bombing of Germany—in other words, the systematic devastation of German cities—after February 1942 was obviously a landmark in the evolution of warfare, and more particularly in the concept of total war. Over the next three years, about three-quarters of the bombs dropped on Germany by Great Britain were against area targets. How is one to account for the adoption of such a momentous course of action?

A rather curious mix of emotional, political, technical, and theoretical considerations seems to have been involved. For some, there was clearly the feeling that the Germans had after all initiated city attacks, first with the bombing of Warsaw, then with the assault on Rotterdam in May of 1940 (which was said at the time to have caused 30,000 fatalities), and finally with the Blitz on Britain itself. Extending in its most intense form from the fall of 1940 to the spring of 1941, the Blitz eventually resulted in some 50,000 tons of bombs being dropped on British cities, which led to about 40,000 civilian deaths. Given this record of events, it was not hard to argue that the Germans had sowed the wind and now were to reap the whirlwind. The Prime Minister himself sometimes seemed to suggest that even though he personally had little desire for revenge, the British people did expect retaliation in kind. In a flight of hyperbole, he commented that the people now demanded that all Germans should be massacred or castrated. He told the House of Commons that "on every side is the cry, 'We can take it', but with it is also the cry, 'Give it them back'."[14] In effect, Churchill's argument seemed to be that in order to sustain the nation's morale, it was necessary to do unto others as they were doing unto Britain.

It is hard to gauge how significant a factor the calls for pure retribution were in the February 14th directive to Bomber Command. As it happens, however, there was a key operational factor confronting the Government in early 1942 that may be seen as pushing the RAF toward a strategy of area bombing quite on its own. It became apparent early in the war that the lack of sufficient fighter support, and the growing effectiveness of German air defenses, presented the RAF with the prospect of prohibitive losses if it attempted to attack German targets in daylight. As a matter of policy, then, by the spring of 1940, Bomber Command had come to concentrate almost entirely on nighttime bombing of the enemy.

Could such raids achieve a sufficient level of accuracy to allow the targeting of precise military objectives? For a time, the analysts at Bomber Command attempted to maintain the fiction that such was possible, but the evidence, as it accumulated, seriously undermined their case and was dealt a particular blow by the so-called Butt report of August 1941. At the behest of Lord Cherwell, Churchill's principal scientific adviser, D.M. Butt of the Cabinet Secretariat undertook a systematic study of the efforts of Bomber Command to date. His analysis revealed that in British air strikes against specific targets in the Ruhr, only one-tenth of the bombers even found their way to within five miles of the assigned target. For other areas, the figure was a still depressing one in three.[15] The inevitable conclusion seemed to be that if Great Britain were to continue its strategic bombing offensive against Germany, the only feasible targets were large urban areas, where the problems of inaccuracy would be much less compelling. Since few if any of the major figures in the Government were inclined simply to call a halt to the bombing offensive—particularly as it was the only major evidence at the time of Britain's determination to carry on the war effort—the turn to indiscriminate bombing followed almost as a matter of course.

Still, it would be somewhat misleading to suggest that those involved simply, and rather mindlessly, adopted area bombing without thought as to its practical military utility and only because it was the one thing Bomber Command could do. There were, in fact, attempts by those in authority to develop a broader strategic rationale for area bombing beyond the limitations that Bomber Command then confronted. Lord Cherwell was a particular contributor to this process, and his ideas reflected one of the standard themes of the prewar airpower theorists. In a famous minute to the Prime Minister on 30 March 1942, Cherwell concentrated on the impact on German morale of a major British area bombing campaign. Based on his analysis of the German bombing of British cities, he argued that "having one's house demolished is most damaging to morale. People seem to mind it more than having their friends or even relatives killed." He went on to estimate that with adequate resources and by concentrating on the fifty-eight major German population centers, Bomber Command could by 1943 render one-third of the German people homeless. "There seems little doubt that this would break the spirit of the people." The concept of the shattering of the German people's morale, and thus of Germany's will or ability to continue the war, was enshrined henceforth as one of the guiding premises of British bombing policy. As the official history of Bomber Command puts it: "Because of the position which he occupied and the time at which he submitted his minute, Lord Cherwell's intervention was of great importance. It did much to insure the concept of strategic bombing in its hour of crisis."[16]

There were, to be sure, other rationales brought forward to justify the bombing of German cities aside from its putative effect on morale. One of these was that it would help to divert German resources from the Russian campaign and the Middle East in order to provide for the air defense of the Reich. Moreover, since German industry was naturally concentrated in and around the major German cities, even so-called indiscriminate attacks on these places were bound to damage or destroy some of the relevant factories. Such attacks would also lead to a shattering of the whole fabric of German civilian life, which in turn would create a basic dislocation in war production and the German home front's ability to support the military machine. Sir Arthur Harris was particularly ardent in advancing these propositions. He went so far as to suggest that if the British government gave its full support to the bomber offensive, Germany essentially could be defeated by airpower alone.[17]

The Evolution of the Area Bombing Offensive

Harris did not wait long after assuming leadership of Bomber Command before he began his long campaign to demonstrate that the theory of area bombing could be translated into a productive reality. The Baltic port city of Lübeck was attacked on the night of 28 March 1942, by 234 RAF bombers. Some two hundred acres or about half of the Old Town was leveled, the German estimate being that over 15,000 people had their homes destroyed as a consequence of the raid. Another old Hanseatic city, Rostock, was given similar treatment later in April. Some 100,000 civilians were forced to evacuate the city as a result of this attack.

Despite these early "successes," Harris was acutely aware that the credibility of Bomber Command as a major, perhaps the major, focus of the British war effort was hardly accepted by everyone in authority. In a rather striking admission of the situation in which he now found himself, Harris recalled that he "had to regard the operations of the next few months as a commercial traveller's samples which I could show to the War Cabinet." He decided that there was a need for a truly spectacular operation that hopefully would lay to rest the doubts of his critics and, in particular, ensure support for Bomber Command from the Prime Minister. It was thus that the plan for Millenium was conceived, the first thousand-bomber raid of the war. The target chosen was Cologne and the results were impressive indeed. Approximately six hundred acres of the city were devastated on the night of 30 May 1942, and as the final wave of bombers approached, the city was burning with such ferocity that the light from the flames could be seen from 150 miles away. More than 45,000 people were rendered homeless, and the roads out of Cologne were clogged with a massive exodus of refugees. When Harris reported the results of Millenium to Churchill, he was gratified by the Prime Minister's reaction. "I knew at once that he was satisfied then.... He wanted above all to get on with the war and no one understood better than he the vast strategic consequences of this operation."[18] Thus, the continuation of a full-fledged area bombing offensive, together with the necessary commitment of resources, had apparently been accepted by the one person whose opinion was decisive.

Even so, there was to be a period of some months before Bomber Command actually entered into a sustained campaign of destroying German cities. One problem was the lack of sufficient numbers of aircraft to sustain such a campaign. Despite the thousand-bomber raid against Cologne (achieved by using every available aircraft at Harris's disposal, including even training units), Bomber Command, on an average day, disposed of only 261 bombers as of the end of 1942. Equally important was the slow introduction of the Lancaster, perhaps the best heavy bomber on all sides in the war, but not available in any quantity until early 1943. There was also the challenge of developing adequate guidance systems for Bomber Command's attacks against the German heartland. Even given the less stringent standards of accuracy required for area bombing, it was not until the end of the year, with the arrival of Oboe and H2S as navigational aids, that the British could feel a renewed confidence about hitting their aiming points in the areas being attacked.[19]

In January 1943, the British Prime Minister and the US President, together with their principal advisers, met in Casablanca to consider the future of the strategic bombing of Germany. The Casablanca Conference, and the subsequent Washington Conference in May of the same year, provided an overall framework for a Combined Bombing Offensive against Germany (codenamed Pointblank). The directives that issued from these meetings were regarded by Bomber Command as final authorization for a general assault against German cities.

The British area bombing offensive against Germany over the next twelve months involved a host of different operations, but it can be summarized by reference to three important episodes in that campaign. After the war, the United States Strategic Bombing Survey offered a rather clinical description of how Bomber Command generally went about its business.

> In determining the aiming point for city attacks, Bomber Command prepared a zone map of the city based on aerial photographs. Administrative and residential areas between 70 and 100 per cent built-up were outlined in red. ... Area attacks on a previously unbombed city were aimed at the center of the red area, while subsequent attacks on the same city were usually directed against the center of the most heavily built-up areas which remained undestroyed.[20]

The first major application of this technique was in the Ruhr Valley, where over a period from March to July 1943, there were a total of forty-three major raids. Virtually all the major urban centers of the Ruhr suffered badly as a result, with the city of Barmen-Wuppertal, for example, experiencing the destruction of almost 90 percent of its built-up area during a raid on May 29. The northern German port of Hamburg was the recipient of thirty-three major air attacks (codenamed Operation Gomorrah) from July to November 1943. The night raids on July 24, July 27, and July 29 represented the apex of the assault on Hamburg. In each instance, well over seven hundred bombers from the RAF rained a combination of incendiary and explosive bombs on the central city area of Hamburg. Approximately 74 percent of the most densely populated section of the city was destroyed. About 50,000 people were killed in these attacks, and around one million refugees fled to safer outlying areas. Perhaps the most noted aspect of the Hamburg raids was the phenomenon of the firestorm, which produced hurricane-type winds of 150 miles an hour and sucked people, trees, and even whole buildings into the center of the flames. The Police President of Hamburg summarized the fate of his city in this way:

> Its horror is revealed in the howling and raging of the firestorms, the hellish noise of exploding bombs and the death cries of martyred human beings as well as in the big silence after the raids. Speech is impotent to portray the measure of the horror, which shook the people for ten days and nights and the traces of which were written indelibly on the face of the city and its inhabitants.[21]

The devastation of Hamburg was henceforward referred to by the Germans simply as *die Katastrophe.*

The final significant event in this phase of the area offensive against Germany was the so-called Battle of Berlin. This began on the night of November 18 and continued for four months until the end of the following March. During this period, some thirty-five raids of more than 500 bombers each were launched against the German capital as well as other cities. Sixteen of the missions were directed at Berlin itself, which represented the greatest single focusing of Bomber Command's efforts since the beginning of the war.[22] Arthur Harris had begun the Battle of Berlin with high hopes. In a typically self-confident communication to the Prime Minister, he had asserted that "we can wreck Berlin from end to end if the U.S. Army Air Forces will come in on it. It will cost between us 400 and 500 aircraft. It will cost Germany the war."[23] As it happened, there was only marginal US participation in this enterprise, and the results of Bomber Command's own efforts proved to be a great disappointment. For various reasons, far less devastation was delivered on Berlin than in the raids against Hamburg (only about one-third of the acreage destroyed as compared to the earlier attacks). Moreover, these results had to be balanced against the increasing losses that Bomber Command was now suffering in its campaign against Berlin and other major cities. The potency of the German night-fighter force as well as their anti-aircraft defenses was reflected in an average loss rate for British bombers on the order of about 5 percent. Sometimes it was even more severe: in an attack on Nuremberg in March 1944, some 94 bombers were lost and another 71 damaged out of a total force of 795 employed.[24]

This level of attrition could not be sustained long, and in view of the rather problematical effect that area bombing seemed to be having on the German ability to maintain the war effort, something of a crisis of confidence developed at Bomber Command and amongst others in authority about the future of the air offensive. As it happened, however, the doubts that had now arisen became submerged in the planning for D-Day, the Allied invasion of Europe. In what under the circumstances may be regarded as a blessing in disguise for Bomber Command, Harris was now ordered to divert virtually all of his aircraft from the bombing of Germany to more direct support for the coming landings in Normandy. Over the next several months, Bomber Command devoted the brunt of its operations to attacks on the German rail system in France and the Low Countries in order to disrupt German transport of reinforcements and materiel to the front after D-Day. They did so with admirable success, and the evidence in fact suggests that the combined British and US assault on these targets played a critical role in the successful Allied invasion. By late May, traffic on the railway network in France had declined to 55 percent of the January figure and, by D-Day itself, it had fallen to only 30 percent of the earlier figure.[25]

By September 1944, Allied forces had not only firmly established themselves in France, but they were making rapid progress against the increasingly shattered German defenses. At this point, a debate resumed over strategy for Bomber Command in its attacks on Germany itself. There was a clear consensus on the part of the Combined Chiefs of Staff as well as most other informed observers that Bomber Command would do best at this point to concentrate on German oil facilities as well as the enemy's communications network. That this was within its reach seemed particularly obvious given the severe deterioration in German air defenses by this stage of the war. The *Luftwaffe* was suffering from lack of fuel, from severe attrition inflicted on it by introduction of the US P-51 Mustang, and from the steady loss of German radar and ground control stations in France. All this made the skies over Germany increasingly comfortable for Allied aircraft. From September onward, in fact, the Allies came to enjoy what the British official history termed "virtual operational omnipotence" in the air, at night and even during the day. The latter point was a key one: daylight bombing, with relatively modest losses, promised a degree of accuracy in hitting targets that was crucial to any precision bombing campaign.

In pondering all this, however, Arthur Harris saw no need to abandon his long-held belief in the essential correctness of the area bombing strategy. As he put it, "I strongly objected to stopping the [area] offensive for which we had worked for five years." He dismissed the earlier success of Allied bombers in attacking oil targets by saying that "what the Allied strategists did was to bet on an outsider and it happened to win the race."[26] He remained skeptical of what he called "panacea targets," that is, supposed chokepoints in German war industry, the destruction of which could be decisive.

In the months that followed, the Chief of the Air Staff, Sir Charles Portal, repeatedly urged Harris to join with the US in a precision bombing campaign against Germany. Harris strongly implied that he would resign rather than accept any significant limitations on his renewal of the area offensive, and he stubbornly continued to stress his own priorities. In the last three months of 1944, the British dropped more bombs on Germany than in the whole of 1943, and some 53 percent of this was delivered on cities compared to 14 percent directed at oil facilities and about 15 percent on transportation targets. Earlier, Harris had established a list of sixty German cities that he intended to destroy, the accomplishment of which, he believed, would effectively end the war. By December, Harris's list of cities ripe for destruction had been pretty well translated into reality. Bomber Command had devastated or seriously damaged 80 percent of all German urban areas with more than 100,000 inhabitants. This exercise in destruction continued even into the spring of 1945, with almost 40 percent of British bombing being directed at city targets.[27]

The most famous (or notorious) of these attacks was undoubtedly the raid on Dresden on the night of February 13, referred to earlier. The ostensible rationale for the raid on Dresden had much to do with the Russians. The attack would help to undermine German resistance on the Eastern front and convince Stalin that despite some recent Allied difficulties, in particular the Battle of the Bulge, his Western partners were still doing their fair share in defeating the Nazis. The British official history described the Dresden raid as "the crowning achievement in the long, arduous and relentless development of a principle of bombing [the area offensive]."[28] At this point, Prime Minister Churchill evidently decided that Bomber Command's "crowning achievement" should be left to speak for itself, and in perhaps the most controversial reference to the area offensive that he offered during the war, he wrote the following to the Chief of the Air Staff:

> It seems to me that the moment has come when the question of bombing of German cities simply for the sake of increasing the terror, though under other pretexts, should be reviewed. Otherwise we shall come into control of an utterly ruined land. ... The destruction of Dresden remains a serious query against the conduct of Allied bombing. ... I feel the need for more precise concentration upon military objectives such as oil and communications behind the immediate battle-zone, rather than on mere acts of terror and wanton destruction, however impressive.[29]

Sir Charles Portal was greatly offended by Churchill's reference to "terror" as a previous goal of British strategy, and in response, the Prime Minister delivered a revised minute that dropped such sensitive references and instead concentrated on the pragmatic benefits to be obtained from a cessation of the area offensive. Having said this, it is striking that whatever qualms were now being felt did not prevent area attacks on German targets being continued virtually to the last days of World War II. Thus, Würzburg was devastated on 16 March 1945, two days later, the city of Witten was two-thirds destroyed, and a month later, there was a further raid on the Berlin suburb of Potsdam by 500 Lancasters, resulting in about 5,000 civilian fatalities.[30] In a sense, all of this could be considered as simply reflexive actions of the vast machine of destruction that Bomber Command had become by this point. At long last, however, the RAF Air Staff issued a directive on April 16 that officially ended Bomber Command's strategic air offensive against Germany. Harris accepted this directive on the practical grounds that there were essentially no more area targets to be attacked in Germany.

An Assessment

In all, Bomber Command launched some 390,000 sorties against Germany in the entire course of the war, with area attacks accounting for about 70 percent of the total effort. Some 8,900 British aircraft were destroyed in the conflict and approximately one million tons of bombs were dropped on the enemy. During the war, about 125,000 men and women joined Bomber Command, either as aircrew or ground support personnel. Of this number, about 56,000 (almost all officers and NCOs) lost their lives, about half of that were injured, and more than 11,000 were taken prisoner, for an overall casualty rate of about 76 percent. The sacrifice in officers alone was greater than what the British suffered in the whole of World War I.[31] As to the destruction visited on Germany, it is estimated that approximately 600,000 German civilians lost their lives to Allied bombing. Perhaps another 800,000 received serious injury. Around three million homes were destroyed. And, of course, Germany lost the war.

The question is how much of a connection there was between the latter outcome and the efforts of Bomber Command as described. Any overall military assessment of the costs and benefits of British area bombing of Germany is necessarily a complex one. Nevertheless, there are certain conclusions about Bomber Command's operations that may be offered with a fair degree of confidence.

The notion that German morale could be shattered by a strategy of devastating German cities proved to be an entirely false premise. "Morale" in this sense basically meant the willingness of the German people to work for and support their government's war effort. For a variety of reasons, the carnage visited on Germany by British bombers never came close to having a real effect in these terms. After the war, the British Bombing Survey Unit (established to study the effects of the bombing campaign) itself conceded the point: "The effects of town area attacks on the morale of the German people were ... very much over-estimated by all other ministries and departments through the course of the war. ... There is no evidence that they caused any serious break in the morale of the population as a whole."[32]

To say that the attempt to undermine German morale by area bombing did not work is actually only one part, and perhaps the least important part, of a critique of this ostensible goal of British air attacks. Far more telling is the almost total lack of any systematic consideration on the part of British decision-makers as to *how* the "undermining of morale" was actually supposed to undercut the German war effort. Indeed, the idea that morale could well be the Achilles' heel of the German war effort can only be regarded as an article of faith rather than the result of a rigorous analysis on the part of those directing Bomber Command's activities.

In a police state such as Nazi Germany, where individuals were executed for offenses as mundane as listening to foreign radio broadcasts, how was a loss of morale to be translated into some sort of mass political activity that would force the hand of the government toward peace? No doubt, as the war progressed, there was growing disillusionment amongst the German people about the prospects for victory, and the devastation of bombing may have contributed to this feeling. At the same time, people had to get on with their lives, produce an income from their jobs, try to sustain their personal relations, and so forth. The point is that for the Germans, as well as for the British during the Nazi bombing of Britain, the expected reaction of human beings under this sort of stress was simply to attempt to survive and hope for an end to the pain. This type of fatalism is reinforced when the state has a capacity and a willingness to employ large-scale coercion to prevent open disaffection.

A second inescapable conclusion about the area bombing offensive against Germany was that it had only a modest impact on German arms production. This is not to say that dropping a million tons of bombs on Germany did not have at least some effect on the German allocation of resources, particularly in diverting such resources from other operations. RAF Air Marshal Sir Arthur Tedder estimated, for example, that anti-aircraft defenses absorbed almost 600,000 men by 1943 and about 900,000 by 1944. He suggests that anti-aircraft guns took around 30 percent of the total German weapons production.[33] Even if we accept these claims, however, the essential fact remains that during the first major phase of Bomber Command's assault on Germany, dating roughly from the spring of 1942 to the spring of 1944, German output of war materiel, far from declining, actually increased steadily. For example, construction of aircraft of all types went from approximately 15,000 in 1942 to about 40,000 in 1944. Production of tanks increased sixfold. Overall, output of weapons and ammunition peaked in the summer of 1944 and was almost three times the level achieved at the beginning of 1942.[34] Production rates declined rapidly after August 1944, but this was due not to the area offensive, but to precision attacks against the German energy and transportation systems.

How is one to account for this quite unexpected outcome (at least from the perspective of Harris and other adherents of the area offensive)? Two factors deserve special mention. The policy of area bombing was based at least in part on the idea that the German economy was fully stretched and that, as Tedder put it, "any general loss to German industry as a whole would have to be borne by the munitions industry." He also admits that this idea proved to be quite fallacious.[35] The notion of a German economy totally mobilized and regimented in support of the Nazi war effort was in fact largely a myth, at least until 1943. In reality, Hitler had always been concerned that a drastic decline in living standards might undermine German support for the war, and consequently he tolerated for quite a while a really extraordinary diversion of German manufacturing capacity to civilian consumption. The point is that there was actually a great deal of slack in German war production until quite late in the struggle, and this meant that Hitler had considerable leeway in meeting any falloff of arms production resulting from the area bombing offensive. Indeed, almost until the end of the war, German factories manufactured more arms than there were German soldiers to employ them.

The second factor militating against the area offensive's having any pronounced effect on German military production was essentially technical. In order for Bomber Command seriously to interrupt output of a particular item of significance, it was necessary for it to undertake repeated raids against a single target. This went against Arthur Harris's tendency to want to deal in turn with all the German cities on his "hit list," that is, the sixty major urban centers that he had originally designated for destruction by Bomber Command. In practice, Harris would order a major strike against one target and then move on to the next, which gave the Germans ample opportunity to restore manufacturing capacity in the areas already attacked.

In sum, the British area bombing offensive against Germany in World War II may perhaps rightly be described in the same terms as those used by the French aristocrat Boulaye de la Meurthe to describe the execution by Napoleon of the Duc d'Enghien: "It was worse than a crime, it was a blunder." This cynical aphorism does not disguise the fact, however, that there are some blunders in the history of military affairs that cannot be accepted as simply the result of honest miscalculation, but rather demand an extensive moral query.

Notes

1. Sir John Slessor, *The Central Blue* (London: Cassell & Co., 1956), 214.
2. Great Britain, 5 *Parliamentary Debates* (Commons), vol. 351 (September 14, 1939): 750.
3. David Irving, *The Destruction of Dresden* (New York: Holt, Rinehart and Winston, 1963).
4. John Pimlott, "The Theory and Practice of Strategic Bombing," in *Warfare in the Twentieth Century*, eds. Collin McInnes and G.D. Sheffield (London: Unwin Hyman, 1988), 121.
5. W.M. Royse, *Aerial Bombardment and the International Regulation of Warfare* (1928), 192, cited in Geoffrey Best, *Humanity in Warfare* (New York: Columbia University Press, 1980), 269.
6. Giulio Douhet, *The Command of the Air*, trans. Dino Ferrari (New York: Coward-McCann, 1942), 83.
7. Ibid., 57–58.
8. Ibid., 14.

9. The full text of Trenchard's memorandum (and his critics' response) may be found in Noble Frankland and Charles Webster, *The Strategic Air Offensive against Germany 1939–1945* (London: HMSO, 1961), vol. IV: 71ff (hereafter cited as SAOG).
10. This type of moral criticism of strategic bombing was widespread at the time. Thus, the *London Times* declared in 1933 that "it would be the bankruptcy of statesmanship to admit that it is a legitimate form of warfare for a nation to destroy its rival capital from the air."
11. John Colville, *The Fringes of Power* (New York: W.W. Norton & Co., 1985), 52–53.
12. Max Hastings, *Bomber Command* (New York: Dial Press, 1979), 84–86.
13. SAOG, vol. I: 323–324.
14. J.M. Spaight, *Bombing Vindicated* (London: Geoffrey Bles, 1944), 45.
15. SAOG, vol. I: 178.
16. Ibid., 331–336.
17. Sir Arthur Harris, *Bomber Offensive* (London: Collins, 1947), 74–75, 113.
18. Ibid., 112–113.
19. Ronald Clark, *The Rise of the Boffins* (London: Phoenix House, 1962), 182–208.
20. United States, *Strategic Bombing Survey* (Washington: Government Printing Office, 1945), Area Studies Division Report No. 31, 4.
21. Martin Caidin, *The Night Hamburg Died* (New York: Ballantine Books, 1960), 9.
22. H.R. Allen, *The Legacy of Lord Trenchard* (London: Cassell, 1972), 149–151.
23. SAOG, vol. II: 47–48.
24. Noble Frankland, *The Bombing Offensive against Germany* (London: Faber & Faber, 1965), 74.
25. John Keegan, *The Second World War* (New York: Viking, 1989), 416.
26. Harris, *Bomber Offensive*, 220–223.
27. Basil Liddell Hart, *History of the Second World War* (New York: G.P. Putnam's Sons, 1970), 609.
28. SAOG, vol. III: 109.
29. Ibid., 112.
30. Martin Middlebrook and Chris Everitt, *The Bomber Command War Diaries* (London: Viking, 1985), 683, 695.
31. Robin Cross, *The Bombers* (New York: Macmillan Publishing Company, 1987), 160; Hilary St. George Saunders, *Royal Air Force 1939–1945* (London: HMSO, 1954), Vol. III: 392.
32. Norman Longmate, *The Bombers* (London: Hutchinson, 1983), 356.
33. John Keegan puts the total number of men and women diverted from other sectors of the German armed forces to air defense at about two million. He goes on to say that this was the one and only military justification that might be given for the area offensive (*The Second World War*, (New York: Viking, 1989), 430).
34. P.M.S. Blackett, *Military and Political Consequences of Atomic Energy* (London: Turnstile Press, 1948), 195.
35. Sir Arthur Tedder, *With Prejudice* (Boston: Little Brown & Co., 1966), 103.

CHAPTER 2

The Bombing Campaign
the USAAF
Douglas P. Lackey

Introduction

In discussions of the bombing of Germany during World War II, the phrase "Allied bombing" is commonly used. But, in fact, the Allied bombing of Germany had two distinct components, the British and the American.[1] American bombing policy was based on different concepts; American plans exhibited different intentions; the Americans had different planes and different equipment; and they executed different missions against different types of targets. American leaders engaged in different debates about bombing policy; the American people had a different experience of what it is like to be bombed; and, the Americans read differently censored news reports about the effects of the bombing in Germany.

One basic contrast frequently stressed by historians between the Royal Air Force (RAF) bombing policy and the United States Army Air Forces (USAAF) bombing policy is that, at least from late 1942, the British were committed to "nighttime area bombing," while the Americans were committed to "daylight precision bombing." It is then argued that American bombing—daytime precision bombing—was morally clean, while British bombing—nighttime area bombing—was immoral. Of the immorality of the British bombing I have no doubt. (I make the case against it in chapter 6 of this volume.) Here, I contest the claim that what the Americans did was morally clean. In reaching this judgment about American bombing, I am not referring only to the horrific raids perpetrated by American airmen against Dresden and Berlin in February and March of 1945. I am referring to what the Americans planned for Germany from the very beginning, even before war was declared in December 1941. My argument has two phases: first, given predictable bombing inaccuracy, there are systematic moral questions that can be raised about precision strategic bombing. Second, "daylight precision bombing" was only a component of a larger American bombing strategy, the ultimate goal of which was the destruction of Germany.

Is Precision Bombing Inherently Clean?

Many people feel, intuitively, that there is a moral distinction between area bombing and precision bombing. In the popular conception, area bombing is wild and vindictive, while precision bombing is rational and morally focused. But the distinction between "area" and "precision" bombing, by itself, carries little moral weight. For example, there could be nighttime area bombing raids over a large area containing only military targets, in the hope that one or more of the military targets would be struck. Such bombing would be imprecise yet morally acceptable. On the other hand, there could be daylight precision bombing raids on enemy civilian hospitals for the purpose of inducing panic in the civilian population. Such bombing attacks would be precise yet morally unacceptable.

Let me explain in a more abstract way why the distinction between "precision bombing" and "area bombing" makes little moral difference. Suppose that the chosen target is the Eiffel Tower. One could design an area bombing raid that would scatter 100 bombs randomly throughout a circle with a radius of one kilometer from the Tower. Studies might show that it is very likely, given such a design, that one bomb would hit the tower and 99 would miss. Alternatively, one might design a precision raid in which 100 bombs are aimed directly at the Tower. Studies might show that, given the available technology, only one bomb is likely to hit the tower and 99 will miss. So with the area raid, 99 bombs will miss the tower and cause collateral damage, and with the precision raid, 99 bombs will miss the tower and cause collateral damage. Notice that the intention behind both raids is the same: "destroy the Eiffel Tower."

The empirical difference between the two raids is this: with the area raid, it is *guaranteed* that most bombs will miss the tower, whereas with the precision raid, it is *not* guaranteed that most bombs will miss the tower. It is possible, but very unlikely, aiming precisely at the Tower, that all 100 bombs will strike the target. This empirical difference cannot, by itself, establish a moral difference. Suppose I locate a murderous enemy in a crowd, and I shoot ten bullets at him, striking several bystanders. No court of law would absolve me on the grounds that all of my bullets *might* have hit the target. The law will decide on what is reasonable and reasonably foreseeable, and in this case of the Eiffel Tower, it is reasonable and foreseeable that some of the bombs will miss.

This is not the place for an extended analysis of the moral rules that should govern strategic bombing. In this chapter, I shall apply two simple and generally accepted rules: first, strategic bombing is immoral if one goal of the bombing is to cause suffering to civilians. Second, strategic bombing is immoral if the harm it causes to civilians is not proportional to the military goals it can reasonably be expected to achieve.

The 1941 American Plan for Bombing Germany

Throughout the war, in the European theater, the American government, in its public statements, publicly endorsed precision bombing as its chosen form of strategic bombing. The American news media repeated and endorsed this stance. In response to Goebbels' accusations that the Allies had adopted terror tactics and to reports that downed Allied fliers were being attacked by enraged German civilians, the *New York Times* editorialized:

> The strategy of the United Nations does not rest, as that of the Nazis does, on atrocities. Civilians do die under our attacks, but not because any allied flier aims at them. The present bombings of Europe have just one objective, and that is to paralyze the Nazi power to fight. ... They can compare the Allied record with the record of German fliers who butchered 40,000 civilians in Rotterdam, machine gunned old men, women, and children as they fled along the roads in France, and who, not daring to come over Britain in the day after the fall of 1940, adopted the strategy of terror bombing.[2]

Even after the bombing of Dresden, when a British Air Commander admitted publicly that one purpose of the raid was to clog the roads with civilians, Eisenhower's headquarters responded: "There has been no change in bombing policy. The United States strategic air forces have always directed their attacks against military objectives and will continue to do so."[3] Such was the declared policy of the United States. The operational policy was different.

The American plan for the bombing of Germany, AWPD-1, was worked out in the summer of 1941, six months before Pearl Harbor and seven months before Hitler, in the first of his many stupendous military blunders, declared war on the United States.[4] President Roosevelt, anticipating American entry into the war, and wanting some estimate of military procurement needs, asked the Army Air Force to prepare a plan for the use of air power against Germany, together with a list of aircraft production requirements. The result was AWPD-1, a plan not just for the use of air power to assist ground forces, but a comprehensive plan for the strategic bombing of Germany. The plan was studied by Roosevelt's trusted aide, Harry Hopkins, and, on his advice, the plan was approved by Roosevelt in September 1941. Bomber production quotas for 1942 were set in accordance with AWPD-1.

Was it permissible for Roosevelt to *ask* for detailed plans for the bombing of Germany, when Germany and the United States were not at war? I affirm it was, for two reasons. First, the decision to develop AWPD-1 and produce long-range bombers did not increase the probability that the United States would go to war with Germany. The generation of AWPD-1 was not intended, in my view, to provoke Germany or to manipulate the American people into war. The plans were secret, and secret plans are not intended to provoke. When they were leaked, apparently by isolationist fanatics, and described in American newspapers in early December 1941, there was no significant reaction on the German side. Hitler had no ideological argument for going to war with the Anglo-Saxon nations—witness his attempts to avoid war with England—or at least he wished to avoid war with England and the US, if he could do so without giving up his other plans for conquest. His decision to declare war on the United States sprung not from his reaction to American war plans, but from the fact that he was allied with Japan and Japan was at war with the United States.

Second, when AWPD-1 was developed in the summer of 1941, Germany was by no means an innocent party. Nations that behave well on the international scene deserve not to be targets of preemptive war plans, but Germany had not behaved well. The United States could have legitimately declared war on Germany in the summer of 1941 under the heading of the collective self-defense of Poland, or Norway, Belgium, the Netherlands, France, or Russia, even in the absence of hostile acts by Germany against the United States.

It was permissible to ask for *a* plan. But was it morally permissible to approve *this* plan? Our judgment of Roosevelt's decision depends on the details of AWPD-1, which we must examine now in some detail. The critical sections relate to targeting policy:

> 3d. The extent of the economic strain [of war] on Germany is indicated by the following: at present there are six and one half million men under arms in the German army, one million in the German navy, and one and half million in the German air force. Behind this armed front there are eight and a half million men engaged in armaments work alone, about half of whom are working the steel industries. Nearly 17 million men are directly engaged in this war, to the exclusion of all normal civil pursuits and production. Hence there is a very heavy drain on the social and economic structure of the state. Destruction of that structure will virtually break down the capacity of the German

state to wage war. The basic conception on which this plan is based lies in the application of air power for the breakdown of the integral and economic structure of Germany. The conception involves the selection of a system of objectives vital to continued German war effort, and to the means of livelihood of the German people, and tenaciously concentrating all bombing towards those objectives. The most effective method of conducting such a decisive offensive is the destruction of precise objectives, at least initially. As German morale begins to crack, area bombing of civil concentrations may be effective …

Possible lines of action are then listed:

(1) Lines of action whose accomplishment will accomplish the air mission in Europe
  (a) disruption of a major portion of the electric power system of Germany
  (b) disruption of the German transportation system
  (c) destruction of the German oil and petroleum system
  (d) undermining of German morale by air attack on civil concentrations
  …
(2) Lines of action representing intermediate objectives
  (a) neutralization of the German Air force
    (i) by attack of its bases
    (ii) by attack of aircraft factories (engines and airframe)
    (iii) by attack on aluminum and magnesium factories.

There follows, after this list, a five-page analysis of the German electrical power grid, the German rail and canal system, and German oil sources, including synthetic oil refineries and oil sources in occupied countries. The level of detail in these bombing plans is startling. For example:

> The vulnerability of the inland waterway system to air attack arises from the fact that the destruction of an estimated 14 targets would neutralize the effectiveness of the east-west canal system of Germany. These fourteen targets consist of three ship elevators, locks at nine points, and the inland harbors at Mannheim and Duisburg. Canal ships and docks are precision targets.

But "precision targeting" can have disseminated effects:

> Crippling of the German transportation system would bring severe suffering to the German people by denying them the necessary coal for heating. The winters in Germany are cold and clothes are becoming scarce. Breakdown of the transportation system would interfere with the orderly distribution of foodstuffs and common utilities.

AWPD-1 then returns to morale bombing in general:

> *Morale.* Timeliness of attack is most important in the conduct of air operations directed against civil morale. If the morale of the people is already low because of sustained suffering and deprivation and because people are losing faith in the ability of the armed forces to win a favorable decision, then heavy and sustained bombing of cities may crush that morale entirely. However, if these conditions do not yet exist, then area bombing of cities[5] may actually stiffen the resistance of the population, especially if the attacks are weak and sporadic. Hence no specific number of targets is set up for this task. Rather it is believed that the entire bombing effort might be applied towards this purpose when it becomes apparent that proper psychological conditions exist.

The text of AWPD-1 demonstrates that the usual story of the relations between the USAAF and the RAF has to be revised. The usual story is that the British were committed to area bombing while the Americans were committed to precision bombing. But in 1941, the British were still sticking to precision bombing, trying (with little success) to hit German submarine pens in France, while the Americans, in 1941, were developing plans for area bombing and for producing mass starvation and hypothermia in Germany by destroying the German electrical and transportation systems. The plan in fact envisages a mixture of strategic bombing and terror bombing.

The strategic bombing discussions of AWPD-1 seem to presume that targets will invariably be destroyed in precision raids. There is no discussion of missing the targets, erroneous identification of targets, or what the circular error probable of B-17 or B-24 raids might be. The Norden bombsight, which worked like a charm in the sunny skies over the training fields in Arizona, was expected to function just as effectively in the drizzling clouds of northern Europe. The predicted scope of destruction is enormous, larger in scale than anything the British had achieved by the end of 1944, even after the destruction of Lübeck and Hamburg. If this is precision bombing, it is precision bombing of apocalyptic design.

AWPD-1 calls for direct attacks on German morale only as the late stage in the plan, only *after* the destruction of the electrical, transport, and oil production systems, or at least only after the enemy's ground forces are stalemated or defeated, and the population is "losing faith in the ability of the armed forces." These objectives, the plan says, can only be achieved subsequent to the destruction of a substantial part of the German air force. The achievement of these preliminary objectives would obviously take several years, during which time, the plan says, area bombing designed to induce terror must be avoided so as not to stiffen resistance. (The reaction of the British to the Blitz is clearly in mind.) In fact, the British began area bombing in early 1942, while the Americans did not engage in area attacks before 1944. AWPD-1 delayed American area attacks on Germany by almost two years. But when the conditions for morale bombing in the plan were met, the Americans began the morale bombing of Germany, right on schedule. AWPD-1 charted the path that led to Dresden. The legitimacy of morale bombing, presumed in AWPD-1, opened the door for the area bombing of Japanese cities from March to August 1945.[6]

Was AWPD-1 a moral plan, given the evils of the Nazi regime? It was not, because it called for attacks on the industrial and transportation infrastructure of Germany, specifically to induce suffering and death among civilians. It was not, because it called for attacks on civilian morale that could only be achieved by direct attacks on civilians. The morale bombing section of the plan should have been discussed and rejected. The strategic bombing objectives should have been redesigned with the exclusive goal, not of causing civilian suffering, but of destroying the enemy's capacity to make war. Instead, no analysis of civilian suffering or terror bombing appears in the plan, and there is no indication that any moral questions were raised about the plan in 1941, or about any of its later revisions. The plan was never vetted for consistency with international law, especially the Hague Conventions, which indicate restrictions on artillery bombardment that could be easily extrapolated to apply to strategic bombing. The seeds of mass destruction were planted in 1941. The only question was when the time would be ripe.

Targeting Policy 1942–43: From Rouen to Schweinfurt

The United States Eighth Air Force, stationed in England, went into action on 17 August 1942, with a series of daylight raids directed at railroad yards near Rouen. For the next year, American targeting policy conformed to the doctrine of daylight precision bombing, consistent with the early phases of AWPD-1. The British were confident, by early 1942, that precision bombing would not work,[7] and made every attempt through 1942 to persuade the Americans to join the RAF in night attacks on German cities. The Americans resisted these arguments and were determined to fight the air war their own way.[8] The tension peaked and subsided with General Ira Eaker's presentation to Churchill at the Casablanca conference in January 1943. Eaker's 1943 memo to Churchill deserves study:

1. Day bombing is more accurate and can destroy obscure but important targets night bombers can't find.

2. Being more accurate, day bombing is more economical because a small force concentrating its bombs is more effective than a large force scattering its bombs.
3. By bombing the devils around the clock, we can prevent German defenses from getting any rest.
4. If the RAF works by night and we work by day, we can prevent airdrome and airspace congestion.
5. Our crews are trained for day bombing. There would be a long delay in re-training them.
6. Our planes and equipment are designed for day operations. They would require extensive modifications.
7. Day bombing permits the destruction of enemy fighters—one of our prime objectives—by exposing them to the B-17s twelve half inch guns.
8. We can co-ordinate day raids with RAF night raids. We can ignite obscure targets by day which the RAF can bomb that night by the light of our fires.[9]

No moral considerations can be found in Eaker's memo. It might be argued that Eaker did not put them in because he believed that moral arguments would have no effect on Churchill. On the contrary, I think moral arguments would have had force, if derived from national traditions, something that Churchill himself wrote about in his books. If Eaker had said, "we Americans don't bomb cities," that might have ended the argument then and there. The fact that he did not include moral arguments is some evidence that he did not have them to give.

As it happened, Churchill *did* accept the practical considerations advanced by Eaker and (reluctantly) agreed to give the Americans their way. The American commitment to daylight raids made for efficient use of the East Anglia airfields: the Americans flew off at night and bombed in the day; the RAF flew off in the day and bombed at night. Furthermore, there were military targets in occupied countries, and bombing in occupied countries required precision so as not to harm "friendly" civilians. The Americans were assigned the delicate task of bombing France without arousing the French.

As American attacks continued through the early months of 1943, problems with the precision bombing campaign emerged. Precision bombing was impossible in bad weather, and bad weather was almost constant. German fighter resistance was stronger than expected and losses were high. Targets were hard to find, hard to destroy, and often easily repaired. Half of the American B-17s were drawn off to support the Allied ground campaign in North Africa, leaving half the planes for twice the work. And, of necessity, repeated raids were directed on German submarine pens, rather than on German war production. Nevertheless, the results were sufficiently promising to prompt the Americans and the British to develop a revised version of AWPD-1, a new plan for 1943–44 that would coordinate British attacks on cities with American attacks on precision targets.

The new bombing plan, developed by the Committee of Operations Analysis in Washington, argued along the lines of AWPD-1: "It is better to cause a high degree of destruction in a few really essential industries or services than to cause a small degree of destruction in many industries. ... The destruction or continued neutralization of some sixty targets could gravely impair and might paralyze the Western Axis war effort."[10]

The British and the Americans settled on seventy-six targets in six systems in the following order or priority: "submarines construction yards and bases; German aircraft industry; ball bearings; oil; synthetic rubber and tires; military transport vehicles."[11] But the fact that the British approved this target list by no means implied that they intended to begin bombing in daylight. They would bomb cities, and the Americans would bomb whatever was left. So in the Hamburg raid on 25 July 1943, the British dropped incendiary bombs on Hamburg at night, while the American Air Force dropped high explosives on the railroad marshalling yards and the docks the next day.

In the summer of 1943, the Americans pursued their attacks on precision targets, raiding into Germany despite the lack of fighter protection. They bombed submarine pens at Wilhelmshaven, ship construction facilities at Kiel, synthetic rubber plants at Hüls, metal works at Heroya, docks at Trondheim, and, as noted, the docks area at Hamburg. The months of August through October 1943 marked the high watermark of the American campaign, with attacks on the oil refineries at Ploesti, in Romania (August 1), the ball bearing plants at Schweinfurt (August 17), and the Messerschmitt aircraft complex at Regensburg (August 17).

In the Ploesti raid, 177 B-24s took off from North Africa and 54 failed to return—41 planes lost in action, a loss rate of 30 percent.[12] In the Regensburg/Schweinfurt attacks on August 17, 376 B-17s took off from England and 60 failed to return, a loss rate of 16 percent. In October, the Americans attacked Schweinfurt again, and lost 77 more bombers, mostly to *Luftwaffe* attacks. Anyone who believes that American bombs were scattered around British-style in 1943 should read the accounts in Leroy Newby's *Target Ploesti* and Thomas Coffey's *Decision over Schweinfurt*.

Clearly, the Air Force had to justify these staggering losses to Roosevelt and to the American people. But the search for a justification revealed a perplexity about precision bombing. When your army advances, you hold more territory and your enemy holds less. But when your air force destroys a factory, how can you measure the effect on the war effort? The economy of a nation is a complex web and cutting the web in a few spots does not destroy the web. The Germans had other oil refineries and rebuilt most of the complex at Ploesti. Ball bearing production was down at Schweinfurt, but never reached zero. Despite Regensburg, the Germans kept producing aircraft. You can say that "the German war effort was impeded by these losses," and that is as far as you can go. The gains were vague. The losses were definite.

In six days in October 1943, the Eighth Air Force lost 179 bombers in the skies over Germany, losses of 10 percent per raid. British Bomber Command, bombing at night, had losses of 4.5 percent. These comparisons led to a crisis of confidence about precision bombing, both inside the military and in the American public. American air force generals had to admit that the losses over Schweinfurt were unsustainable. They also had to admit that although each raid was a "success" in terms of targets destroyed, the entire effort was a failure in that German war production roared on. They did not know, until Speer's memoirs were published after the war, the degree to which the raids of 1943 had in fact hurt the German war effort: directly in loss of material, and indirectly in the energy expended on dispersing war production out of the cities. Instead, the official history of Air Force operations in World War II reports bleakly of November 1943: "The fact was that the Eight Air Force had for the time being lost air superiority over Germany."[13]

The months of August through October of 1943 marked the most intense efforts of the USAAF to implement the early stages of AWPD-1 and cripple the German economy. The effort had failed, or so they believed. In 1999, W.G. Sebald wrote that the Germans brought the destruction of their cities upon themselves.[14] For the Americans in 1943, it was clear which "Germans" had brought this about. The Americans were forced to abandon precision bombing because of the courage of the fighter pilots of the *Luftwaffe*, who had defended Germany in 1943 with the zeal and tenacity with which the Spitfire pilots defended London in 1940. If Germany had been less well defended in 1943, its cities might have been spared by the Americans in 1944 and 1945.

The Americans Move to Terror Bombing

As American air force losses mounted in 1943, air force commanders found it increasingly difficult to remain loyal to precision bombing and the earlier section of AWPD-1. For one thing, so far as the American press was concerned, there was little or no moral distinction between area bombing and precision bombing: they were both praiseworthy. Neither was equated with terror bombing. American newspapers reported both types of operations side-by-side, usually under the rubric of "slamming the Germans." Consider the first *New York Times* article on the July 25 Hamburg attack:

> United States heavy bombers struck deep and hard into Germany by daylight yesterday, hammering aircraft factories at the Baltic port of Warnemünde and showering hundreds of tons of high explosives into the smoking ruins of Hamburg, gutted by the British Royal Air Force's night bombers twelve hours earlier in the greatest bombing assault of the war ... Paced by the Flying Fortresses major raids, medium bombers delivered many other blows at the Nazis in the occupied low countries and France.[15]

When Goebbels on the radio described the Hamburg raid as "terror bombing," the *Times* replied on July 26: "Berlin angrily denounced [the attack on Hamburg] as the heaviest 'terror raid' Germany has suffered. Hamburg, with its twenty-two miles of quays, is the greatest seaport in Continental Europe. Its shipyards make it the cradle and the refuge of German submarine power. As an industrial center it is a target as important as Düsseldorf or Cologne."[16]

One sympathizes with the reluctance of the *New York Times* to believe anything said by Joseph Goebbels. But the quotes around the phrase "terror bombing" surely are belied by the content of the news story in the same issue, and the argument that Hamburg is "as important a target as Düsseldorf or Cologne" indicates a slippage from choosing targets *in* cities to making targets *of* cities. No distinction is made between British area bombing and American precision bombing in the follow-up news story printed on July 31, which does not distinguish the American contribution from the British contribution in the annihilation of Hamburg.[17]

A small but articulate group of Americans wanted *more* area bombing and *less* precision bombing. In early 1943, Allan A. Michie, a reporter for *Reader's Digest*, argued that daylight precision bombing was getting American airmen killed in large numbers with no discernible results. The war can be won quickly by bombing Germany, Michie argued in his book *The Air Offensive Against Germany*, published in mid 1943:

> German morale is starting to crack under the terrific weight of the explosives and fire bombs the RAF has poured into the Reich ... 1,000,000 Germans have been driven from their homes ... More than seven square miles in nine German cites have been wiped off the map. It is my personal conviction that so far the performance of American bombers in the European theater has been disappointing ... The fact that night bombing is carried on by the British is no reason for Americans to scorn it.[18]

As losses mounted in the fall of 1943, an increasing number of Americans were coming to think that Michie was right. The British, with their area bombing, could point to results comparable to traditional military victories: by destroying Hamburg, they had denied territory to the enemy, something that armies had done from time immemorial. The Americans, with precision bombing, were reduced to talk about destroying ball bearing machines, hardly as psychologically compelling as "destroying Hamburg."

What of the moral superiority of precision bombing? What of the tens of thousands of civilians killed by the RAF in one night in Hamburg? The American people could not see the distinction in 1943. First, there was the unpleasant fact that large numbers of Germans civilians were also killed by precision raids, when "precision raids" in 1943 meant that 50 percent of bombs fell further than a thousand feet from their targets, and one bombing run in three missed their targets by 3,000 feet or more.[19] Second, there was the even less pleasant fact that precision bombing, the bombing of choice in occupied countries, often killed friendly civilians. The initial raids in the precision bombing campaign against Rouen killed 170 French civilians and destroyed many medieval buildings in the cathedral area.[20] By the time the Allies landed in Normandy in June 1944, 15,000 French civilians had been killed by American bombs. If it is morally permissible to kill a certain number of friendly civilians in precision raids, why should it not be morally permissible to kill a larger number of unfriendly civilians in area raids? "Why be nice to undefended towns and cities?" the *Boston Herald* editorialized. "The time-honored system of tit for tat is the only one which Hitler and the Germans can understand."[21] American sympathy for German civilians killed by American bombs was close to nil, despite the fact that Germans were the largest ethnic group in the United States. The Americans in 1943 agreed with Sebald in 1999: the Germans brought these miseries on themselves.

But now, if area bombing inside Germany was permissible, what is the difference between area bombing, the presumed target of which is the capacity to make war, and terror bombing, the target of which is the desire to make war? Certainly, area bombing causes terror, and I cannot find a single person in these years who supported area bombing and yet regretted the terror that area bombing caused. The terror was welcomed; it, too, was helping to end the war. And I cannot find a single person who criticized terror bombing who also did not criticize area bombing. When criticism of American bombing policy surfaced for the first time, in March of 1944, the critics wrote in protest of "obliteration bombing," a label that comprehended both terror attacks and area attacks.

The military planners in late 1943 seemed to be caught in an irresistible inference chain: if precision bombing was morally indistinguishable from area bombing, and if area bombing was indistinguishable from terror bombing, then precision bombing was morally indistinguishable from terror bombing. Why then should the USAAF persist with precision bombing, which caused so many more American casualties? Terror bombing, which had been unthinkable in 1942, became thinkable by the end of 1943. Various military planners, strategists, and psychologists in early 1944 set about devising plans to break German morale, including plans to launch unmanned B-17s loaded with explosives careening into Germany, plans for attacks on hundreds of smaller Germans towns, plans for dropping booby traps like explosive toys, and plans for strafing German civilians along the roads.

In the end, little came of these ideas. The main agency of terror was simply more area bombing, sometimes on cloudy days, sometimes using radar rather than the Norden bombsight to locate targets. In January and February of 1944, the USAAF bombed Kiel, Wilhelmshaven, Emden, and Frankfurt. In March, American planes began to bomb Berlin. The huge increase in the number of bombs dropped on Germany (10,000 tons in one "big week" in February 1944) betrays the shift from the destruction of specific targets (still often officially assigned) to the devastation of areas. In Italy, American planes bombed Rome. Later that spring, American planes bombed Belgrade, Sofia, and Bucharest. In the summer, they laid waste to central sections of Milan and Padua and the suburbs of Florence. The effect of American bombing in these non-German territories was a developing hatred for Americans. In Serbia, Bulgaria, and Romania, the people bombed by the Americans welcomed the Red Army with open arms. In Italy, reports my CUNY colleague Claudia Corradini, who as a child experienced the bombing and destruction of her house in the Campo di Marte section of Florence in 1944, good will among the Florentines toward the Americans was wiped out in one day. Area bombing produces terror, but terror produces resentment.

The shift to area bombing, as noted above, was forced upon the USAAF by the efforts of the *Luftwaffe*. Bomber losses in October 1943 were unsustainable. But a large fraction of the losses of 1943 were due to a lack of fighter escort when the bombers flew over Germany. This very problem was solved in February 1944 with the arrival (at long last) of the P-51 fighter with auxiliary fuel tanks attached to the wings, which enabled fighter aircraft to accompany the bombers deep into Germany and back. The availability of the P-51 created a moral problem for the Americans in 1944. In 1943, the USAAF practiced precision bombing when they could ill afford it. In 1944, when they could afford it, they ceased to practice it. The American area raids of 1944 and 1945 could not be justified on the grounds that precision bombing was unsustainable given the strength of the *Luftwaffe*. In fact, the less opposition American bombers received, the more indiscriminate their bombing became. It is as if German weakness inspired American contempt.

American Protests Against Terror Bombing

After Pearl Harbor, there had been little domestic criticism of American conduct in the war. There was a pacifist movement in the US, but that movement opposed war as such and not any particular methods used in the war. But as the Americans veered towards area bombing in 1944, opposition to the new tactics surfaced. In early March 1944, the Quaker magazine *Fellowship* published an article by Vera Brittain entitled "Massacre by Bombing." Brittain wrote: "Hundreds of thousands of helpless and innocent people are being subjected to forms of death and injury comparable to the worst tortures of the middle ages ... Nothing less than absolute certainty [that these bombings would shorten the war] entitles even the most ardent of the war's supporters to use these dreadful expedients."[22]

Brittain's article, in a pacifist publication, might have been dismissed as another critique of war in general. But the article was preceded by a public statement signed by twenty-eight leaders of American Protestant churches, churches by no means linked to pacifism. The declaration by twenty-eight religious leaders was front-page news in the *New York Times* (6 March 1944) under the headline "Obliteration Raids on German Cities Protested in U.S." "In our time," the signers wrote,

> war is showing itself in its true colors. ... The contesting parties pay little heed to the former decencies and chivalries, save among their own comrades. Christian people should be moved to examine themselves concerning their participation in this carnival of death—even though they be thousands of miles away. Here, surely, is a call for repentance: that we have not acquainted ourselves with the verities and realities of what is being done in our name in Europe.[23]

Brittain's article and the clergymen's preface provoked considerable commentary, including surprisingly sympathetic remarks in the Catholic Press.[24] But since Brittain's article mainly described the effects of British bombing, American readers might still have concluded that these criticisms did not fully apply to what the USAAF was doing. This idea that area bombing American-style was "clean," while area bombing British-style was "dirty," was challenged in September 1944 by John Ford, a Jesuit priest, in an article entitled "The Morality of Obliteration Bombing."[25]

Ford defined "obliteration bombing" as "strategic bombing ... in which the target to be wiped out is not a definite factory, bridge, or a similar object, but a large section of a whole city, comprising one-third to two-thirds of its whole built-up area, and including by design the residential districts of workingmen and their families."[26] This obviously includes an attack on life, limb, and property of many civilians. Ford went on to inquire whether obliteration bombing could be morally defended.

One way of defending it was to argue that in modern war, hardly any civilians remained uninvolved in their country's war effort, and that therefore hardly any civilians were morally protected against harm. Ford granted that civilian involvement in modern war was greater that in earlier ages, but denied that this development had made the very notion of innocent civilians obsolete. He proceeded with a detailed calculation of what fraction of a nation's population could be considered as directly and significantly contributing the war effort, and concluded that "even in a most totally war-minded country in the world the certainly innocent civilians far outnumber those whose status could be considered doubtful."[27]

As indicated above, the American news media and the USAAF consistently denied that American bombers were "aiming at innocent civilians." The argument, which seems to assume the principle of double effect, was that the bombing was aimed at military installations, war-related industries, and communications of the enemy; that is, it aimed at a good effect. It also had a bad effect, namely the injury and death of civilians and the destruction of their property. But the latter effect was not intended, but only foreseen; it was not a means to the production of the good effect, but merely an incidental, side-effect of the bombing. Ford endorsed the principle of double effect, but argued that in this case it was being misapplied. Its misapplication resulted in a much too simple solution, "advising the air strategist to let go his bombs, but withhold his intention."[28] Yet, in view of the nature of obliteration bombing, its strategist could not honestly claim not to be intending to harm civilians. Ford's conclusion concerning obliteration bombing was that "it is impossible to adopt this strategy without having a direct intent of violating the rights of innocent civilians. This intent is, of course, gravely immoral."[29]

The Path to Dresden

Vera Brittain and Father Ford's *cris de coeur* had some effect. Roosevelt himself responded to Brittain through a letter from his secretary, Steven Early, published in the April 1944 issue of *Fellowship*. Early reported that the President was disturbed by civilian casualties, but the best remedy for civilian casualties was to win the war, and then abolish the "philosophy" that would lead to future wars.[30] Administration spokesmen were reminded to reiterate that American planes aimed only at military targets.

In the late summer of 1944, a battle raged inside the Roosevelt Administration and inside the USAAF as to whether the Air Force should make a full conversion to area bombing. General Lawrence Kuter, the assistant chief of staff for USAAF war plans, stated that "it is contrary to our national ideals to wage war on civilians,"[31] which would imply that American "national ideals" were directly in conflict with AWPD-1. By the fall of 1944, the protests against obliteration bombing had subsided and dissenting voices within the USAAF had been marginalized. How did this happen? In his book *Wings of Judgment*, Ronald Schaffer suggests that the change in bombing policy came from Roosevelt, who is reported to have told Secretary of the Treasury Henry Morgenthau in August of 1944: "We have to get tough with Germany, and I mean the German people. We either have to castrate the German people or treat them in such a manner so they can't just go on reproducing people who want to act the way they have in the past."[32] But the suggestion that American bombing policy was significantly influenced by Roosevelt is hard to believe. Roosevelt had never involved himself in details of military operations; he left these matters either to military professionals or to subordinates. According to General Hansell, Roosevelt signed AWPD-1 without ever reading it, and there is no record of USAAF staff responding to directives from the White House. But if we return to AWPD-1, we discover that the plan calls for terror raids against cities when it is apparent to the enemy that the war is lost, and that certainly must have been the case for most Germans by the fall of 1944. Thus, we do not really have to account for a "change" in bombing policy in early 1944. What happened was in the plan from the beginning.

What the American People Knew

By 1943, the RAF began to destroy German cities, one after the other, while the Americans, in the earlier phases of AWPD-1, were sticking with daylight precision bombing. The contrast between the effects of British bombing and American bombing, in 1943, are clear in retrospect. But war coverage in American newspapers lauded British efforts as much as the American; indeed, as the interest in Michie's book suggests, newspaper editorials wondered why the Americans were not more like the

British. To demand that the British act more like the Americans might be perceived as an insult to an ally.

Consider the *New York Times* coverage of the raid on Hamburg in July 1943, the source of the first man-made firestorm in history. As previously noted, the RAF struck against the center of Hamburg, while the Americans aimed their bombs at the docks and waterfront. Nevertheless, the headline "Biggest RAF-U.S. Raids on Reich blast Hamburg, Hit Baltic Cities" lumps the two attacks together, and the article proceeds:

> The RAF night bombers in fifty blazing minutes blasted Hamburg with 2,300 tons of explosive bombs, a far greater weight of bombs than ever before had been dropped in a single operation. ... The RAF dropped an average of fifty-two tons of explosives and incendiaries every minute on Hamburg harbor and its shipbuilding yards and vital industrial plants, smashing ground defenses and scattering them ... Large formations of American Flying Fortresses staged the follow-up daylight raid on Hamburg, raining hundreds of 500 pound bombs in mid afternoon through great clouds of smoke rising thousands of feet from the fires started by the RAF armada. The Hamburg assault [said Brig. Gen. Frederick Anderson of the US Eighth Air Force] involved "coordination with the RAF, both in planning and execution."[33]

In an accompanying editorial, the *New York Times* rejected German claims that the raid on Hamburg was designed to cause terror, claiming that the city was a major seaport and an important industrial center.[34] Nevertheless, the destruction in Hamburg was so extensive that the paper stopped short of describing the devastation as collateral damage. On July 31, six days after the initial article on the Hamburg raid, the *New York Times* reprinted a U.P. dispatch from London:

> The great German port of Hamburg, smashed by 8,000 tons of bombs in six days and nights of merciless Allied air assault, was described by eyewitnesses today as a city of smoke-blackened ruins, with more than 31,000 of its people dead or wounded and the Nazi authorities preparing to evacuate the mass of the civilian population. ... Fires started by the RAF and American bombers have caused widespread damage in the inner harbor area ... Destruction in other areas of the city was said to be indescribable ... More than 130,000 homeless refugees were reported to have been sent into eastern Germany.[35]

The July 31 article, carried on page six, prompted no accompanying editorial. I have found no American newspaper editorial directed specifically at the destruction of Hamburg. Apparently, no newspaper in the United States thought that the killing of 31,000 people in a single day was worth editorial reflection. Note, furthermore, that the article refers to "Allied bombing" and does not distinguish the American from the British contribution.

The conflation of British bombing with American bombing also characterized the coverage of Dresden. The initial headline in the *New York Times* read "Rail City Blasted: 500 U.S. Heavies Bomb Town in Direct Path of Red Army Troops." The article proceeded: "The great aerial offensive in support of the Russian front ... surged into its third day today. ... The day-and-night bombing pattern, started off by the Royal Air Force and the United States Army Air Force Tuesday and Wednesday, was repeated."[36]

It is almost as if the *New York Times* wanted to blend British and American bombing policies rather than distinguish them. The suggestion that the raid had as its main result the killing of civilians and the destruction of art was rebuffed: "The Germans pulled out all the stops on the sympathy propaganda, reporting that Dresden 'has been turned into a heap of ruins' and that 'irreplaceable art treasures have been transformed into smoking, pulverized rubble.' However, a previous announcement indicated that as in Britain and France, portable art objects had long since been removed to safety vaults."

So the first thrust of newspaper reportage contended that Dresden was a strategic target. But the military purpose of bombing Dresden remained vague. How could bombing Dresden help the Red Army? The idea was that the roads would be clogged with terrorized civilians, disrupting the German retreat. About the terror the *New York Times* made no excuses: "German Terror Mounts" proclaimed a sub-headline. "The latest attacks created manifest terror in Germany ... Reports from Sweden told of 'huge oceans of fire' raging in that city ... Swedish radio reported 20,000 to 35,000 people had been killed in the first 24 hours of the Allied assault. It added that 200,000 residents had fled in panic."[37]

And even if one argued that the Dresden attacks were not intended to cause this panic, the destruction of Dresden was wholly out of proportion to any conceivable military gain. The British and the Americans, starting from different strategic premises, converged over the skies of Saxony in an attack, not against German troops, but against the German people, contrary to basic principles of just war. As the *New York Times* editorialized, or confessed, two days after Dresden:

> From east and west, and most devastatingly from the skies, it is being brought home to the German people that they are merely making the cost of their defeat heavier to themselves by continuing a hopeless resistance. If in that resistance more landmarks of European culture and Germany's own better past must be wiped out, the Germans may, as they were drilled to do, thank their Fuehrer for the result.[38]

Conclusion

The text of AWPD-1 shows that American military leaders, even before the war with Germany began, chose as the primary goal of the war effort the destruction of German infrastructure. Detailed plans for the destruction of the German canal system, the electrical grid, and heating oil supplies were drawn up in the summer of 1941. But the goal of "producing mass hypothermia" by precision daylight bombing is just as immoral as the British goal of destroying German cities by nighttime area bombing.

What the air-raids meant for the German people was made clear to the American public in reports in major American newspapers in 1942 and 1943. No murmur of disapproval can be found in the American press about either precision bombing or area bombing in 1942 or 1943. What was happening on the ground in Germany simply did not register with the American people.

A debate in the United States about the morality of American bombing in Germany began in 1944. The American people were given a moment to reflect on what their country was doing. But the argument against the bombing was generally rejected, and as a result, the American people, as well as the military leadership, should be held accountable for what was done. The American participation in the Dresden raid was not an irrational aberration from the general design of American bombing. It was part of the policy from 1941. Given that the public criticism of American bombing, begun by American church leaders in spring 1944, fizzled out soon after D-Day, it must be concluded that mass killings of German civilians in air attacks were implicitly endorsed by a large majority of the American people. The old legal principle applies: silence implies assent.

Notes

1. All references to "American" or "America" within this chapter refer to the United States of America or the citizens thereof and do not include any other country in North or South America or the citizens thereof.
2. *New York Times*, 1 June 1944, 18.
3. Quoted in Ronald Schaffer, *Wings of Judgment: American Bombing in World War II* (New York and Oxford: Oxford University Press, 1985), 99.
4. The story of the development of AWPD-1 is most completely told in Haywood Hansell Jr., *The Air Plan that Defeated Hitler* (Atlanta: Higgins-McArthur/Longino & Porter, 1972). All direct quotations from the plan are taken from Appendix IV of this book.
5. This is, to my knowledge, the first time that the phrase "area bombing" appears in an American military document.

6. This is a broad conclusion stated in very broad strokes. The historical details involve many ironic shifts. Hansell, the principal author of AWPD-1, in fact opposed the area bombing of Japanese cities in January 1945. Mainly for this reason, Hansell was relieved of his command in February 1945 by Curtis LeMay, who had no qualms about bombing Japanese cities.
7. For the British decision to abandon area bombing for precision bombing see Max Hastings, *Bomber Command* (New York: Dial Press, 1979), 135–157.
8. The best account of this intense British pressure is in Thomas M. Coffey, *Decision over Schweinfurt* (New York: David McKay, 1977), 133–157.
9. Memo quoted in Coffey, *Decision over Schweinfurt*, 168.
10. Wesley Frank Craven and James Lea Cate, *The Army Air Forces in World War II* (Chicago: University of Chicago Press, 1949), vol. 2: 355.
11. Ibid.
12. See Leroy W. Newby, *Target Ploesti* (Novato, CA: Presidio Press, 1983).
13. Craven and Cate, *The Army Air Forces*, vol. 2: 705.
14. "The majority of Germans today know, or so at least it is to be hoped, that we actually provoked the annihilation of the cities in which we once lived" (W.G. Sebald, *On the Natural History of Destruction*, trans. Anthea Bell (London: Hamish Hamilton, 2003), 103).
15. *New York Times*, 25 July 1943, 1.
16. *Boston Herald*, 4 July 1944.
17. *New York Times*, 31 July 1943, 6.
18. Allan A. Michie, *The Air Offensive Against Germany* (New York: Henry Holt, 1943), 1–10, passim.
19. Ibid., 344.
20. Ibid., 218. The effects are still visible in Rouen today. Compare the splendid limestone of the cathedral with the squalid concrete of nearby structures built to replace those destroyed by the USAAF.
21. *Boston Herald*, 4 July 1944.
22. *Fellowship* X, March 1944, 50. Brittain's article consisted of excerpts from her book *Seed of Chaos* (London: New Vision, 1944), which she began writing in 1943. The book does not distinguish between British area bombing and American precision bombing, but the examples of destruction in her book are taken from RAF raids.
23. The signatories included Rev. Dr. George Butterworth, Madison Avenue Presbyterian Church, and Rev. Dr. Harry Emerson Fosdick, Riverside Church (Episcopalian), both nationally prominent Protestant leaders.
24. James M. Gillis, "Editorial Comment," *Catholic World* 159, May 1944: 97.
25. John C. Ford, S.J., "The Morality of Obliteration Bombing," *Theological Studies*, vol. 5 (1944): 261–309. An abridged version is reprinted in Richard A. Wasserstrom, ed., *War and Morality* (Belmont, CA: Wadsworth Publishing Co., 1970). My references are to the reprinted version.
26. Ibid., 24.
27. Ibid., 22.
28. Ibid., 27.
29. Ibid., 32.

30. Early, *Fellowship* X, April 1944: 79. Brittain replied that Early's letter was "irrelevant, unjustified, and destructive of the very ideals with which the American people went to war" (*Fellowship* X, June 1944: 1).
31. Schaffer, *Wings of Judgment*, 81.
32. Ibid., 88. Apparently, Roosevelt believed that if the Germans were frightened by bombing, their children would also be likely to be frightened by bombing. The doctrine that acquired characteristics are inheritable dies hard.
33. *New York Times*, 26 July 1943, 7.
34. Ibid., 26 July 1943, 18.
35. *New York Times*, 31 July 1943, 6.
36. *New York Times*, 16 February 1945, 1.
37. Ibid., 6.
38. "Doom Over Germany," *New York Times*, 16 February 1945, 22.

CHAPTER 3

Under the Bombs
Earl R. Beck

The four months from May through August of 1943 were marked by a series of major setbacks for Germany's war efforts both at home and on the battlefronts. They began on May 12 and 13 as the German armies in North Africa surrendered to the British. The radio report from the famed and once victorious Africa Corps read: "Munition exhausted. Weapons and war materials destroyed. The German Africa Corps has fought as ordered until it is no longer capable of fighting. The German Africa Corps must be born again! Heia Safari!"[1]

The "desert fox," Field Marshal Erwin Rommel, had been called home prior to the end of the fighting. Some Germans speculated that the news of his "illness" that circulated two months after the actual recall was just an excuse to save him from the same fate as Field Marshal Paulus at Stalingrad.[2] The term Tunisgrad began to circulate for this second defeat, but there was none of the deep pathos associated with the tragedy in Russia.[3] The number of those taken prisoner, some 130,000 German soldiers, was larger than that of those captured by the Russians, but there was not the same last desperate (senseless) fighting as in Stalingrad and reports circulated that the Germans accepted the end of their desert hardships with relief, even cheerfully.[4] At least there were letters home from these prisoners. Prisoners of war in Canada wrote that things there went "exceptionally well" and that they were "especially well fed."[5] There was not the cold, heart-wrenching silence that covered the fate of those who had fallen into the hands of the Russians.[6]

The defeat in Tunis was followed by Allied attacks on the Italian islands of Pantelleria and Lampedusa and Allied landings in Sicily on July 10. Mussolini fell from power on July 24, and by August 17, the German and Italian forces had given up the struggle in Sicily and evacuated to the Italian mainland. And to many Germans, especially those in southern Germany, it seemed likely that the road northward into the homeland would be covered quickly.[7]

Meanwhile, a quiet period on the eastern front was broken with the opening of Hitler's planned *Fall Zitadelle* (Operation Citadel), designed to breach Soviet tank forces in the Ukraine and create a new dynamism for the German forces stalled since Stalingrad. The great tank battle around the city of Kursk began on July 4. By the twelfth, the Russians were in control of the battlefield. The new German *Panther* tanks had proved faulty and Soviet defensive strategy had foiled the German plans for a new offensive. Although Soviet losses were more serious than German losses, the Soviets' recovery was rapid—their operational tanks on July 5 numbered 3,800; by July 13, they had shrunk to less than 1,500; but by August 3, they were back to 2,750.[8] Citadel was to be the last great German drive on the eastern front. From this point on, it was the Russians who seized the initiative, who began to push the Germans out of hard-won gains, and who moved grimly westward toward the German homeland. Citadel symbolized a coming defeat—the only hope was for a stabilization of the front, not for great victories.

The news from the battlefronts weighed heavily on the home front. But those at home confronted increasing peril from bombing raids that became more numerous, attacked new as well as old targets, and wreaked ever more havoc and destruction. The months of May and June of 1943 were a shocking prelude to the even more shocking catastrophe visited upon Hamburg in July. In sixteen major raids, the British dropped over 24,000 tons of bombs on German cities, most of them within the industrial zone along the Rhine and Ruhr rivers. In each of these raids, an average of 1,500 tons of bombs were dropped. But these cold figures give little comprehension of the destructive combination of thousands of incendiary bombs and hundreds of enormous explosive bombs and land mines that blasted whole city streets into ruins. Dortmund, in two visits, came under 3,500 tons of bombs; Düsseldorf, in two raids, suffered almost 4,000 tons of bombs. Bochum, in two raids, was hit with 2,500 tons and Cologne in two visits, received 2,200 tons of bombs. Duisburg, Essen, Wuppertal, Emden, Oberhausen, Krefeld, Mülheim, Gelsenkirchen, Kiel, and Bremen were also attacked during this two-month period.[9]

In this "battle of the Ruhr," many of the cities were close enough that the inhabitants of one city could see the raids taking place in neighboring cities. Josef Fischer watched the destruction of Wuppertal exactly a year after the thousand-bomber raid on his own city, Cologne. Two days later, he traveled there to see the results—"an ash heap around which the ruins of the houses provide the background scenery." In the streets, he wrote, there was total silence except when another stone dropped from the wall of a house. A new phase in the bombing war had been opened,

Fischer thought—the total destruction of a city.[10] And to his nagging self-questioning of how he might protect his own home in his own city—water, he decided, was the answer. Every floor of his home was loaded with water, in cans, tubs, the bath tub, everything possible, and sand, stone, and cement were placed in the cellar to repair damages there."[11]

Goebbels was still the only major Nazi leader brave enough to visit the devastated cities. He visited Dortmund, where he found the destruction "virtually total." The raid on that city on the night of May 23/24 was, he thought, probably the worst ever directed against a German city (over 2,000 tons of bombs had been dropped).[12] Again Goebbels expressed his concern for the survival of Germany under these circumstances. The only bright spot he could find was the fairly "respectable" number of planes shot down.[13] The only difficulty with this was that canny Germans multiplied the number of planes destroyed by ten to get the probable number of enemy planes involved in a raid, and the result did not help to boost popular morale.[14] The rumors of heavy death tolls were supported by army reports that changed the earlier phrasing "the population suffered losses" to "the population suffered heavy losses." Figures of 15,000 deaths in Dortmund, 17,000 in Düsseldorf, and 27,000 in Wuppertal were circulated.[15] Adding to the horror of these numbers were stories of people turned into living torches by the phosphorus bombs, of others getting stuck in the hot asphalt of the streets, and of many throwing themselves into the nearby rivers only to find that the fire rekindled when they emerged into the air.[16]

The spectacular and partially successful British raids on the Eder, Sorpe, and Möhne dams in the same period (16/17 May 1943) resulted in some flooding in the Ruhr valley and caused great temporary concern among the population. Complete success would have resulted in considerable loss of life as well as a major reduction of production.[17] The obvious possibility that other dams might be breached added to the worries of the population. But neither the raids on the cities nor those on the dams produced the loss of life that was anticipated by the attackers and rumored among the victims. The total wartime losses of the three cities named above were far below the estimates current at the time: Dortmund, 6,341; Düsseldorf, 5,863; and Wuppertal, 7,150.[18] The relatively modest losses underscore the success of the air-raid shelters provided, the effectiveness of the instructions for air-raid precautions, and, most of all, the courage and determination of the people themselves.

The personal accounts of bombing raids by the pilots concerned far outnumber the personal accounts written by the bombed. Perhaps the best of the relatively rare accounts by the victims is that of Josef Fischer, an inhabitant of the city of Cologne, who remained in that heavily bombed city until the very end of the war. On June 17, the city received its first attack of this period, a mild one since the weather was bad, most planes were recalled, and some of the bombs were simply dumped into the fields around the city. A modest death toll of 146 was scored from the bombs that were dropped, including 80 women and 34 children. But only 25,000 of the previous 250,000 homes were left undisturbed and streetcar service was completely disrupted. By now, food for those bombed out was reduced largely to potatoes. Ration cards were given out for products no longer obtainable. Placards and handbills warned the population that in the event of being buried in the next raid, one should knock on the walls with some hard object or even scratch with one's fingernails. The rescue crews were now provided with listening devices that could detect these sounds, and efforts to get attention by shouting or calling simply used up the available oxygen too rapidly. Fischer found himself a chisel that he placed in his cellar. This would allow him to take apart the cellar walls. He also heeded the advice of having rags and water cans with covers placed there so that in the event of close strikes, one could breathe through moistened rags to filter out the dust and dirt.[19]

The test of these preparations was not long in coming. On the night of 28/29 June 1943, Cologne suffered under another raid.[20] This time the weather did not save the city. Five hundred and forty British planes dropped 1,614 tons of bombs. The anti-aircraft guns kept up an unceasing fire. Around Fischer in his cellar fell explosive bombs in an unbroken series, producing the succession of pressure-suction-pressure-suction that became familiar to Germans during the bombings. Fire bombs fell on the grounds about the house. Those waiting in the cellar should have left the shelter to extinguish the fires that were probably starting overhead, but exploding bombs prevented it. They waited fearfully in their shelter. Only by sound could they distinguish what was occurring—every bomb had its own peculiar sound. If there was a rustle like a flock of doves flying up, it was a bundle of small stick bombs breaking apart, with each stick finding its own target. If there was a short, sharp explosion, it was a 12-kilogram firebomb, which could spread fire eighty meters in all directions. If it was like a bucket of water splashing in the street, it was a 14-kilogram liquid firebomb, which could spread liquid rubber and benzine fifty meters around the impact area. If it plumped down like a wet sack, it was a fire canister holding twenty liters of benzol, somewhat cruder but as effective as benzine. If it cracked like an explosive bomb as it hit, it was either a 106-kilogram bomb that threw out rags soaked with benzine or heavy oil or a 112-kilogram firebomb, which covered nearby houses with a thousand "cowcakes" of benzol and rubber. And there were still, of course, the explosive bombs and mines, which tore out the doors and windows to provide air to feed the flames and surpassed the effects of an earthquake, so that those in the cellar thought of themselves as perched in the heart of a volcano.

In the midst of all this destruction, a sound came from the cellar of Fischer's neighbor. A hole was opened in the wall between the houses. When they were asked what was wrong, the neighbors answered that the cellar stairs were on fire and that the fire was in the cellar itself already. The hole was opened wider—women, children, a soldier, a civilian, suitcases, and a cradle with a crying baby made their way through the aperture. One great suitcase fell open to reveal only a woman's black straw hat and a jar of marmalade—its owner was undoubtedly mentally unsound. A woman was crying because her husband was still next door, but refused to leave the remnants of his home. Soon they discovered that the fire next door would shortly set afire a coal supply there—the oxygen supply in both cellars would be rapidly used up. The old man had to come over so that the hole could be closed. Eventually, they persuaded the recalcitrant old fellow to give up his lost home. The piece of sheet iron that Fischer had stored for such purposes was placed over the hole and covered with sand. The soldier, almost a civilian since he had left his rifle and knapsack next door, told them it was better in Russia than here.

The sound of falling bombs ceased. They crept above, fighting smoke and dust to extinguish the fires there. Fischer's use of flame retardant had helped to save much of his house. But no door could be opened without a fearsome in-pouring of heat. Every house in the neighborhood was burning. Every window, every corner, every tree, every bush was lit in the colors of the flames—sometimes yellow, sometimes red, sometimes white. At six in the morning, the firestorm came. The air was sucked in from the surrounding areas to feed the flames until they soared to the clouds. Seventy or eighty people were now in this one cellar. All waited to see whether the fire would die down or bring them death. Fischer moved his little family into a supply cellar where the air was better. He and others fought the fires in the house and waited. By noon, the fires had died down. One by one, the people in the cellar picked up their most cherished possessions and trudged off to seek new homes—probably, thought Fischer, in the surrounding area, but not in Cologne itself.

Those in the cellar had survived. But many others had not been so lucky. Hundreds of scarcely recognizable remains, merely identified by fragments and by the location of the bodies, were laid out in great halls and tagged for the information of anxious relatives or the always needed public records. Some had died in fearful fashion. The body of a pregnant woman was found on the sidewalk outside a hospital. In the midst of the bombing, she had given birth before reaching the hospital, but both mother and newborn infant were consumed by the flames. In sixty minutes of bombing, the lives of 3,460 people were snuffed out and 400,000 people lost their homes. But the army distributed bread, fat, sausage, and milk. For the weary survivors, life went on. And many people in Cologne still wanted to stay "at home."

In the margins of this story, we find various attempts at an organized response to the crisis, sometimes successful, sometimes not. There are the air-raid regulations, written, says Fischer, by a man working in the daylight, sitting quietly at his desk in a clean and comfortable room—regulations that make no sense when put into practice in the darkness of the night with the heat of the flames all around. There is the fire-retarding treatment, which does work. There are the firefighters called in from an area one hundred kilometers around Cologne, but refusing to help until the proper orders come and sleeping while the fires burn merrily around them. There is the distribution of supplies, which helps to soften the harshness of events. And there is the careful collection and labeling of the bones of the dead.

Two of the rare diaries of the war period present cogent appreciations of the popular mood in this time of trial. Gottfried Benn wrote that "the situation becomes ever more enigmatic; it is in the long run only mythologically to be experienced and understood, if one wants to try to deal with it."[21] And in similar fashion, Horst Lange confided in his diary: "How much is everything placed in question! Every plan of life and every kind of tie [to the past]." But he added that one could always begin again and that "the people are astoundingly calm.—One endures everything; one would even endure the end of the world calmly, I believe, so weary is one already."[22]

There were, undoubtedly, some Germans who still believed in the magic weapons of which Goebbels spoke, closer to reality than the propaganda minister knew, or in the possible success of that last desperate effort of the marathon runner who might break the tape before his rivals. But the great masses carried on because there was nothing to do but to carry on, with the hope that somehow they would be among those who survived. *Überleben* (survival) became the motif of life—not to be burned up in a firestorm, killed on the battlefront, or executed by a dying regime. In sorrow, in weariness, in dull anxiety about the future, one continued to farm, to make guns and tanks and planes, to search for food, to "party" if one had a chance, to sit in the air-raid shelters as the bombs landed ever closer, to listen to the foreign radio broadcasts even if this was dangerous, because they told more about what was taking place than the official reports of the regime did, to hold on to what possessions one could as the fragility of ownership became ever more apparent, and, most of all, to survive—not to see the glorious new world pictured by the Nazis but to take on the future, however it might come. In this attitude, there was both courage and resignation, morale and lack of morale. Where Benn wrote that the period could only be understood "mythologically," one might, perhaps, substitute the word "primordially," with emotions, objectives, hopes, and fears reduced to the most elementary of expression.

There was, indeed, in the bombing of Hamburg much of the "mythological" or "primordial," although the British planners of the attacks gave the operation the biblical designation "Gomorrah." The stated objective, "to destroy Hamburg," carries one back to the days of the Greeks and the Romans and the destruction of Troy and Carthage, except that instead of the Roman Senator Cato demanding the eradication of Carthage, this time it was the British commander of the Royal Air Force Bomber Command, Sir Arthur Harris, who set in motion on 27 May 1943, "the process of elimination" of Germany's second largest city.[23] Harris was, of course, doing no more than what Hitler himself had threatened to do in respect to British cities on 4 September 1940. In his speech at the Sportpalast in Berlin in that more optimistic period, he had promised that the German *Luftwaffe* would reply to British air attacks every night in increasing measure and that it would "eradicate their cities."[24] But that a British general should follow in the footsteps of the *Führer* was not greatly to his honor, and that he could accompany this move with the use of a biblical title that suggested that he was the omnipotent God Almighty raining down fire and sulfur on the evil inhabitants of a modern Gomorrah underscores a megalomaniac character. There is in any war that blighting of sensibilities that allows those on the battlefront to fire bullets against the enemy that may kill or simply maim, to send cannon shells that tear at the viscerals or lop off the foe's arms or legs, and to direct the flame thrower that engulfs the enemy tank and sends its occupants screaming in agony from its oven-like interior. But to contemplate the blanketing of a great city of well over one million inhabitants with explosives and fire in order to destroy thousands (in planning conception, hundreds of thousands) of women and children along with the male soldiers or armament workers who might be there was a return to the most primitive conceptions of warfare.

To a considerable degree, the British were prisoners of the weapons they possessed and of the exigencies of the war they were fighting. Unable as yet to attack Germany by land, with the fighting in Italy still far from the German borders, and with the German submarines now virtually eliminated from the scene, the British had only one way to bring the war home to Germany—from the air. To do this more effectively, they had built more and better bombers and constructed larger and more effective bombs. To justify these expenditures, to maintain morale at home, and (they hoped) to sabotage the morale of the enemy, the bombers had to destroy more houses, buildings, and factories, and kill more of the enemy. For this purpose, the "destruction" of a city would provide a clear symbol of the effectiveness of the weapons employed. Hamburg lent itself well to this objective—as Harris stated at the time, "I had always wanted to have a real dead set at Hamburg. It was the second biggest city in Germany and I wanted to make a tremendous show."[25]

As this quotation indicates, it was the size of Hamburg that governed Harris's plan more than the status of the city as a producer of submarines or its role as Germany's major seaport. A little later, Harris was to look to Germany's largest city, Berlin, as a goal and to suggest optimistically that "we can wreck Berlin from end to end if the USAAF will come in on it. It will cost between us 400–500 aircraft. It will cost Germany the war."[26] By this time, he was also keeping an account of the effects of aerial bombardment in terms of the degree of destruction of the cities bombed and the number of persons killed. "Total destruction" was to answer Germany's concept of "total war."

Hamburg, of course, fulfilled several other qualifications attached to target goals at this particular stage of aerial warfare. By careful planning, it could be reached without an excessively lengthy flight over German-held territory. Its location on the coast and the easily recognizable water areas in and about the city would facilitate the identification of target areas. And portions of the city lent themselves to the effective use of the bombing weapon that had increasingly demonstrated its destructive capacity—fire. There was, of course, contrary to what some inhabitants of the city had hoped, no consideration of the fact that the city had once been a stronghold of anti-Nazi Social Democrats or that it had had significant business and commercial relationships with both England and the United States.

Tactically, too, the planning for the raids on the city provided an opportunity for significant trials of new procedures. First of all, the raids were to be accompanied by the first use of "Window," the dropping of thousands of pieces of tin foil colored black on one side to produce "snow" on the German radar, thus confusing those directing opposing fighter planes seeking to intercept the bombers and rendering ineffective the radar-directed German anti-aircraft batteries. Secondly, the target-marking procedures were greatly improved with the "pathfinders," who located and marked the aiming point with red indicators and who were provided with a back-up force, which renewed these target indicators with green flares dropped at specified intervals. Instructions were also given that those planes that came in later should overshoot the markers by two seconds, a device intended to prevent the customary "creep back" of the bombs from the targeted area that had occurred in previous raids because of the tendency of bomber crews to try to get rid of their bombs as soon as possible when they were in areas heavily protected by anti-aircraft fire.[27]

Finally, Hamburg was to be the target of the largest concentration of British bombers since the thousand-bomber raid on Cologne. The plans called for repeated attacks on the city with the American Eighth Air Force now operative from English airfields cooperating with the British night raids through follow-up daytime missions. These plans were to eventuate in seven air-raids on Hamburg, beginning with the British night raid in the early morning hours of Sunday, 25 July 1943, followed by two American daylight raids on the same day and on Monday, July 26, a British harassing raid with light mosquito bombers on the night of Tuesday, July 27, followed by the most damaging British raid on the night of Wednesday, July 28, and two more British night raids on Friday, July 30, and Tuesday, August 3.

These raids were not the first launched against the city on the Elbe. The official records of Hamburg's police chief counted the raid of July 25 as the 138th raid on the city.[28] The city had been included among the ninety-four places in Germany designated as those in most danger of enemy air attacks.[29] Its organization and planning for air-raid defenses, although by no means fully adequate, were better than those of many German cities. Although the construction of the bunker- or tower-type shelters that offered protection against the direct or near hit of high explosive bombs had lagged behind needs, every inhabitant of the city had access before the July raids to at least the kind of shelter that protected against the flying fragments of bombs or of buildings struck by bombs. Where private cellars were to be employed, connections to adjoining cellars had been provided, equipped with heavy iron doors allowing escape in two directions and the sealing off of damaged sections. Air-raid services, fire-fighting forces, special repair crews, and first-aid services had been well planned and equipped. The only problems arising in these areas resulted from the intrusion into these functions of party agencies acting with more arrogance than efficiency.[30]

Even before the war, fire-fighting experts in Hamburg had realized the dangers of prospective fire bombing for German cities.[31] The early wartime bombing had spurred efforts to secure new equipment. By the time of the July bombings, the city had 305 new fire engines, 935 portable power pumps, 49 fire boats, and 312 kilometers of fire hose—enough to have reached from Hamburg to Berlin.[32] Efforts had been made, as elsewhere, to clear the attics of old furniture and other burnable materials, but often this resulted in the storing of this kind of property in empty stores used as a kind of warehouse, which created a whole new and perhaps more dangerous fire hazard.[33] Moreover, Hamburg fire authorities had discovered from earlier raids that the small, four-pound stick bombs, which the British used in large numbers, did not simply lodge in the upper stories as had been anticipated. Planning procedures had called for those in the cellar air-raid shelters to check periodically for fires in the upper stories and extinguish them before they could set the house or building completely on fire. However, experience showed that these small firebombs fell with such force that they could often penetrate several stories.[34] Moreover, the British had adopted the practice of fitting a portion of these stick bombs with an explosive charge, which made the prescribed "self-help" measures to extinguish them increasingly perilous.[35] These relatively cheap weapons were overall probably the most effective bombing weapon employed in World War II prior to the development of the atom bomb.

The British raid on the night of July 24 was a severe one. It came just after midnight, hence early on the Sunday morning of July 25. Seven hundred and forty of the original 791 bombers leaving England arrived over the target. The dropping of "Window," the strips of foil designed to confuse enemy radar, proved very effective in diminishing the accuracy of enemy fighter activity and of the anti-aircraft defense of the city. There was the customary inaccuracy of the pathfinder "markers," who laid the target indicators for the main body of bombers, but these were not so severe as they had been in some of the earlier raids. Although only 306 of the bombers released their bombs within a three-mile radius of the goal, the heavy loads of bombs were concentrated in a closely built-up section of the inner city and adjacent areas. They caused, as a consequence, fires of unprecedented size and scope. Even the late-arriving bombers, which tended to drop their bombs before reaching the main target area, created much havoc in the northwestern sections of the city.[36]

In spite of all the preparations, the city's fire-fighting forces were challenged beyond their capabilities. In many places, the extinction of the fires was made more difficult by the fact that supplies of coal and coke, stored for the coming winter months, caught fire. The central police station burned down, but the command center in its underground bunker survived. The streets were filled with rubble, and fire engines could not traverse them. Those that tried lost their tires and some were caught in the bombing. Gas, water, and electricity lines were damaged. Water for the fire services had to be brought from storage basins or open waterways. Although help was brought in from Lübeck, Kiel, and Berlin, the Hamburg firefighters for the first time found themselves unable to extinguish the fires by nightfall on the day of the attack. At 4:15 on the morning of July 26, the weary fire chief was summoned out of bed to the headquarters of the chief SS officer of the city to explain his incompetence in not having put out the fires and was told that all fires had to be out by noon of that day. The firemen were able to curtail open flames by that Monday evening, in spite of the two US daylight raids that took place on Sunday afternoon and Monday morning.[37] Both of these attacks concentrated on the harbor area. The first destroyed an unfinished ocean liner, the *Vaterland*, which was being used for lumber storage, and both raids damaged docks and business establishments in the harbor area. As in several later US daylight raids, a considerable number of planes were lost in the operations, but the mere fact that the enemy could venture to attack in broad daylight had a significantly depressing effect on German morale.[38]

But the recovery in Hamburg from the first raid was relatively rapid. Free editions, combining the efforts of the local newspapers, were distributed on Sunday. Special three-day food rations were made available along with 50 grams of real bean coffee, 10 extra cigarettes, 125 grams of sweets, and half a bottle of spirits to calm the nerves of the survivors. The news reports paid more heed to the fall of Mussolini than to the raid on Hamburg. Orders were issued forbidding workers to leave the city, but some had already begun to seek safer havens.[39]

On Tuesday, six British mosquito bombers engaged in a few "bites" over Hamburg, doing little damage but demonstrating their virtual invulnerability from the German defenses. Perhaps they also warned the people of Hamburg that it was not over yet. The water tanks were full. The fire hoses were back in order. The people who remained in the city went to the best air-raid shelters possible, filling them beyond reasonable capacity. Thousands had already decided that security lay somewhere else than in Hamburg.[40] All of their apprehensions became justified on the night of Wednesday, July 28, the "firestorm night," when Hamburg suffered the most devastating raid inflicted on any German city.[41]

The horrors of this raid have been retold many times. One major German study and two English ones have appeared within the last five years. What occurred quickly became a matter of myth as well as fact. The memories of the hundreds of thousands who survived were barely sampled. Rumors had as much effect both at home and abroad as did the official reports.

There were almost the same number of British planes involved as on the early morning of July 25. Seven hundred and twenty-two bombers arrived over the city. There was the same marking procedure—the targeted point was somewhat east and south of the point that had been laid down for the first attack. There was a little less "creep back" of the bombs from the target area this time. A slightly higher percentage of planes dropped their bombs within the three-mile circumference around the aiming point.

The weight of the bombs dropped was approximately the same as in the first raid.[42] But this time, the results were far more catastrophic. Partly this was due to the more accurate bombing, partly to the atmospheric conditions, which converted what might have been an ordinary firestorm into a much more severe one. The days prior to these raids had been part of a long period of hot, dry weather. The temperatures during the first part of July had risen as high as 90°F (32°C) in the shade. Night temperatures also remained abnormally high. The moisture content of the air on this particular night was as low as 30 percent. Remnants of smoke and dust from the earlier bombings tended to preserve ground temperatures. At the same time, a low-pressure area lay north of Hamburg along the coastline, in close proximity to the high-pressure area that had covered the city.

Any firebombing raid tended to create rapidly rising heat drafts. In many bombed cities, these created firestorms of varying intensity. But the unusual climatic conditions in Hamburg created very abnormal circumstances. As the incendiary bombs fell, the heated air rose much more rapidly than usual—the smoke rose to observable heights of four to five miles. The air brought in from the areas surrounding the major fires attained cyclonic force. Ground-level Hamburg became the fire pan of a gigantic oven. The heat level in large portions of the city reached completely unbearable heights.[43] The fires were fed from the previously existing rubble and the new damage done by the explosive bombs that accompanied the incendiaries. The winds tended to change direction quickly, sometimes completely reversing themselves, so that the extinguishing of fires in one area could be foiled by a new rush of flame from a totally different starting point. Moreover, the rapidity of the spread of the firestorm meant that the firefighters' efforts had to be mostly devoted to extricating people from the most seriously affected areas rather than to combating the raging flames.

Death took thousands of Hamburgers during this night. Some died softly, smothered by carbon monoxide within the air-raid cellars. Some died in agony, caught in the streets as the fires raged among those fleeing. Women found the thin summer dresses they wore aflame and tore them off as they ran. Some of them stumbled alive into the air-raid shelters—a completely naked woman in the advanced stages of pregnancy lurched through the door of one of the main fire department shelters and shortly afterwards delivered her child in the bunker. Other naked women lay among the dead on the streets, seemingly untouched by the flames but dying from the effects of the excessive heat. There were stories of the shrinking and mummification of those who died, of the horrible distortion of male sexual organs by the heat, of the reddened or browned faces of the victims. Condemned as rumors at the time, these accounts were verified by official police reports.[44] Thus, the oft-repeated stories of demented Hamburgers carrying bodies of deceased relatives in their suitcases—a man with the corpse of his wife and daughter,[45] a woman with the mummified body of her daughter,[46] or other women with the heads of their dead children[47]—gain some substance, together with the reports of autopsy efforts that could not pierce the skin of some dead bodies without the use of a saw or bone-cutters.[48] There were, of course, gross exaggerations. The common story that the asphalt of the streets melted and entrapped fleeing persons, in the most extreme form leaving them so engulfed that relatives came to place pillows under their heads and to feed the slowly dying captives until police bullets ended their misery, finds no factual support.[49] On the other hand, there seems to be ample evidence that phosphorus bombs were more heavily employed than the British were willing to admit.[50]

No brief resume can suggest the conduct of the Hamburgers during this enormous catastrophe. The confrontation of death measures personal, and not collective, character. There were heroes and non-heroes. There were those who died of carbon monoxide or heat exhaustion in their shelters when a dash to safety might have been possible. There were the heroes: the firemen who made perilous journeys through the fire-ravaged areas to help the escape of those trapped within them and the civilians who kept their heads when others were losing them and led or sometimes forced their fellows to move from certain death to security. The enormous courage necessary for those who sought to move through the streets ravaged by the cruel winds of the firestorm stands above and apart from any consideration of the political philosophy of those involved. There is no evidence that the heroes were Nazis giving their all for the sake of the *Führer*. On the other hand, there is no evidence that those who placed themselves in peril to save friends, neighbors, or unknown helpless women and children were non-Nazis or anti-Nazis. There was much evidence of panic—not surprising in view of the nature of events—and of irresolute apathy and surrender to fate. But any evidence of widespread disorder or rioting seems totally lacking.[51] Basic discipline was apparently upheld, although the firestorm night spurred an increasing evacuation of the city.

But the British had not completed their work with the firestorm night. Two nights later, on Friday, July 30, over seven hundred bombers again attacked the city. The area of main destruction completed a semi-hemispheric devastation of the city's center.[52] The Barmbek area was set aflame, but this time there was no great firestorm. Nevertheless, town authorities at the time believed that the raid was even more intense than the previous one. One of the most tragic episodes of the bombing occurred on this night as the exit from the public air-raid shelter of the building housing the great Karstadt department store was blocked and 370 persons died of carbon monoxide poisoning.[53] In this raid, it was also demonstrated that even the great tower bunkers, supposedly secure against direct hits, were not completely safe—a heavy explosive bomb penetrated the bunker in the Wielandstrasse, but miraculously only two women were killed, while the other two thousand occupants emerged frightened but unhurt.[54]

Over the weekend, the British gave the Hamburgers a rest while they blasted Remscheid and Düsseldorf. But on the night of Monday, August 2, seven hundred and forty bombers again started for Hamburg. Perhaps the Almighty felt Gomorrah had gone far enough. Thunderstorms prevented the arrival of more than half of the planes and rendered the dropping of bombs by those that did arrive scattered and uncertain. The state opera building was hit, but the food supplies stored in its foyer were saved. Otherwise, the loss of buildings and of people was relatively small.[55] By this time, a large part of the population had sought refuge outside the city. It took a while for them to return. They had no way of knowing that for the British their "Battle of Hamburg" was over.

Hamburg was the most serious victim of this hot summer of 1943. But other German cities suffered too. Cologne continued to be a frequent target of British attacks, but the cathedral, although damaged, survived and the railroad station still served its purpose.[56] The Währd section of Nuremberg was twice blanketed with bombing "carpets," and those beneath them suffered under the phosphorus bombs, with the same scenes as those in Hamburg of naked people who had torn off the clothing affected by the phosphorus and crowds of people black with dirt and sweat as they sought escape from the fire areas. For those who suffered, the only semi-comic relief came when the Gauleiter Karl Holz started his speech for the funeral of those who had lost their lives in this raid and was interrupted by a new alarm so that he had to talk of the "final victory" while the bombers flew over the city toward nearby Regensburg.[57]

The cities of the Ruhr were also repeated targets—along with Remscheid and Düsseldorf, named above, Duisburg, Essen, Gelsenkirchen, Wuppertal, and Leverkusen were continuously hit. There was even a kind of competition for the accolade of "worst-bombed city." The mayor of Duisburg pointed out in a memorandum that his city had, as early as September 1942, suffered a loss of 98.2 percent of its dwelling places whereas Cologne had only had 50 percent damaged.[58] Berlin, the capital, was not yet a significant competitor for such dubious honors. It was not until late in August that its days of trial began.

The US strategy of daylight bombing received several severe shocks during this period. The raid by the "Flying Fortresses" and "Liberators" on Schweinfurt on August 17 was far from successful—60 of the 376 planes that started for the attack were lost because of the German anti-aircraft and fighter attacks, and many of the bombs fell outside the target area. This was a prelude to an even more serious setback two months later on October 14.[59] But the records indicate that the flight of a great mass of US bombers across Germany in broad daylight had an enormous impact on German public opinion. Many Germans who saw this fleet of US planes above them waved cheerfully to the pilots, assuming that they had to be *German* planes.[60] And another mission, much too costly at this point, the US B-24 attack on the Rumanian oil fields at Ploesti on August 1, was still a harbinger of the dangers implicit in the US partnership with the British—the German people knew, according to an observer, how vital these oil fields were.[61] Only the German children profited from the US air-raids. The steel gasoline canisters they dropped were gathered up by the youngsters, cut in half, and used for boats on ponds and streams.[62] But the British, too, paid a heavy but worthwhile price for one of their raids. Although their attack on the night of August 17/18 on the German rocket installations at Peenemünde cost a loss of forty bombers, the operation forced a fatal postponement of the development of the V-1 and V-2 weapons designed for vengeance against the English. These not-so-secret vengeance weapons were delayed an entire year in production.[63]

Beneath the bombs, Germany became a seething anthill of people on the move. The numbers of evacuees from the larger cities multiplied enormously. Women and children, the aged, and the feeble were encouraged to leave the endangered cities. Everywhere, they were seen carrying packsacks on their backs and whatever family treasures they could manage to take with them. The Jews, wrote one anti-Nazi, were getting some revenge now, although these refugees were not going to extermination camps.[64] Places for their reception were designated by the government, special trains provided, and public welfare agencies of the party were entrusted with their reception and the provision of housing.[65]

Unavoidably, inordinate difficulties were attached to this vast internal movement of people. If the evacuees could find some place of refuge with relatives or close acquaintances, difficulties were manageable. Even then life could be trying. In spite of comfortable housing, good meals, and quiet nights in good beds, Mathilde Wolff-Mönckeberg complained about the hostess's rules requiring her guests to take off their shoes before entering the house and to refrain from smoking indoors and about her propensity to decide which of her guests she would deign to talk with. It was not long before Frau Wolff-Mönckeberg and her husband were back in bomb-torn Hamburg.[66] But for many other evacuees, things were much worse. They were quartered in parts of Germany where the style of life was very different from that at home. Food was differently prepared and sometimes seemed less adequate than what they had had at home. Their quarters were often narrow and uncomfortable because they were crowding into areas where there was not that much extra room. They had not been able to carry the necessary household equipment, so they had to use the cooking utensils of the hostess if they tried to prepare their own food.[67] Many came to feel that those who lived in the less-bombed areas of Germany did not realize the real consequences of the air-raids. Reports came back to their home cities that the evacuated women were called "bombing women" and treated so unfairly that they would prefer to go back and live in the ruins. The newspapers, said the evacuees, ought to portray the effects of the raids more fully so that those who gave them shelter would better appreciate their reasons for having to accept shelter from strangers.[68]

The hosts, of course, resented this enormous invasion of outsiders. They complained that many of the women did nothing but sit around, instead of helping with the housework or the farming. Although they were duly impressed by the horror stories of the raids, they did not feel that their past hardships justified these women in ruining the daily lives of the host families. Since these evacuated women did not have to work, they could afford to stand in line for hours and buy up available food supplies. Some of them, with a number of children, were entitled by their "Muki cards" (ration cards for mother and child) to go to the front of the food lines and buy what they wanted. The visitors always seemed to have plenty of money, so they were also blamed for the rising prices of food. And they were always complaining and demanding special privileges and attention. Some went even further. One report from Munich accused evacuees from Hamburg of stealing eggs and killing chickens and related the story of one woman who took down her farmer-host's curtains to make a dress for her daughter. There were also assertions that the morality of any of these visitors was not above reproach.[69]

Obviously, the mood reports tended to exaggerate the level of complaints. Many of the hundreds of thousands who left the bomb-damaged cities during this summer must have rejoiced at the feeling of security and the freedom from the continuing air-raid alarms. Christobel Bielenberg discovered that the accommodations her family was supposed to have in the little town of Rohrbach were completely unsuitable, but she managed to get one of the private rooms of the local innkeeper, so that she and her family remained there comfortably for the rest of the war, helping with the chores and making friends with the local residents.[70] Erich Kuby and his wife lived on a farm—he worked, she paid pension, all went well, and the food was much better than they would have had in the city.⁷¹ But many of the evacuees did return when they were able to, seeking even in the ruined remnants of their homes some sense of identity from the past.

Many people in the bombing zones were concerned about their school-age children, who were evacuated separately from their parents (the whole school, teachers and children, was moved as a unit). Some of these children were sent a long way from home. Those in Nuremberg and some other parts of southern Germany, for example, were sent into the Czech protectorate, where they were endangered by future Russian drives. And, of course, there were stories that the children were not treated well, had insufficient food, suffered from sickness and attacks of lice and scabies, and so forth. In some areas, the parents threatened the use of force to keep their children at home.⁷²

There is no doubt that the ever more devastating bombing greatly increased the nervousness, fear, and depression of the Germans.⁷³ The process of evacuation spread, especially from the evacuees from Cologne and Hamburg, the horror stories of agonizing deaths. Everywhere the question was, "Will our city be next on the line?" Grim preparations had to be made. Frankfurt a. M., not yet attacked, stored up two thousand plain wooden coffins for the inevitable day.⁷⁴ There was, of course, and remained through the rest of the war, the hope and expectation of retaliation against the English. Thus, one man from Essen expressed the feelings of many when he said that "the hour of vengeance is now the only hope of the bomb victims. If this hour does not come and that still during this year, then there will be sooner or later a revolution in every great city, since the mood of the bomb victims in regard to the government is frightful. Many say that they have nothing to lose, at the most their lives, but before then other heads will roll."⁷⁵

The anger of this man and of many others was directed at the absence of adequate fighter defense, the transfer of anti-aircraft guns from the endangered cities to the eastern front, and the inadequacy of air-raid shelters.⁷⁶ Both Field Marshal Erhard Milch, the Reich director of air armament, and Albert Speer, the minister of munitions, were convinced after the effects of the bombing of Hamburg were seen that greater attention must be paid to the defense of the homeland. The key, in Milch's view, was an increase in the fighter forces defending Germany's cities even if battlefront air cover had to suffer. With an all-out production of the Messerschmitt 262 jet fighters and the V-1 flying bombs, Milch hoped to change Germany's fortunes. The complete fulfillment of his plans was to be shattered by Hitler's interference and Göring's incompetence, but fighter strength and tactics did improve in the months that followed.⁷⁷

The public mood also turned strongly against Goebbels's propaganda approaches. Most criticized was his harping on the damage to Germany's cultural heritage, notably the attack on the cathedral at Cologne. From all over Germany came the response that it was the human losses that should be emphasized, not the material ones. "Better the cathedral at Cologne destroyed than one hundred men killed" was one trenchant comment.[78] The people, said one report, were tired of Goebbels's "club-footed fairy stories" and Göring was asleep.[79] Anger was also directed at the speech of Robert Ley, the minister of labor, who suggested that evacuation problems could easily be solved since Germany had two million vacant rooms that could be occupied. Perhaps this was true, was the response, but most of these were in the possession of the wealthy and the well-off, who were not going to share them with ordinary people.[80]

Goebbels himself was aware that many Germans were commenting on Hitler's failure to visit the scenes of the bombing and on the fact that he was not even shown on the newsreels. He was happy with his own reception in the bombing areas, but one Sicherheitsdienst report pictured him as visiting the Ruhr with a caravan of fifteen luxury cars and another said that he could only travel in an armored car through these areas.[81] When Hitler was finally shown on the newsreels in his command bunker, the shots were fuzzy and some critics suggested that close-ups were avoided for fear of showing how worn and depressed-looking he was.[82] One of the most often quoted jibes against the government in this period was the verse, usually attributed to the miners in Düsseldorf and addressed to the British bomber pilots: "Dear Tommy, please fly further on your way; spare us poor miners for today. Fly instead against those people in Berlin; they're the ones who voted Hitler in."[83]

The party, of course, continued to display the accustomed bureaucratic stance of feverish activity designed to deal with the myriad problems occasioned by the air-raids. There were local collections to aid bombing victims and numerous contributions to funds set up for this purpose by Goebbels's Reich Ministry of Propaganda.[84] Party agencies sought to provide more information on how to deal with phosphorus bombs in order to reduce the fears of these weapons.[85] Efforts were made to speed up the building of additional air-raid shelters, to increase the use of fire-retardant chemicals, and to streamline the organization of air-raid protection.[86] Local party leaders were now given independent authority to issue the war service crosses that denoted heroic civilian action during air-raids.[87] Party leaders sought to discourage rumors of the evacuation of party offices from Berlin and of any seizure of hospital space due to the needed shifting of party offices elsewhere.[88]

Some of the evacuees returned to their homes after the temporary cessation of raids on a particular area. Sometimes this was due simply to nostalgia for "home," frequently combined with the fear that if living quarters were left unoccupied, someone else would take them over. Cramped and crowded quarters still contained familiar belongings. The dirt and grime from smoke and soot could be removed with hard work, and flowers were still available to lighten the gloom. And often it was less strenuous to live within the ruins than to trek long distances from a place in the suburbs to work in town.[89] But both Cologne and Hamburg faced the menace of droves of vicious rats, grown strong by feeding on the corpses that were left unburied within the rubble as well as the potatoes and other food supplies lost beneath the broken buildings. A great poisoning action in Cologne disposed of many of the nasty animals, but in their nests beneath the surface, they survived, procreated, and constituted a vermin army until many months after the war.[90] Percy Ernst Schramm wrote of the rats in Hamburg, which "scurried fat and fresh on the streets," but added that even more disturbing were the flies—"great, shining green, such as no one had seen before. In clumps they rolled about on the pavement, sat on the remnants of the walls procreating with one another, and warmed themselves tired and satisfied on the splinters of the window panes. When they could no longer fly, they crept through the smallest crevices, besmirched everything, and their rustling and humming was the first thing we heard as we awoke." Only the cold wind of October put an end to these pests.[91]

Life in the ruins became a common part of the scene and one of the more popular articles, "How We Live" (*"Wie wir leben"*) in *Das Reich* stood out from the usual propagandist publications for its more realistic contents.[92] Difficulties with transportation, failure of utilities, infrequency of rubbish collections, a decline in the number of food stores, and the inadequacy of their supplies were often a part of the scene.[93] Although propagandist, the accounts of cooperation in the bomb-ravaged cities and of a recovery of some sense of their original identity by those who returned to their homes, seemed to reflect the reality of the day.[94] For most of those who lived among the ruins, the bare quest for survival (*Überleben*) became the motif. As Ursula von Kardorff expressed it, "The thing is to have as many parties as possible and to make the most of one's house while it is still there."[95]

* * *

Grumbling, mumbling, complaining, no longer full of the joy of living, no longer expecting a quick victory, even increasingly dubious of any victory, crouching in fear under the bombs, working to exhaustion in the factories or on the farms, the Germans continued their daily tasks and daily duties. A movie, a concert, an extra pair of eggs or some fresh fruit, some fresh flowers on the table, a party with the last remnants of some long-saved liquor—all of these provided some relief from the humdrum desperation of war. This time was, as Gottfried Benn wrote on 7 August 1943, "the day when summer ends.—For it is a time of finality; a new beginning from the start is not possible even if one remains alive in a country in which there is not and will not be one piece of cloth, one pair of bootlaces, or one bucket more. Astounding everything, but above all astounding until my last moment of life: this people!"[96]

* * *

[In 1944] the bombing war continued to be the primary focus of attention for the Germans at home. For those in the great cities, the frequency of raids began to convert the experience of living under the bombs almost into a routine, although each new raid carried new perils by virtue of new bombs and new bombing techniques. Those in smaller places had their first taste of the terror that their countrymen in the big cities had experienced during the last three years. The appearance of large numbers of US bombers by day added to the horror of nighttime attacks. The Germans were impressed by their perfect formations (adopted for the vain efforts at defense against fighter attacks) and the rapidity with which bombs were dropped in the "carpet" pattern. But they soon came to realize that the British bombers carried the larger and more destructive bombs. In this period, according to Josef Fischer, the British began to use a bomb between the size of a land mine and an ordinary explosive bomb (probably the 4,000-pound explosive bomb), which had an even more serious effect than the mines. The latter were in light casings and, when they exploded, exerted pressure over a large area. This was a regular bomb that tended to penetrate more deeply before exploding. The most noticeable effect of this bomb was the force of the vacuum or suction created by the explosion. It will be recalled that all of the explosive bombs exerted first a pressure outward and then, as the blast effect passed over a particular area, a suction effect. The suction in this case was so strong that it penetrated the slightest crevices of the air-raid shelters and literally pulled the hair of the women present aloft, so that the words, "their hair stood on end" became a physical description and not just a literary one.[97]

In spite of Cologne's already long "road of sorrow," one-half million people still lived in the city, many of them simply sleeping in the bunkers at night and going to work in the daytime. A bride and groom were married in a bunker and then rode on a bicycle to their honeymoon refuge across the city. The air-raid warning system became useless with the constant threatening of the city as bombers moved to many other destinations in Germany. People listened to the plane trackers on the radio to know when the raids were really meant for Cologne. After the Fischers had gone to their shelter, their little dachshund provided a second warning. When his sharp ears caught the sound of the coming bombs, he wet the floor and rolled in fear.

After air-raids, emergency first-aid stations tried to handle the multitude of lesser complaints quickly. Many people helped themselves—Fischer and 130 of his neighbors worked together to add to the security of their own air-raid shelter, carrying dirt, stones, and sand from wherever they could find them to bolster up the sides and top of their refuge. By the end of this period, Cologne could no longer count on the help of hundreds from outside the city as had been true in the earlier raids. The evacuation of those trapped in air-raid shelters had to be carried out by mechanical means, often with the danger of completely burying those trapped below.

In Berlin, a dozen new attacks joined those begun in November. The city was still a difficult target, requiring a long flight to the goal, and was always heavily defended by anti-aircraft fire and usually by strong fighter forces as well. Each raid took a heavy toll on the attackers and only too frequently the bombs fell more than three miles from the aiming point.[98] Neither the factories located in the city nor the government offices there were fatally damaged. The bureaucrats continued to find some place from which to carry out their assigned roles, and the people of the city ruefully watched the loss of more and more of their apartments, but somehow most of them stayed in the city. The use of heavier bombs made the great tower bunkers more popular. Hundreds crouched along the winding staircases that led ever higher into the structures—most people thought the lower floors were "safer." Even anti-Nazis now used the opprobrious "they," which designated those who threatened their peaceful existence, for the British enemy pilots as well as the German secret police and the Gestapo. But if Ursula von Kardorff's diary reflects a reasonable sampling of the scene in Berlin, many of those who were stuck in the city danced on the edge of the volcano, looking for anything that might relieve the dullness and tensions of daily life.[99] The long, cold, and sunless winter finally moved to an end by April, but the bombings did not. The city continued to be the prime target of air-raids until the end of the war. But among Berliners, as the Sicherheitsdienst reports frankly said, "the majority of our people are also firmly of the opinion that we must endure all difficulties and 'set one's teeth.' One does it because one must and because there is nothing else to do."[100]

In Hamburg, half a year after its great catastrophe, life had returned to some semblance of normality. Traffic in the main streets had been restored. Many of those who had left the city had returned. Somehow, somewhere, they had found shelter, however primitive, in order to be back "at home." People were, of course, not "optimistic" and "happy." Most assumed that new raids would come and previous experience engendered almost universal fear. There were shortages and surly officials dealing with the public. The only real hope lay with the prospect of vengeance, which was "dressed up in mystical dimensions."[101]

Notes

From: Earl R. Beck, *Under the Bombs: The German Home Front, 1942-1945* (Lexington, KT: The University of Kentucky Press, 1986), 57-77, 82, 108-110. Copyright © 1986 by The University of Kentucky Press. Reprinted with permission.

Abbreviations used in the notes:
Hq = *Hauptquartier* (Headquarters)
OLGP = *Oberlandesgerichtspräsident* (President of the Higher Regional Court) reports
Rs = *Rundschreiben* (Circular)
SD = *Sicherheitsdienst* (Security Service of the SS)
T = Records of the Natonal Socialist German Workers' Party, Martin Bormann's Office
VI = *Vertrauliche Informationen* (Confidential Information) sent to party officials from Martin Bormann's office

1. W. Paul, *Der Heimatkrieg, 1939 bis 1945* (Esslingen am Neckar: Bechtle Verlag, 1980), 152.
2. SD, Linz, May 21, 1943, T 81, reel 6; cf. M. Domarus, ed., *Hitler. Reden und Proklamationen, 1932-1945* (München: Süddeutscher Verlag, 1965), 2, pt. 2: 2014. He was recalled March 11; the news was released May 11.
3. U. von Kardoff, *Diary of a Nightmare: Berlin 1942-1945*, trans. E. Butler (London: Rupert Hart-Davis, 1965), 25 Apr. 1943, 39-40.
4. SD, Bad Brückenau, 4 June 1943, in M. Broszat et al., eds., *Bayern in der NS-Zeit* (München: R. Oldenbourg, 1981), vol. 1, pt. 7: 642.
5. Ibid.
6. Rs 83, 29 May 1943. T 580, reel 16.
7. SD, Schwerin, 20 July 1943, T 81, reel 6: Hq. SD to Party Chancellery, 22, 30 July 1943.
8. A. Clark, *Barbarossa: The Russian-German Conflict, 1941-1945* (New York: Morrow, 1965), 329-345.
9. From A. Hillgruber and G. Hümmelchen, *Chronik des zweiten Weltkrieges* (Düsseldorf: Athenäum/Drosche, 1978), 169-174.
10. J. Fischer, *Köln '39-'45. Der Leidensweg einer Stadt* (Köln: J.P. Bachem, 1970), 122-124.
11. Ibid., 124.
12. L.P. Lochner, ed. and trans., *The Goebbels Diaries, 1942-1943* (Garden City, NY: Doubleday, 1948), 393, 397.

13. Ibid.
14. SD, Linz, 29 June 1943, T 81, reel 6.
15. SD, Linz, 23 June 1943; SD, Schwerin, 29 June 1943, ibid.
16. Ibid.
17. See Goebbels's comments in Lochner, *Goebbels Diaries*, 382–384.
18. E. Hampe, ed., *Der zivile Luftschutz im Zweiten Weltkrieg* (Frankfurt/M.: Bernard & Graefe Verlag für Wehrwesen, 1963), 166.
19. Fischer, *Köln*, 125–131.
20. The story that follows is based on ibid., 135–137.
21. G. Benn, *Briefe an F.E. Oelze, 1932–1945* (Frankfurt/M.: Fischer Taschenbuch, 1975), 30 July 1943, 338.
22. H. Lange, *Tagebücher aus dem Zweiten Weltkrieg* (Mainz: Von Hase und Koehler, 1979), 3 Aug. 1943, 117.
23. Martin Middlebrook, *The Battle of Hamburg: Allied Bomber Forces Against a German City in 1943* (London: Cassell & Co., 2000), 95.
24. Paul, *Heimatkrieg*, 67–68.
25. Middlebrook, *Battle of Hamburg*, 97.
26. C. Webster and N. Frankland, *The Strategic Air Offensive against Germany, 1939–1945* (London: HMSO, 1961), vol. 2: 190.
27. Ibid., 150–151.
28. Hans Brunswig, *Feuersturm über Hamburg* (Stuttgart: Motorbuch Verlag, 1979), 195.
29. Ibid., 12–13.
30. Ibid., 166–189.
31. Ibid., 30.
32. Ibid., 173.
33. Ibid., 180–182.
34. Ibid., 48.
35. Ibid., 172.
36. See map, ibid., 189–199.
37. Ibid., 199–206.
38. Ibid., 208–210. Compare Middlebrook, *Battle of Hamburg*, 175–233.
39. Brunswig, *Feuersturm*, 206–208.
40. Ibid., 216.
41. With the later reduction of the number of casualties involved in the raid on Dresden late in the war, it appears that Hamburg still retains this dubious honor.
42. Ibid., 211–220; Middlebrook, *Battle of Hamburg*, 234–251; Gordon Musgrove, *Operation Gomorrah: The Hamburg Firestorm Raids* (London: Jane's, 1981), 65–82.
43. The description of the meteorological conditions is from Brunswig, *Feuersturm*, 264–273, and Musgrove, *Operation Gomorrah*, 102–116.
44. See police reports cited in Percy Ernst Schramm, *Neun Generationen. Dreihundert Jahre deutscher "Kulturgeschichte" im Lichte der Schicksale einer Hamburger Bürgerfamilie (1648–1948)* (Göttingen: Vandenhoeck & Ruprecht, 1964), vol. 2: 572.
45. F.P. Reck-Malleczowen, *Diary of a Man in Despair*, trans. P. Rubens (London: Macmillan, 1966), 188–189.
46. SD, Kitzingen, 30 Aug. 1943, in Broszat, *Bayern in der NS-Zeit*, vol. 1, pt. 7: 649.
47. SD, Summary Report, 6 Aug. 1943, T 580, reel 875.

48. Schramm, *Neun Generationen*, 2: 573.
49. Brunswig, *Feuersturm*, 244–246; circulation of rumor seen in von Kardoff, *Nightmare*, 51.
50. Middlebrook, *Battle for Hamburg*, 146–147.
51. There are in later Sicherheitsdienst reports comments on anti-Nazi shouts and actions in Hamburg, but these seem to be scattered and unverified.
52. See map, Brunswig, *Feursturm*, 254–255.
53. Ibid., 256.
54. Ibid., 257–258.
55. Ibid., 261–263.
56. Fischer, *Köln*, 162–166.
57. F. Nadler, ed., *Eine Stadt im Schatten Streichers. Bisher unveröffentlichte Tagebuchblätter, Dokumente und Bilder vom Kriegsjahr 1943* (Nürnberg: Fränkische Verlagsanstalt, 1969), 170–174.
58. OLGP, R22, 3363, Düsseldorf, 30 July 1943.
59. T.M. Coffey, *Decision over Schweinfurt: The U.S. 8th Air Force Battle for Daylight Bombing* (New York: David McKay, 1977), 259–281.
60. SD, Bad Neustadt, 20 Aug. 1943; SD, Friedberg, 22 Aug. 1943; SD, Bad Brückenau, 23 Aug. 1943; SD, Lohr, 23 Aug. 1943, in Broszat, *Bayern in der NS-Zeit*, vol. 1, pt. 7: 645–646.
61. SD, Schwerin, 3 Aug. 1943, T 580, reel 875.
62. Z. Kruk, *The Taste of Fear: A Polish Childhood in Germany, 1939–1946* (London: Hutchinson, 1973), 108.
63. SD, Schwerin, 24 Aug. 1943, T 580, reel 875, reveals that the people of the area knew the nature of experimentation at Peenemünde.
64. R. Andreas-Friedrich, *Der Schattenmann. Tagebuchzeichnungen, 1939–1945* (Berlin: Suhrkamp, 1947), 118.
65. VI 438, 443, 28 July 1943, T 81, reel 4.
66. M. Wolff-Mönckeberg, *On the Other Side: To My Children, from Germany, 1940–1945*, trans. and ed. R. Evans (London: Peter Owen, 1979), 67–68.
67. For views of these matters see SD, Schwerin, 24 Aug. 1943, T 580, reel 875; OLGP, R22, 3358, Breslau, 31 July 1943.
68. OLGP, R22, 3363, Düsseldorf, 30 July 1943; 3374, Köln, 30 July 1943.
69. OLGP, R22, 3379, München, 21 Aug. 1943; 3358, Breslau, 31 July 1943; SD, Berchtesgaden, 30 Aug. 1943, in Broszat, *Bayern in der NS-Zeit*, vol. 1, pt. 7: 648; Regierungspräsident von Oberbayern, 9 Aug. 1943, ibid., 3, pt. B: 629.
70. C. Bielenberg, *The Past Is Myself* (London: Chatto & Windus, 1970), 120ff.
71. E. Kuby, *Mein Krieg* (München: Nymphenburger Verlag, 1975), 342ff.
72. Nadler, *Stadt im Schatten*, 158–159; Kreis School Office, Fürth, 31 Aug. 1943, in Broszat, *Bayern in der NS-Zeit*, vol. 1, pt. 7: 582.
73. See reports, SD, Schwerin, 3 Aug. 1943, T 580, reel 875,; SD, Halle, 15 July 1943, T 81, reel 6; OLGP, R22, 3385, Rostock, 31 July 1943.
74. OLGP, R22, 3364, Frankfurt/M., 27 July 1943.
75. SD, Kitzingen, 30 Aug. 1943, in Broszat, *Bayern in der NS-Zeit*, vol. 1, pt. 7: 649; cf. SD, Linz, 6 July 1943; SD, Hq., 9 July 1943, T 81, reel 6.
76. SD, Hq., 15 July 1943, ibid.; SD, Bad Neustadt, 20 Aug. 1943, in Broszat, *Bayern in der NS-Zeit*, vol. 1, pt. 7: 645–646.

77. D. Irving, *The Rise and Fall of the Luftwaffe: The Life of Field Marshal Erhard Milch* (Boston: Little, Brown & Co., 1973), 231–237.
78. SD, Weimar, 9 July 1943, T 81, reel 6; see also SD, Schwerin, 13 July 1943, ibid.; SD, Friedberg, 18 July 1943, in Broszat, *Bayern in der NS-Zeit*, vol. 1, pt. 7: 643.
79. SD, Schwerin, 3 Aug. 1943, T 580, reel 875.
80. SD, Schwerin, 13 July 1943, T 81, reel 6; cf. SD, Friedberg, 22 Aug. 1943, in Broszat, *Bayern in der NS-Zeit*, vol. 1, pt. 7: 646.
81. Lochner, *Goebbels Diaries*, 404; SD, Weimar, 9 July 1943, T 81, reel 6; SD, Bad Brückenau, 16 Aug. 1943, in Broszat, *Bayern in der NS-Zeit*, vol. 1, pt. 7: 645.
82. SD, Berlin, 12 Aug. 1943, T 580, reel 875.
83. Not a literal translation, but reflecting the tone of the German verse. SD, Bad Brückenau, 16 Aug. 1943, in Broszat, *Bayern in der NS-Zeit*, vol. 1, pt. 7: 645; cf. SD, Weimar, 9 July 1943, T 81, reel 6, which attributes it to Zeiss factory workers. ["*Lieber Tommy, fliege weiter, hier sind alle Bergarbeiter. Fliege weiter, nach Berlin, da haben alle 'Ja!' geschrien.*" – editor]
84. For example Nadler, *Stadt im Schatten*, 174–184; see letters to Goebbels, 15 July, 12, 27, 29 Aug. 1943, T 580, reel 589.
85. VI 468, 13 Aug. 1943, T 81, reel 4.
86. Rs 110, 3 Aug. 1943; 35g, 14 July 1943, 104, 22 July 1943, T 580, reel 16.
87. Rs 110, 3 Aug. 1943; 126, 27 Aug. 1943, ibid.
88. Rs 50g, Sept. 1; 112, 14 Aug. 1943, ibid.
89. See stories of Wolff-Mönckeberg, *On the Other Side*, 75–76; Andreas-Friedrich, *Der Schattenmann*, 121ff.
90. Fischer, *Köln*, 162–163.
91. Schramm, *Neun Generationen*, 572–573.
92. SD, Linz, 6 July 1943, T 81, reel 6.
93. See Wolff-Mönckeberg, *On the Other Side*, 76; in Essen, the air raids in March destroyed 210 food stores and that of July 25 another 545. See H. Schmitz, *Die Bewirtschaftung der Nahrungsmittel und Verbrauchsgüter, 1939–1950. Dargestellt an dem Beispiel der Stadt Essen* (Essen: Stadtverwaltung, 1956), 458–459.
94. See *Münchener Neueste Nachrichten*, 7/8, 21/22 Aug. 1943.
95. Von Kardoff, *Nightmare*, 49–50.
96. Benn, *Briefe*, 339.
97. Description of affairs in this period from Fischer, *Köln*, 170–178.
98. See diagram in Martin Middlebrook, *The Nuremberg Raid, 30–31 March 1944* (London: Allen Lane, 1973), 81.
99. von Kardoff, *Nightmare*, 82–102.
100. 3 March 1944, T 580, reel 878.
101. OLGP, R 22, 3366, Hamburg, 31 Jan., 12 Apr. 1944; cf. Wolff-Mönckeberg, *On the Other Side*, 87–96.

CHAPTER 4

Firestorm

Martin Middlebrook

Few people in Hamburg had been surprised when the sirens sounded for the second major RAF raid. During the past three days and nights, the city had already been struck by one heavy RAF raid and two light Mosquito raids by night and by two US daylight raids. Most of the population now realized that they were caught up in a major attempt by the Allied bomber forces to destroy their beloved city.

The evacuation of the civilians whose homes had been bombed in the first RAF raid had continued smoothly. Many other people who had not lost their homes also tried to leave and some succeeded in doing so but the authorities tried to restrain this type of evacuation because of the strain on transport services and because too many workers leaving the city would affect industrial output. The flak authorities had made a major attempt to bring help to the city and several railway flak batteries had clanked their way into Hamburg and taken up position at various railway sidings. It is not known how many such batteries arrived before this second RAF raid, but seventeen railway batteries, containing sixty-eight of the heavy 105- and 128-mm guns, are known to have arrived in the city by 31 July, four days later.

The last two nights had been uneasy ones and most people had spent them sleeping in their shelters. The public shelters had been left open and these two warm summer nights had seen many civilians sleeping on the grass outside, ready to go inside the shelter in case of a raid. Then, after all danger of a raid had passed, the civilians had dispersed back to their homes.

> On one of these nights my husband was not at home and I went to the public shelter at the railway station. I didn't want to be alone; I wanted company. But, to return home through the city at 3.30 or 4.00 a.m., when foreigners and thousands of sinister people are creeping past you and when you are carrying your last few valued possessions in a suitcase which could be quite easy for someone to snatch—that was something I wouldn't want to experience again. (Anne-Kaete Seiffarth)

The fires started by the RAF three nights earlier still had not all been extinguished. A particular problem was the innumerable stocks of coal and coke, which could hardly be seen burning during the day, but which glowed brightly at night. Only a few hours before the second big RAF attack, Gauleiter Kaufmann had ordered that an all-out effort be made to put out these fires completely. Thus, nearly every fire appliance in Hamburg was sent to the western part of the city to fight these smoldering coke and coal fires and they were still there when the RAF put down their concentrated bombing attack on the other side of Hamburg a few hours later.

The sirens had sounded in Hamburg at twenty minutes to midnight, but the longer flight of the bombers round to the east of Hamburg meant that there was a lull of more than an hour before the first aircraft appeared over the city. A lady in the district of Hamm, which was soon to be bombed, remembers standing in front of her house during this period of calm. "It was completely quiet. No planes. No flak. It was an enchantingly beautiful summer night." Then, just before 1 A.M., the sound of many aircraft was heard approaching; to everyone's surprise the noise came from the east. The first golden-yellow markers were seen in the sky and the bombs started dropping.

* * *

Fifteen Pathfinder aircraft dropped their loads of markers in the first five minutes of the raid. From the evidence of photographs taken by the bombers at that time, no less than twelve of these loads of markers cascaded over one limited area. These crews were all Blind Markers and they were aiming their loads solely by means of their H2S radar sets. This all-radar primary marking had never before been successful when employed by the Pathfinders. Even now, although the early marking was concentrated, it was not particularly accurate. No markers appear to have been released over the designated Aiming Point in the city center. The concentration of markers was approximately two miles east of the correct place and was over the Billwärder Ausschlag and Hammerbrook districts, just north of the Elbe. This failure to mark the Aiming Point was due to the difficulties experienced by the radar-set operators in the bombers in establishing their exact position in those early days of radar marking. The Bomber Command interim report on this raid says: "It is understood that many of the Y [H2S] aircraft did not follow the correct procedure of using Harburg—an isolated built-up area south of Hamburg—to check their positions."[1] It is probable that an unexpected crosswind had carried the Pathfinders slightly southeast of their planned marking run and that, just before the echo of the wide River Elbe came through the center of their radar display screens, they released their markers at that point.

The two-mile error was not a serious one; there was plenty of built-up city around the area marked. The Main Force bombers arrived promptly and, finding this one prominent group of markers, they bombed it with unusual accuracy. There was never more than that one bombing area, starting in Billwärder Ausschlag and Hammerbrook and moving back only slowly northeastwards into the districts of Borgfelde, Hamm, and, finally, into Wandsbek and Horn. Parts of the bombing had even fallen beyond the main area marked, into the Sankt Georg area toward the city center and south of the Elbe into the dock area. This was an unusual example of Main Force bombing moving *against* the creep-back and the credit for it is due to the doggedness with which the Pathfinder Recenterers and Backers-Up applied to their task.

The RAF men had not been mistaken in their belief that they had carried out a raid of unusual concentration and ferocity. The majority of the bombs had not quite fallen into the area of Hamburg chosen by the Bomber Command planners, but, because Hamburg was so large, these bombs had hit an equally valid part of the city. That was the nature of area bombing.

It is worth taking a closer look at those parts of Hamburg that were so heavily bombed on this night. The southernmost limits of the bombing area were the districts of Billwärder Ausschlag and Rothenburgsort, both on the north bank of the Elbe. Rothenburgsort did not have a large population, being small in area and semi-industrial in character. It did, however, contain the largest children's hospital in Hamburg. Billwärder Ausschlag was a densely crowded working-class area, which could claim the distinction of having produced the lowest pro-Nazi vote—22.9 percent—in Hamburg in the 1933 elections. The earliest bombing of the night had fallen in these two districts but the greatest weight of the attack had fallen a little further north. Here was located the old district of Borgfelde, one and a half miles from the city center, and Hamm, a little further out. Hamm was an extensive area split into Hamm Nord, Hamm Süd, and Hammerbrook.

These main bombing areas were "layered," in that they were split up by a series of prominent roads and two canals, all of which ran from west to east through Borgfelde and Hamm, a main road, the Hammer Landstrasse, being a particularly prominent dividing line. South of this road was a reclaimed area of former marsh, now the home of many thousands of workers and their families. The forebears of these people had been farm-workers who had been drawn into Hamburg when the city's port and industry had been modernized half a century earlier. Now they lived, almost without exception, in that peculiarly German type of property, the low-rental, multi-storey block of flats run by *Wohnungsbaugesellschaften*— non-profit property companies often owned by local authorities, business concerns, trade unions, or any combination of these. Street after narrow street was comprised of these six-storeyed buildings, each block usually housing eighteen families. There were many children. These areas were not slums, but they were densely crowded and their streets had certainly seen much poverty during the years of depression. The people who lived in such areas were often called *Proletarier*—"common workers"—by those who lived only a few streets to the north, across the Hammer Landstrasse. Here, in slightly less crowded conditions, was to be found a more middle-class population: the families of skilled tradesmen, office workers, and minor officials. These people paid a higher rent for their flats, which were usually owned by private landlords.

The bombing had also spread into the areas of Sankt Georg, Hohenfelde, Eilbek, Barmbek, and Wandsbek. Serious damage and casualties were caused in all of these places but the reader will soon understand why attention must remain in the Borgfelde, Hammerbrook, and Hamm districts. It is important to remember that these areas were predominantly residential—although there were a number of small commercial premises of back-street type—and that they were densely populated with families of the middle and lower brackets of Hamburg society. Most of the streets were narrow and there was an almost complete absence of open spaces.

It is sometimes claimed in Hamburg that, on this night, the RAF destroyed those parts of the city that were the least sympathetic to Hitler and his National Socialist cause. The 1933 voting figures do not support this. Although, as has been said, Billwärder Ausschlag had the lowest Nazi vote in Hamburg, Borgfelde and Hamm produced voting figures for that party that were fractionally higher than the Hamburg average. The average Nazi vote in the city was 38.7 percent. The figures for Borgfelde and Hamm were 39.9 and 42.2 percent respectively.[2] The truth is that most of the people of Hamm and Borgfelde had never been politically active. They were simple working people, many of whom had voted for Hitler because he had promised them work. "When you were only getting 8 marks and 50 pfennigs a week, there was no other way." That sum of money, paid to a workless husband and father in the depression years, had been worth ten English shillings or two US dollars at that time. The hapless people of Hamm and Borgfelde were about to pay dearly for the votes they had cast ten years earlier.

The bombing lasted for no more than an hour. During the first part of that period, the effects on the ground were not greatly different in character from those experienced in the previous raid, three nights earlier, although the bombing was more concentrated and the fires more numerous. Few people in the city were out in the open and had the opportunity to view events during this time, but one witness had a good view. Hermann Bock had been a secondary-school teacher in Hamburg until he was called up for military service. Now he was back in his native city as commander of a railway flak battery, which had just arrived from Mönchen-Gladbach and taken up position at a railway siding on the Mühlenhagen in Rothenburgsort on the southern edge of the bombing area. On his arrival, Bock had been "not happy to be in Hamburg, as a Hamburger, as everyone knew the seriousness of the possibility of more air-raids but, trusting fully in our comradeship and sense of duty, we will protect our home city despite all the danger." Leutnant Bock goes on to describe the opening of the attack as viewed from his battery position.

> Hamburg's night sky became in minutes, even seconds, a sky so absolutely hellish that it is impossible even to try to describe it in words. There were airplanes, held in the probing arms of the searchlights, fires breaking out, billowing smoke everywhere, loud, roaring waves of explosions, all broken up by great cathedrals of light as the blast bombs exploded, cascades of marker bombs slowly drifting down, stick incendiary bombs coming down with a rushing noise. No noise made by humans—no outcry—could be heard. It was like the end of the world. One could think, feel, see and speak of nothing more.

The guns of this flak battery fired for twenty minutes but then bombs bursting in the battery position cut every electrical cable providing power to the guns.

By contrast to the experienced flak officer, Elli Nawroski was a sixteen-year-old girl worker in a small paint factory in Bankstrasse, Hammerbroook. On this night, it had been her turn to sleep in the factory air-raid shelter as part of the works' fire-fighting team. When the sirens sounded, the members of the team had gone to various parts of the factory, ready to deal with incendiary bombs.

> It wasn't long before we had to go down to the shelter. The houses opposite had no basements and the women and children there ran across into our shelter also. Above this shelter was our paint factory in which there were stored several tons of highly explosive liquid nitrogen.[3] We were all sitting on the floor, where we thought it would be safer, heads bowed, praying. The civilians who had come thought that we air-raid people, with steel helmets and some sort of uniform, were fully trained and that they would get some protection in the company of such people. This was not true. I didn't even know where the water hose was. I was just a sixteen-year-old girl with such a uniform and a steel helmet.

> The earth shook, the walls cracked and the plaster came down like flour until the whole basement was one cloud of dust. We thought that it was like an earthquake. No one spoke a word.

Then, the nerves of one of my colleagues snapped. There was complete silence in the shelter when this girl suddenly started to laugh. There were obviously heavy bombs bursting near by and, maybe, this girl thought that her house had been hit. Someone said, "This is nothing to laugh about," to which the girl replied, "This is all I have ever wanted." She really had no idea what she was saying. Her mother and grandmother were both killed that night.

Hermann Kröger was more experienced. He was a foreman and the leader of the fire-fighting team in a small coffee factory in the Wendenstrasse, also in Hammerbrook, but closer to the center of the main bombing area. After the alarm had sounded, he had ordered all the fire hoses to be rolled out. When this was done, he had posted four men in various parts of the factory, one on each floor, and taken the other five down to the shelter, outside the doors of which stood their mobile fire pump.

Then came this hail of bombs and we all had the impression that our factory was being constantly hit. The building next door certainly got a direct hit and our own building went up and down like a lift but we found out later that we were only hit by incendiary bombs and phosphorus. Five minutes after the opening of the bombing, two men came down from the upper storeys and said that they would be killed if they stayed upstairs any longer. After ten minutes, a third man came back, absolutely frantic. Then the fourth man, Hartmann, came in. We all stayed on the steps of the shelter, ready to leap into action when the bombing stopped and get the motor pump going from the yard.

Suddenly, there came a rain of fire from heaven. We tried to get out to the pump but it was impossible. The air was actually filled with fire. It would have meant certain death to leave the shelter and it would have been impossible under these circumstances to save the factory, even if we could have reached the pump. Also, we couldn't open the doors without endangering the neighbors who had come into the shelter. The fire around us became even more concentrated. Smoke seeped into the shelter through every crack. Every time you opened the steel doors, you could see fire all around.

The joinery works next door had also caught fire. There was not sufficient water in the cellar so we used Minimax hand fire-extinguishers to try to hold back the fire. Then a storm started, a shrill howling in the street. It grew into a hurricane so that we had to abandon all hope of fighting the fire. It was as though we were doing no more than throwing a drop of water on to a hot stone. The whole yard, the canal, in fact as far as we could see, was just a whole, great, massive sea of fire.

"A storm ... a hurricane ... a sea of fire." Everything experienced in the Battle of Hamburg before this time had been seen in other bombed cities, although not often on the same scale. But what coffee-factory foreman Hermann Kröger saw, in his little corner of Hammerbrook, was a small part of a completely new and most horrific result of aerial bombing. This "storm of fire" later became the subject of intense scientific study and it was concluded that not even the most severe natural fires, such as forest fires, ever reached the intensity of the occurrence experienced in eastern Hamburg during the early hours of Wednesday, 28 July 1943. The German word "*Feuersturm*" was immediately coined and brought into use to describe this phenomenon; that word was recorded in the main log of events being kept by the Hamburg Fire Department a little over one hour after the storm started. The English word "firestorm" is a simple and adequate translation.

The firestorm started through a combination of three main factors. Hamburg had an efficient meteorological station and its records show that there had been an unusual combination of very high temperatures and low humidity during the day preceding this raid. At 6 o'clock in the evening, six hours before the RAF bombs fell, the temperature had been 30° Centigrade (86° Fahrenheit) and the humidity only 30 percent, compared with an average of 40–50 percent for a normal midsummer's day.

The second factor was the unusually concentrated marking and bombing of the RAF. Once this had been achieved, the standard RAF area bombing bomb-loads had achieved their purpose. The large 4,000-lb blast bombs had blown in doors and windows. A multitude of small 4-lb incendiaries had started fires in roofs; the larger 30-lb incendiaries had penetrated deeper inside buildings. High-explosive bombs, which were mixed in with the incendiaries all through the attack, had cratered roads, blown debris into streets and discouraged fire-fighting. A great number of fires had thus been started in a relatively small area of a densely built-up district of Hamburg.

The third factor was that Gauleiter Kaufmann's order the previous evening, that the three-day-old fires smoldering in the western part of the city should be extinguished, had resulted in nearly all of Hamburg's firefighting appliances being on the wrong side of the city. The prominent position of the Alster lake meant that these fire units had to use the few roads in a bottleneck of the city between the Alster and the Elbe or take the longer route round the north of the Alster to redeploy their fire-engines in the new bombing area in the east. Many of these roads were blocked by recent high-explosive bombs. By the time the fire units reached the east, they were too late to prevent a catastrophe. The block wardens, factory fire teams, and other semi-amateur firefighters in the east—like Fräulein Nawroski in her paint-works and Herr Kröger in his coffee factory—had had no chance to stop the spread of fire on their own.

Within fifteen minutes of the first bombs being dropped, hardly any of the many fires were being tackled and they were rapidly becoming out of control. The apartment blocks of Hamburg mostly had good, strong brick walls between each block. The fires did not spread through these walls but, as each individual fire became stronger, it consumed the timber floors and burst through the roof of that block to become a fiercely burning torch. All fires, as a matter of natural course, draw in fresh air in order to consume its oxygen. The strongest of fires in Hammerbrook literally struggled for air and not only did they draw in fresh air from the narrow streets outside, they also dragged heated air out of surrounding buildings that had smaller fires. This hot air brought with it sparks and burning brands which, in turn, started fresh fires in those buildings not already alight. Soon, several extensive groups of buildings were on fire, each requiring more and more air. This was repeated again and again, until the whole of that area that had been bombed in the first phase of the raid was one complete sea of fire, greedily sucking air out of the surrounding areas where the bombing had not been so concentrated. The final part of the process of the joining up of the fires probably took place in a matter of seconds. The area filled with fires became a roaring inferno, the center of which is estimated to have reached a temperature of 800° Centigrade and into which air was being sucked from all directions at speeds that may have reached hurricane force. This was the firestorm.

It is generally agreed that the firestorm started at 1:20 A.M., twenty-three minutes after the first bombs had fallen. In its first stage, the firestorm area was probably about one square mile (two and a half square kilometers) in extent and was confined to the Borgfelde and Hammerbrook districts. Hans Brunswig, in 1943 a senior fire officer in Hamburg, has written a history of the city's bombing experiences during the war that contains a map showing the estimated center of the firestorm as being near the junction of two narrow canals: the Mittel Kanal and the Hochwasser Bassin.[4] It may only be a coincidence that on the Normannen Weg, close to this point, there was a large timber-yard and sawmill, owned by a Herr Nienstadt, but it is possible that blazing stacks of timber here may have been the core of the firestorm.

The tremendous updraught from the firestorm and the fierce winds coming into it from all sides at ground level completely overwhelmed the effects of the light natural wind that had been blowing. Because of this, there was none of the normal windborne spread of fire. Left to itself, the early firestorm area would have remained static and eventually would have burned itself out. But the firestorm was not left to itself. The RAF bombing continued for a further half an hour after the firestorm became established. This bombing spread slowly back along the line of the bombers' approach, more fires were started, and the firestorm was thus extended by the RAF into a new area. This eastward expansion of the firestorm probably measured at least two miles, engulfing the remainder of the extensive Hamm residential district and extending into the less densely populated districts of southern Wandsbek and Horn. It was this extension eastwards of the firestorm that caused the sudden changes of the storm's wind direction mentioned by so many survivors. The original firestorm also spread itself north and west, toward the city center, partly because of further bombing in these areas and partly through the radiant heat effect of the firestorm, but this movement was only slight and probably extended the fire area by no more than a few hundred yards in each direction. The large St George's Hospital, near the Alster, just escaped both the bombing and the firestorm. There was little southern expansion of the firestorm, the River Bille—a fairly wide tributary of the Elbe—and the extensive railway marshalling yards in that area combining to form a fire-break.

The final extent of the true firestorm area was an irregular rectangle measuring approximately one and a half miles from north to south and nearly three miles from west to east, perhaps making an area of four square miles or nearly ten square kilometers.[5] For comparison purposes, this is roughly the same area as that part of central London extending from Euston and King's Cross stations down to the River Thames and from Hyde Park Corner across to the Tower of London. A similar area in New York would be almost the whole of Lower Manhattan from Madison Square Park to Battery Park. But neither of these city areas is of the same character as was the Hamburg firestorm area. The tenement buildings of London's old East End or of New York's Harlem were more the type of building in that area of Hamburg subjected to the firestorm. It has been estimated that 16,000 apartment-block buildings on street frontages totaling 133 miles were ablaze during the firestorm.

The height of the firestorm was reached some time between 3 and 3:30 a.m., more than an hour after the raid ended, so that no RAF man witnessed its climax. The four men who bailed out of crashed bombers near Hamburg that night and survived were all, fortunately for their skins, several miles away, either already locked up or hiding in fields.

Most buildings in these older parts of Hamburg had basement shelters and nearly every member of the civilian population was in one of these when the firestorm started. Even above the crashing noise of high-explosive bombs, the people could hear the howling of the storm in the streets outside, "like the devil laughing," one survivor says. At the same time, the temperature in the shelters started to rise, smoke or very hot air entered and the houses above their heads caught fire. The authorities had always stressed that there was no safer place during a raid than one's air-raid shelter, but thousands and thousands of ordinary people, nearly all old folk, housewives or children, now had to make the most important decision of their lives: stay in their shelters, filling as they were with smoke and burning air and in danger of being buried by the ruins of a burning house above, or venture out into the crazed world of the firestorm streets and try to find safety elsewhere. There are survivors to describe the scene in those streets. They all talk of the tremendous force of the hot, dry wind against which even strong men were sometimes unable to struggle and which forced doors of houses open and broke the glass in windows. Anything light was immediately whipped away, bursting into flames as it went if it was burnable. Branches were torn off trees; even whole trees were forced over and their roots dragged out of the ground. What appeared to be "bundles of flames" or "towers or walls of fire" sometimes shot out of a burning building and along a street. There were "fiery whirlwinds," which could snatch a person in the street and immediately turn that person into a human torch while other people, only a few yards away, were untouched. The wind was always accompanied by clouds of sparks that looked like "a blizzard of red snowflakes," and all survivors remember the shrieking and howling of the storm as it raced through the streets.

The choice whether to stay or to move was a terrible one. Most fortunate were the single, able-bodied people. Most agonizing was the state of mind of mothers with babies or young children. We can follow the fortunes of a few of those people who did decide to leave their shelters.

Traute Koch was a fifteen-year-old girl in Hamm.

> Mother wrapped me in wet sheets, kissed me, and said, "Run!" I hesitated at the door. In front of me I could see only fire—everything red, like the door to a furnace. An intense heat struck me. A burning beam fell in front of my feet. I shied back but, then, when I was ready to jump over it, it was whirled away by a ghostly hand. I ran out to the street. The sheets around me acted as sails and I had the feeling that I was being carried away by the storm. I reached the front of a five-storey building in front of which we had arranged to meet again. It had been bombed and burnt out in a previous raid and there was not much left in it for the fire to get hold of. Someone came out, grabbed me in their arms, and pulled me into the doorway. I screamed for my mother and somebody gave me a drink—wine or schnapps—I still screamed and then my mother and my little sister were there.

About twenty people had gathered in the cellar. We sat, holding tightly to each other and waited. My mother wept bitterly and I was terrified.

Rolf Witt was one of the few men of military age still living at home; he had suffered from having a faulty heart valve since childhood. His home—on the Wendenstrasse in Borgfelde—was only 250 yards from the estimated center of the firestorm.

Word of what was happening in the street must have spread to the people at the back of our shelter because they broke down the wall to the next-door basement. That was a great mistake because, when they did this, they found that they were looking into a furnace. The street door was half open and, with the air being drawn out of our basement, the smoke and fire came pouring through the break in the wall. Everyone became severely affected by smoke. I heard people screaming but this became less and less; I believe they were suffocating.

You must realize that we were within seconds of death. I could not speak to my parents because of the gas mask I was wearing. I tapped father on the shoulder as a sign that I was going. I thought they would follow me. A few seconds before I would have suffocated, I must have had a tremendous burst of strength. At a moment when the door was open and when no burning debris was falling down, I sprang out into the street but against the wind. I think I must have remembered that there was a small park near by and that, in that direction, there might be safety.

The flying sparks of phosphorus were burning my hands. I had an old winter coat and I pulled this over my head. I threw away my briefcases with all my papers in. Everything was done on impulse and I must have had tremendous luck to get out of that steel shelter door and to avoid the falling debris as I crossed the street. I am not a religious man but I believe that God gave me a push just at the right moment.

I ran eighty or a hundred meters to a railway bridge and I lay down under this, behind a steel tube, to protect myself against the sparks. I had a small thermos flask in my jacket. I took off my gas mask and had a little drink of tea. I had a terrific thirst. A second man came and took shelter with me; his clothes were burning. I took off my coat and beat out the fire on the other man. It was then that I looked back at my parents' house and saw that it had already collapsed and was only a heap of ruins. I ran on and managed to reach a football pitch and I found a small ticket kiosk, miraculously saved from the fire. I got inside it and spent the rest of the night there. I saw no one else all night.

I never found my parents and was never sure where or how they died. I have always felt guilty that I abandoned them. Later, when their shelter was cleared, they found fifty-five bodies—at least they found fifty-five skulls. There had only been about twenty-five people there originally. I think the others had maybe come in from the house behind. I never met another survivor from my home or the houses at the back.

The death certificates for Rolf Witt's parents, issued on 20 May 1944, record the time of their death as 1:40 a.m. on 28 July. Witt's own exertions in the firestorm caused no ill effects to his diseased heart and, toward the end of the war, he was declared fit for service with the Volkssturm.

Käte Hoffmeister was a nineteen-year-old milliner whose home was in the Grevenweg in Hammerbrook:

> We came to the door which was burning just like a ring in a circus through which a lion has to jump. Someone in front of me hesitated. I pushed her out with my foot; I realized that it was no use staying at that place. The rain of large sparks, blowing down the street, were each as large as a five-mark piece. I struggled to run against the wind in the middle of the street but could only reach a house on the corner of the Sorbenstrasse, the ground floor of which had not yet caught fire and where I was able to rest for a little while in the entrance to regain my breath and to get out of that shower of sparks.
>
> My mother, my Aunt Emma and myself had all left the doorway of our house at about the same time. While I was resting, my aunt came and stood with me. I had a little bag with my papers and jewelry but my hands were already burnt by the sparks and I dropped the bag. My aunt told me to leave it there. I was terrified but she was so calm and determined to get out through the fires to find a safe place. I didn't want to go out into the fire again but she dragged me out and we set off up the street, still against the wind. We knew the area very well and we decided to go to the place known as the Löschplatz—a piece of open ground on the other side of the Mittel Kanal, about 200 yards away. It was an old quay where ships had landed goods years ago. We thought that we could reach there first and then go on to the football pitch on the Eiffestrasse.
>
> We got to the Löschplatz all right but couldn't go on across the Eiffestrasse because the asphalt had melted. There were people on the roadway, some already dead, some still lying alive but stuck in the asphalt. They must have rushed on to the roadway without thinking. Their feet had got stuck and then they had put out their hands to try to get out again. They were on their hands and knees screaming.
>
> Aunt Emma and I stood by a row of four big trees that were on fire and again we discussed what we were going to do. I suggested that we roll down this bank; it was too steep to get down any other way. I took

my hand out of my aunt's and went. I think I rolled over some people who were still alive. I lost my aunt at that point. By then, my face and arms and legs had been burnt so that I could only act by touch but my burns had not yet started to hurt. I felt a thick woolen blanket; I knew, by instinct, that it would be safer under that blanket. We had always been told, over and over again, that a woolen blanket would protect us against fire because wool does not burn but only smolders. I got under it and stayed there.

Next morning, Käte Hoffmeister, although badly burnt, went to look for her relatives. She found the body of Aunt Emma, identifying it by a blue-and-white sapphire ring that she always wore. Her father and two uncles died, but she later met her mother, by coincidence, in the same hospital near Kassel, 160 miles from Hamburg.

The Chief of Police's Report contains several eyewitness accounts from civilians who survived the firestorm. Two of these are from people who also reached that little canalside quay where Käte Hoffmeister survived. Frau Erika Wilken and her husband had taken shelter, with a crowd of other people, in some public toilets built under the nearby roadway of the Grevenweg. Herr Wilken had stood on a toilet seat, wetting cloths in the tank above for other people to bathe themselves in the fierce heat.

> But the worst was yet to come. To our misfortune, a large phosphorus bomb fell directly outside the toilet. The people nearest the door now gave way to an indescribable panic. The inner toilet doors were torn off and used as shields in front of the bomb. After a few minutes, these doors too were burning brightly.
>
> Terrible scenes took place, since all of us saw certain death in front of us, with the only way out a sea of flames. We were caught like rats in a trap. The doors were thrown on to the canister by screaming people and more smoke and heat poured in. In the meantime, the water in the tank had been used up. My husband was completely worn out and we crouched next to the bowl. The other people here sat down too; some collapsed and never woke up again. Three soldiers committed suicide. I begged my husband to beat back the flames with our blanket but he was no longer able to do so. So I did it. My hair began to singe and my husband extinguished it.
>
> What now? Our hearts were racing, our faces began to puff up and we were close to fainting. Perhaps another five or eight minutes and we will be finished too. On my question, "Willi, is this the end?," my husband decided to risk everything and try to reach the outside. I took the blanket and he the little suitcase. Quickly, but carefully so that we would not slip on the corpses, we reached the outside. One! Two!

Three! We were through the wall of fire. We made it. Both without burns; only our shoes were singed. But our last strength and courage had gone. We lay down on the ground at the side of the canal. People swimming in it kept wetting our blanket for us.[6]

The other account from this place[7] is by Johann Burmeister, a greengrocer:

> Many people started burning and jumped into the canal. Horrible scenes took place at the quay. People burned to death with horrible suffering; some became insane. Many dead bodies were all around us and I became convinced that we, too, would perish here. I crouched with my family behind a large stack of roofing material. Here we lost our daughter. Later on, it transpired that she had jumped into the canal and almost drowned but was saved by an army officer and she returned to us early next morning.
>
> Please spare me from having to describe further details.[8]

Herbert Brecht, a fifteen-year-old boy in a *Schnellkommando* unit, was one of the few people who had to be out on the streets on duty. His small team had been sent from its post at the Osterbrook school, in Hammerbrook, along the Süderstrasse into what became the main firestorm area.

> I was in the wooden trailer with two other lads. The heat from the surrounding houses, which were on fire, was unbearable. We whimpered and cried from the pain of it. Our car got stuck behind a burning tramcar but we freed ourselves with a push. After another 300 meters, a man suddenly clamped into the trailer and pressed his hot steel helmet against my face, but not on purpose. We shook him off and he remained lying in the road. Burning people ran and staggered after us. Others were lying on the road, dead or unconscious. At the junction of Süderstrasse and Louisenweg, our trailer got stuck in a bomb crater. We unhitched it and jumped into the car which was still running; there were six of us crammed inside. After another 200 meters we were forced to a halt between the trams standing in front of the tram depot. Our car caught fire immediately. We all managed to get out and we stood there in those fires of hell. The storm pulled me, unwillingly, into an enormous bomb crater in the middle of the road. Those of us who did not get into this crater had no chance of survival. One of my group was never seen again. The noise was like that of an old organ in a church when someone is playing all the notes at once.
>
> There was a smashed water main in the bomb crater. Although there was no pressure left in the pipe, the water still ran into the crater and we had to fight against a flood. Some people drowned or were buried

when the sides of the crater caved in. Above, there was this terrible heat but I was lying safely in the water. Because I always wore my goggles on duty, I could see everything very clearly. The burning people who were being driven past our bomb crater by the storm could never have survived. Eventually, there were about forty people lying in the crater. There was a soldier in uniform near me with a lot of medals. He tried to take his life with a knife. He showed me his bleeding breast and said, "I can't do it."

About that time, I noticed that a car had driven into our crater and had buried some people beneath it. Because one is only half conscious in such a situation, I hadn't seen this happen. It was only through the crying of a small boy that I noticed it. He was lying with the front bumper of the car on top of him. We managed to pull him out with a lot of effort but I can't say whether he survived.

The screams of the burning and dying people are unforgettable. When a human being dies, he screams and whimpers and, then, there is the death rattle in his throat, not at all bravely and not as beautifully as in a film.

The car that had driven into Herbert Brecht's bomb crater by mistake was that of a Herr Dehler of the Hamburg Water Department. Herr Dehler survived the firestorm and his report of the incident was later filed in the papers of the Chief of Police.

The number of people who were able to save themselves from the firestorm area was surprisingly large. However terrifying and formidable the circumstances, the will in the human spirit to survive drove the brave and resourceful to almost superhuman efforts. But even this was not enough unless luck also played its part. The successful survivors had to have avoided the falling timbers and bricks—and even bombs in the earlier stages of the firestorm; and they had to have been within reach of a place suitable for survival. The people whose experiences have been quoted above made use of a house burnt out in a previous raid, a football pitch, a low-lying piece of ground by the side of a canal and a deep and partly flooded bomb crater. Many others saved themselves by jumping into the canals of the area, preferring the risk of death by drowning to that of death by fire. Exhausted and often badly burnt, the survivors of the firestorm waited for its end.

There were many, many thousands who did not have that combination of will-power, courage and luck necessary for survival and the firestorm caused death on a scale never seen before in aerial bombing. Even a high proportion of those bold enough to quit their shelters and attempt flight through the streets perished. Many who took to the streets allowed themselves, in their confusion, to be carried along by the storm of wind toward greater danger. It needed a clear head and much physical strength to turn and battle against the wind. And even the taking of the correct path was no guarantee of survival. The distances to safety were often too great and only those, similar to the cases already described, who were fortunate enough to find a place where a little air and temporary salvation from the flames could be found, survived. People were hit by flying timbers or falling bricks. Babies or little old people were simply dragged bodily by the storm into burning buildings. Many others became exhausted; they staggered and fell. Sometimes they crawled to the gutters, hoping to find a little air there but, within seconds, their clothes and very bodies caught fire. Perhaps the worst ends befell those who ran on to a roadway where the asphalt surface had melted. All these methods of meeting death in the streets were observed and later reported by survivors.

The bodies of the victims were later found where they had died—nearly always face downwards, one arm thrown around the head. Most of the bodies were blackened and shriveled to half their normal size, like mummies, but others were unburnt, although all of their clothes, except their shoes, had disappeared. This unusual sight was probably the result of victims attempting to flee while clad in little more than night clothes, which were torn off by the storm or were dissolved in the intense heat without the bodies of their owners being burnt.

There was a far greater loss of life, however, among those who had heeded all the advice given about air-raids and who remained in their shelters. The exceptions were those fortunate people who were in the purpose-built public *Bunker* shelters. These shelters had gas- and smoke-tight doors and, once these were closed, those inside had a good chance of survival and there were no examples of any large loss of life in these shelters. One survivor says, "The people of Hammerbrook were not often given to praying but they certainly prayed hard that night." When she emerged, many hours later, this person had to step through the fat of the molten bodies of those who had come to the shelter too late.

But there were few public shelters in the areas where the firestorm raged. Nearly every block of flats had its basement shelter. It was to these that the vast majority of the population had gone when the raid started and it was here that the citizens of those districts died in their thousands. I have received no personal contribution nor seen any written record from any person who remained in a basement shelter and survived from that area where the firestorm burnt at full intensity. The manner in which these people died can only be guessed from the condition in which their bodies were found when the ruins cooled several days later.

The firestorm had, first, drawn the good air out of these shelters and replaced it by smoke or, sometimes, by colorless gases from which the oxygen had all been burnt. Autopsies established that the overwhelmingly predominant cause of death was poisoning by carbon monoxide, rarely by burning. At some stage during this process, the apartment block above would have burnt down and the brickwork of its roof, its internal walls, and its stairways would have collapsed to cover the basement shelters, rarely crushing the roof of the shelter but usually blocking all exits. It was in these brick-covered tombs that so many deaths occurred. The bodies were sometimes found heaped up around the blocked exits, indicating that the occupants had realized that they were trapped and in danger of death. But most of the dead were found sitting at tables or against walls, in the most peaceful of positions, as though they had fallen asleep, and, in a way, they had, for they had breathed the invisible and odorless carbon monoxide into their bodies without realizing the danger. Such victims were usually fully clothed, although parts of the clothing would have scorched away, and the intact bodies were always baked a brownish colour. All such bodies were considerably shrunken; the Germans called them "*Bombenbrandschrumpfleichen*"—the shrunken bodies of fire bombing. Some bodies were found lying on the floor of shelters, in the coagulated black mess of their own molten fat tissue.

There was a final category of body. In some shelters, nothing more was found than a thin layer of ash on the floor. In these places, fresh air had penetrated after the firestorm had blown out but while fires were still burning. These bodies had then been incinerated, but only several hours after the deaths of their owners.

Approximately 40,000 people—nearly all civilians and mostly old folk, women, and children—died either in the streets of the firestorm area or in their shelters.

The terrible furnace of the firestorm started to subside about three hours after it started. The first lessening of the wind and fire was observed in the western part of the now two-mile long firestorm area and it started to die down only when nearly all of the flammable material had been consumed in that area where the storm had started. Tentative estimates say that this stage was reached at about 4 a.m. The wind gradually dropped and, although there were still some fires where more durable material continued to burn, they burned now in a more conventional manner. This process spread steadily eastwards and it has been estimated that the last signs of the firestorm disappeared between 6 and 7 a.m. The five-hour period in which the firestorm had raged would prove to be a turning point in the history of the city of Hamburg, as a great divide in the pattern of human life and in the physical appearance and condition of the city.

The great heat in the center of the firestorm area remained. It would be two days before rescue workers could penetrate to the hottest areas, but there was no hurry; there was no one there to rescue. It would be two weeks before safe and comfortable passage could take place through such areas. But, now, as the new day of Wednesday, 28 July appeared, the air at least became breathable, although the sun did not appear. Smoke from the ruins of Borgfelde, Hamm, and Wandsbek would continue to blot out the sun for several days. Rescue workers started to penetrate the edge of the fire area and, there, they met the survivors of the firestorm. It is not over-dramatic to describe it as a meeting with those who had come back from the very edges of death.

Hermann Kröger was the leader of the fire-fighting team in the Wendenstrasse coffee factory.

> Between six and seven in the morning, we dared to open a few tiny steel windows at the side of the canal. Fresh air streamed in and our breathlessness vanished. Although we could not leave the shelter, we knew one thing—that every soul in there had been saved and would be able to leave that shelter alive. All the people in the surrounding buildings had died. We pulled in some people out of the canal. They had jumped into it from the other side, which was burning fiercely, and they had swum across to us. There were large patches of fire on the water, just like when you pour inflammable spirits on to water and put a match to it. We thought it might have been caused by the liquid phosphorus that the bombers had dropped. These people kept smacking their hands on the water, while they swam, trying to push the flames away. A police patrol appeared on the opposite side of the canal and we called out and told them about our condition. It was decided that those who could not or would not leave the shelter through the yard should go by boat. Unfortunately, this did not happen and everyone had to leave by way of the Wendenstrasse.

> After we had convinced ourselves that we could not put out the roaring fire in the factory, the garages and the offices, we left. It was painful that we men, with all our equipment, were quite powerless to fight the fire. It was hell let loose in that night. All the coffee in the factory—about five tons of real coffee for the armed forces and a lot of *Ersatz*—had burnt but there was so much fire that we didn't smell it burning.

> At 8.30 a.m., with several other men, we walked along the Wendenstrasse towards our homes, climbing over rubble and bodies as we went—in order to discover whether our families and homes had survived.

Traute Koch was the girl who had taken shelter in a house that had burnt out in a previous raid.

> After endless hours, one of the men came and made it clear to us that it was no longer burning in the streets and that we should try to get out

of this hell. With great apprehension we stepped out on to the street. There was only one way, in front of us, but what a way! There was a great heat and a leaden gloom over us. Where there had been houses only a few hours before, only some single walls with empty windows towered upwards. In between were large heaps of rubble, still glowing. Torn overhead wires were hanging everywhere.

There was not much rubble on the streets and, after about a hundred meters, we came to the place which, only a few hours earlier, had been our home. The wall between the dining-room and the staircase was still standing. I could still see the radiator and I remember thinking that the Meissen porcelain group that I had loved so much ought to be standing on it—a fleeting thought. We couldn't stay there long; the soles of our feet were too hot. All the time I thought that I would start burning.

We came to the junction of the Hammer Landstrasse and Louisenweg. I carried my little sister and also helped my mother climb over the ruins. Suddenly, I saw tailors' dummies lying around. I said, "Mummy, no tailors lived here and, yet, so many dummies lying around." My mother grabbed me by my arm and said, "Go on. Don't look too closely. On. On. We have to get out of here. Those are dead bodies."

Herbert Brecht was the *Schnellkommando* boy who had sheltered in the partly flooded bomb crater.

At midday—it never got light—a man came and pulled some of us survivors out of the crater. He was an elderly man who also had a burnt face. When he pulled me out by the hands, my skin stuck to him in shreds. He looked at me—I cannot describe his look—and he could only say, "*Junge! Junge!*" I cannot say how many of us survived in that crater. I had been given a new, brown uniform only three weeks earlier and been told that it was flame-resistant. I feel that this saved my life. My old uniform had been a captured French soldier's uniform with some old First World War boots.

I set off in the direction of Hammerbrook because everything was still burning in the direction of the school where our post was. The air was hardly breathable and my injuries hurt hellishly. Dead lay everywhere. Most were naked because their clothes had been burnt away. All had become shrunken, really small, because of the heat.

I stumbled on as far as Heidenkampsweg but the way was blocked here. I tried to retrace my steps but then I collapsed. I must have been picked up by someone I never saw because I woke up in a *Bunker* shelter with a woman trying to put little pieces of food into my mouth.

The fire brigade had been able to do little fire-fighting, being overwhelmed by the scale of the fires. Instead, their men had worked during the raid at saving as much human life as was possible, but only on the edges of the firestorm area. The Fire Department Headquarters, at the Berliner Tor Fire Station, was at the northwest corner of the firestorm area and had become a major place of refuge where hundreds of people took shelter. A fireman who does not wish to be named, being concerned for some reason over his pension, had helped look after these people. Now he set out into Hammerbrook to look for his brother—a disabled soldier—and his family.

> I only got to the Heidenkampsweg. In the entrance to the Maizena Haus (a large office building) I saw a lot of dead, naked people on the steps. I thought that they had been killed by a blast bomb and been blown out of the basement air-raid shelter. What surprised me was that the people were all lying face downwards. Only later did we find out that these people had died there through lack of oxygen.
>
> I climbed over the ruins, further into the damaged area. There were no people alive at all. The houses were all destroyed and still burning. In the Süderstrasse, I saw a burnt-out tramcar in which naked bodies were lying on top of each other. The glass of the windows had melted. Probably these people had sought refuge from the storm in the tram.
>
> I eventually reached my brother's home on the Grevenweg; it was just a heap of smoking bricks. I helped to clear their shelter five weeks later. There was only charred bones and ash. I found a few objects that belonged to my relatives—their house keys and some coins that my nephew was always playing with.

The area that had suffered from the firestorm was soon declared a prohibited zone to ordinary civilians, and those people who tried to enter, seeking to know the fate of relatives, were turned away by armed guards. Anne-Lies Schmidt had walked in from the country and, later that day, she tried to find her parents in Hammerbrook.

> My uncle and I went on foot into this terror. No one was allowed into the devastated district but I believe that one's stubbornness becomes stronger at the sight of such sacrifice. We fought bodily with the sentries on duty and we got in. My uncle was arrested.
>
> Four-storey-high blocks of flats were like glowing mounds of stone right down to the basement. Everything seemed to have melted and pressed the bodies away in front of it. Women and children were so charred as to be unrecognizable; those that had died through lack of oxygen were half charred and recognizable. Their brains tumbled from their

burst temples and their insides from the soft parts under the ribs. How terribly must these people have died. The smallest children lay like fried eels on the pavement. Even in death, they showed signs of how they must have suffered—their hands and arms stretched out as if to protect themselves from that pitiless heat.

I found the bodies of my parents but it was forbidden to take them because of the danger of epidemic. Nothing to remember them by. No photographs. Nothing! All their precious little possessions they had taken to the basement were stolen. I had no tears. The eyes became bigger but the mouth remained closed tight.

The first instinct of so many of those civilians who were able to escape from the bombing area without serious injury was to flee, if possible to get clear out of the city. Ingeborg Reifkogel, a young teacher living in Hamm, actually started her flight during the raid when smoke started to pour into the shelter of her home.[9]

All the houses were on fire in the Sievekingsallee and it was very hot. But I had poured a bucket of water over myself, put on a pair of motoring goggles which protected me from the flying sparks and I held a wet cloth in front of my face. I found this more comfortable than the gas mask which I had hanging round my neck. I also had a head scarf on and, on top of that, a wet old felt hat. Dressed like that, I got through on the tramrails in the middle of the street until I reached the Autobahn. This was full of dense red smoke from the blaze on both sides, but smoke doesn't burn, of course. The main thing was not to panic. If one could keep wet and the sparks didn't start to burn, it would be possible to get through all right.

I kept on walking along the Autobahn, quite calm, in spite of the explosions all around me. In one place the road was covered with water; probably a dud bomb had burst a water main. The embankment was blazing and I couldn't go up and round that way, so I waded through. The water only came up to my knees and my shoes and socks didn't take long to dry in the heat. There was still so much smoke that it was impossible to breathe without the wet cloth.

Shortly before reaching Jenfeld, I met some people by an air-raid shelter built into a bridge over the Autobahn. I dipped my cloth in water again there. They asked me to stay with them but I couldn't bear the thought of sitting beside two dead children. The only other people I had met up till then had been a party of prisoners who were running around, unguarded, and who warned me in broken German about the phosphorus that was still smoldering everywhere. I was so calm, almost cheerful, that I grinned as I thought of the picture on the cover of the book, *Gone with the Wind*. At least Scarlett O'Hara had a wagon, whereas I had to walk.

Then I passed through an area where delayed-action bombs were exploding and some friendly people who were living in their garden houses offered me shelter and gave me a piece of bread. I started out again at 5 o'clock in the direction of Rahlstedt. The whole of Jenfeld was on fire; the barracks were badly damaged. In Tonndorf, only windows were broken. Rahlstedt was all in one piece. When I got there, I sat down in the Diffring's garden so as not to wake them up. At seven o'clock, Frau Diffring looked out of the window and took me upstairs. I was able to wash, have breakfast and go to bed.

Fräulein Reifkogel had walked just four and a half miles, from the edge of the firestorm area to this peaceful village outside Hamburg. She must have been one of the first of what was to become a mass exodus of people fleeing from that part of the city that had been bombed, out along the roads leading to the east. This flight soon received a boost when Gauleiter Kaufmann ordered that an official announcement be made appealing to all those inhabitants of Hamburg who were not needed for essential work to leave the city. (No documentary copy of this appeal seems to exist. It was probably issued in the late morning or early afternoon of that day and was mainly made known to the public by the use of loudspeaker vans.) The news that a massive and horrible catastrophe had occurred in one part of the city had already flashed around the remainder of Hamburg. There could not be the slightest doubt, now, about the RAF's intention to destroy Hamburg and that other areas could receive the same treatment, perhaps in the next night. The flight now became general and it has been estimated that 1,200,000 people—nearly two-thirds of the total population—left their homes by nightfall of that day.

The early fugitives simply left the city on foot and kept going until they reached open country, but some sort of order was established to the evacuation process as the day progressed. Hermann Matthies, the city's Director of Public Welfare, remembers that his carefully prepared catastrophe plan proved entirely inadequate. "I threw it into the corner of my office and we improvised everything from then on." This is where the Nazi Party organization came into its own. Brooking delay, excuse, and objection from no one, party officials gradually imposed a limited order out of chaos. It had always been expected that the railways would be used for any mass evacuation, but bomb damage to stations or hallway lines had rendered fifteen of Hamburg's eighteen stations useless for this purpose. Four huge collecting places were designated: at the Moorweide Park, at the Horn and Farmsen racecourses, and at an open space in Billstedt. It was at the Farmsen racecourse that the important *Preis von Deutschland* race meeting was to have been held only three days earlier. To the dazed and frightened people now resting on the grass with their last few possessions, such innocent pleasures as horse-racing must have seemed a lifetime away.

Herculean efforts produced food and drink. Half a million loaves of bread, 16,000 liters of milk, beer, coffee, and tea were all made available during that first day of the big evacuation. Every spare motor vehicle—private and military—was pressed into service to take people to railway stations outside the city. The students of Hamburg University, for example, are credited with transporting 63,000 people in this way. From the country stations, the evacuees spread all over Germany, taking with them news of the recent happenings in Hamburg. Ships on the Elbe were also used, often to carry wounded, and it is reported that Junkers-52 transport planes were taking off from Fuhlsbüttel airport "ceaselessly."

It would be many days before the last evacuees could be taken from Hamburg. The accounts of Frau Anne-Kaete Seifarth, who set out on foot with her husband and son from Eilbek, can speak for the thousands who did not wait for official transport.

> Father fetched a cart from his workshop and we commenced the most ghastly journey of our lives. We loaded the possessions that we had been able to save on it. Joe got some bread from the Kreffts' house; they happened to be away and their parents had fled. Uncle Waldemar suddenly stood in front of us. His anxiety had driven him to us. His house had fortunately been spared. He brought us his last helping of cold meat. Good old uncle! He cried and cried bitterly as he saw us set off with our cart. Joe was pushing the cart; father pulled it with a rope. I pushed my heavily laden bicycle.
>
> For our flight, we tried to find a safe route, near the canal where the houses were more widely spaced, in the direction of Friedrichsberg. Everything was burning there as well. Prams, bicycles and carts and such like—all heavily laden—were being pulled by some of the fleeing people but most of them didn't take anything; they only wore their night-clothes. Firemen, soldiers, lorries—all mingled together and everyone silent and stunned, their faces almost delirious. Why? Why? What was the reason for all this?
>
> One man has gone mad. He's standing in front of a mound of bricks from a collapsed wall, on top of which he has erected the swastika flag. He is screaming at the fugitives with a steel helmet on his head—his face mad—and he is bombarding the fugitives with bricks. Father screams at him and he is taken aback enough to let us pass. We con-

tinue, by large bomb craters, over the ruins of collapsed house fronts. The Tommies have also been here, house after house hit, the fire hoses are everywhere in the road.

Gradually we reach the town boundary of Wandsbek; here we also find bombs everywhere. Slowly the day becomes clearer; the dense clouds of smoke are behind us now. We are in the great stream of fugitives on the Lübecker Chaussee now. Old people, small children—everyone is creeping along under the sun; it is hot now. Every village that we come to is full to bursting point. Compassionate farmers give out some coffee and milk but what can that do for thousands of people. The evening approaches and, completely exhausted, we can go no further. We all have blisters on our feet. We look like stokers. No beds, no barns, no stables to be had. People have settled and are lying down on lawns, in woods. By chance, our tent had been ready to hand in the cellar and father and Joe had wisely brought it along, thinking that it might be needed. We get some water from a farm and, finally, the three of us settled down in the tent. We were at Stapelfeld.

Another account describes the exodus as seen through the eyes of an inhabitant of the area outside Hamburg into which these refugees were trudging. Margot Schulz lived in Bergedorf, the first small town on the broad main road to Berlin.

It was the most pathetic sight I had ever seen. If I think back on it now, I don't think it can have been true. They were in their night dresses—half burned sometimes—and pajamas, sometimes a coat thrown over their shoulders. They pushed their belongings in a pram, still with the baby in. Sometimes they had a lot of those little carts—"*Handwagen*" we called them—little four-wheeled carts; I don't think you have them in England. You have to imagine the hysteria, with some of the people burnt and crying. It went on for days. It was just endless.

My sister and I got some fruit juice that we had from our garden and a bucket of water. We stood there all day giving drinks to these people. The other people in Bergedorf were doing the same but we ran out in the end and had to give up.

I remember a woman suddenly collapsing on the pavement across the road from where I lived and giving birth to a baby. The baby came after about a quarter of an hour or twenty minutes of moaning and groaning; it must have been a "shock birth." Fortunately they took her into a house. There was another woman, sat on the pavement near by, breast-feeding her baby. She was only dressed in a nightdress and all her hair was burnt away. And, all the time, the exodus went on. It was a constant stream of misery.

This great flight by the citizens of Hamburg, given official blessing by the leading official in the city, was, in strictly military terms, the most significant event of the Battle of Hamburg. It was the culmination of Bomber Command's success. The RAF bombing had caused so many problems to Gauleiter Kaufmann and his subordinates that he had been forced to close down all normal life in his city. Death and destruction, although widespread, were not the most serious of Kaufmann's problems. They were simple factors that had to be accepted and dealt with in the course of time. Hamburg was faced with the problems of the living: the rescuing of bomb victims, the putting out of fires, the disarming of hundreds of unexploded bombs, the tending of the injured and homeless, the fear of epidemic, of looting, and the restoration of all the public services that had been disrupted. The city of Hamburg, even under the firmest of directions and the most brilliant of organizations, simply could not cope with all these problems and, at the same time, keep any semblance of normal life. Those people, packed in buses and cars or tramping in their misery out of Hamburg, were the visible evidence that area bombing operations had stopped the normal life of a major city.

Notes

Martin Middlebrook, *The Battle of Hamburg: Allied Bomber Forces against a German City in 1943* (London: Cassell & Co., 2000), chapter 15: Firestorm, 252–281. Copyright © Martin Middlebrook 1980. Reprinted with permission.

1. Public Record Office AIR 14/3012.
2. The Hamburg *Statistisches Jahrbuch 1932/33*, 240–241.
3. The liquid nitrogen would not have exploded, but would have evaporated quickly causing skinburns, damage to eyes, and suffocation.
4. The map is in Hans Brunswig, *Feuersturm über Hamburg* (Stuttgart: Motorbuch Verlag, 1978), 218–219.
5. The Hamburg Chief of Police's Report says that the firestorm area was twenty-two square kilometers, but that figure is probably too high and covers many fringe areas in which there were many fires and strong winds but no true firestorm.
6. Appendix 10 of the American translation of the Chief of Police Report, 82–83. (The report has not been published, but translations are available through the National Technical Information Service, US Department of Commerce, Springfield, Virginia, and Microinfo Ltd., Alton, Hants.)
7. This canalside area, the Löschplatz, is now the garage and lorry park of a Mercedes-Benz dealer. Only one of the four trees burning that night now remains. The public toilets under the Grevenweg, where so many people died, are now a small lock-up store.
8. The Hamburg Chief of Police's Report, American translation, 102.
9. This account and the one following, from Frau Seifarth, are from letters written immediately after the evacuation.

PART II
THE MORAL ISSUES

 CHAPTER 5

Can the Bombing Be Morally Justified?

Igor Primoratz

In this chapter, I look into the main ways in which the bombing of German cities and towns in World War II has been, or might be, morally defended. I argue that all these attempts at justification fail. If my argument is correct, the bombing was an unmitigated moral atrocity.[1]

Rejecting Civilian Immunity

The bombing of Germany's cities and towns is a moral issue because it was a deliberate attack on the civilian population. It killed some 600,000 civilians and seriously injured another 800,000. Its aim was to undermine German civilians' morale and terrorize them into pressuring the Nazi government to halt the war and accept unconditional surrender. Civilians are normally considered innocent and therefore morally protected against such an attack. The bombing campaign was a violation of the centerpiece of the *jus in bello* prong of just war theory (and any other plausible ethics of war): the principle of civilian immunity.[2] Those who propose to defend the bombing usually accept this principle, and try to show that there were good reasons for not adhering to it in the case at issue so that the bombing was justified, all things considered. But one might also try to exculpate those who designed and implemented the strategy by rejecting the point of departure of most of the debate—the idea that in war, civilian life, limb, and property are, at least *prima facie*, off limits. To my knowledge, this position has not been advanced by philosophers. But it has been espoused by two writers who were very much concerned with the moral issues of the day. Interestingly enough, both had been at the receiving end of attacks of enemy air force on civilians in World War II and accordingly might have been expected to have some appreciation for the idea of civilian immunity.

The first is George Orwell. He had personal experience of the bombing of London by the German air force. Yet, in his column in *The Tribune* published on 19 May 1944, he utterly rejected the objections to the bombing of German cities advanced by Vera Brittain. Brittain's was one of the very few prominent voices raised in Great Britain at the time against the bombing. She was a pacifist; however, her criticism of the bombing was not couched in pacifist terms, but was rather based on the principle of civilian immunity and the view that "it is better to suffer disadvantage in war than to descend to the lower levels of barbarity," such as "the slaughter of civilians by bombing or starvation, and the avoidable destruction of humanity's cultural heritage."[3] Orwell has some understanding for pacifism, but none for the distinction between barbaric and civilized ways of waging war. The idea of constraining warfare by some such rule as civilian immunity, and indeed all talk of limiting or humanizing war, is "sheer humbug." Orwell cannot see why it is worse to kill civilians than to kill soldiers. "Obviously one must not kill children if it is in any way avoidable," he writes, "but it is only in propaganda pamphlets that every bomb drops on a school or an orphanage." While "legitimate" warfare kills "the healthiest and bravest of the young male population," a bomb dropped on a city kills a cross-section of the population. That is a preferable outcome, because

> war is not avoidable at this stage of history, and since it has to happen it does not seem to me a bad thing that others should be killed besides young men. I wrote in 1937: "Sometimes it is a comfort to me to think that the aeroplane is altering the conditions of war. Perhaps when the next war comes we may see that sight unprecedented in all history, a jingo with a bullet hole in him." We haven't seen that yet … but at any rate the suffering of this war has been shared out more evenly than the last one was. The immunity of civilians, one of the things that have made war possible, has been shattered. Unlike Miss Brittain, I don't regret that. I can't feel that war is "humanised" by being confined to the slaughter of the young and becomes "barbarous" when the old get killed as well. … War is of its nature barbarous, it is better to admit that. If we see ourselves as the savages we are, some improvement is possible …[4]

Orwell's argument has two prongs: it consists of a deontological and a consequentialist component. At this stage of history, at least, war is inevitable, like a natural disaster, rather than a matter of someone's responsibility. It is therefore better, for it is more just, that the suffering it brings should be distributed more evenly, rather than inflicted for the most part on healthy young men in the field. Moreover, as long as we cling to our illusions about "civilized" warfare, we will continue to wage wars. Only if war is allowed to play itself out in all of its destructiveness and barbarity, and if it is clearly perceived and acknowledged as such by all, do we stand a chance of progress toward a world without war.

We can understand, perhaps, how Orwell came to argue along these lines against the background of trench warfare in World War I, in which an entire generation of young men had been decimated. The soundness of his argument is another matter. War is not at all, or at least not entirely, something that descends on human beings like an earthquake, completely unrelated to human choice and responsibility. Orwell, too, knew this. If it were, one could not think it a good thing to see "a jingo with a bullet hole in him." What people choose to do and not do does matter. To be sure, if one advisedly helps bring about an unjust war, or supports such a war, one deserves to pay a price for it. But it is not obvious that one deserves to pay the *ultimate* price. And in any case, not all civilians are jingoes.

Children, in particular, are not, and indeed cannot be, jingoes. Any large civilian population is bound to include a significant proportion of children. If distributive justice requires that the killing and destruction in war be distributed evenly across the entire civilian population, independently of individual choice and action, as Orwell claims, then it is not obvious, nor indeed true, that "one must not kill children." Yet Orwell is unwilling to accept this implication of his argument. Instead, he points out that not every bomb dropped on German cities and towns hit a school or an orphanage. That is true, but not to the point, given Orwell's position. The remark is also disingenuous: the bombing did kill some 100,000 children.

The other author is Hans Magnus Enzensberger. He, too, had spent endless nights in a cellar, hoping to survive an air-raid on his city. Yet he, too, has no time for civilian immunity. But his reasons are different from Orwell's.

> I well remember the ... terrors of the air-raids. And the grown-ups who cowered on the benches in the cellar, at whom these "terror raids" were aimed; they were the "innocent civilians." ... But it wasn't always like this. A strange transformation had occurred in the "innocent civilians" who sat in the cellars while all around them phosphor bombs turned the city into a sea of fire. I remember how their eyes lit up every time the Führer spoke and let them know what he had in mind: "a titanic and unprecedented struggle," a fight to the bitter end. ... Without their enthusiastic support the Nazis could have never come to power.[5]

Wars always start with jubilant masses applauding the warmongers leading them. These leaders are often elected; sometimes their position is confirmed in subsequent elections. They, and the soldiers they send off to war, are acting as "representatives of their society who feed on its rage, its cruelty, its lust for revenge."[6] If so, civilians are not really innocent, but rather responsible for what their military do to the other side. Accordingly, when attacked by the other side, they are merely facing the fatal repercussions of their own actions and omissions.

Surely Enzensberger is being much too harsh on his fellow Germans. No doubt they or, more accurately, many of them, could properly be blamed on several counts. Still, the Nazis never received the majority of German votes in free parliamentary elections.[7] The platform that elicited the support that the Nazis did receive, whether enthusiastic or not, spoke of prosperity and peace, not of starting a world war. They did not come to power on a landslide vote, but rather through coalition politics of a rather crude sort: as William L. Shirer puts it, Hitler became chancellor "by way of the back door, by means of a shabby political deal with the old-school reactionaries he privately detested."[8] Once in power, the Nazis replaced liberal democracy with a one-party police state, and then took Germany to war. Is the fact that many civilians' eyes lit up and that they cheered at rallies organized by an extremely brutal totalitarian regime in wartime reason enough for them to be blown to pieces or incinerated in their cities and towns? Surely no thoughts and feelings in themselves can make one deserve, or become liable to, such an extreme fate. Nor can support for an unjust war, which was manipulated or coerced by a totalitarian state.

What of the claim that the government and the military are "representatives" of their society? This, I take it, means that the killing and destruction the military wreak on the enemy in the course of an unjust war somehow "represent" what civilians in the rear are thinking, feeling, and saying. That certainly shows those civilians and their society in a very bad light. But, again, surely that is not enough, in itself, to justify killing and maiming them, whether as deserved punishment or as a measure of military exigency.

Both Enzensberger's judgment of his compatriots and his sweeping rejection of the idea of civilian immunity, then, are wide of the mark.

Rejecting *Jus in Bello*

Orwell and Enzensberger defend the bombing by rejecting the principle of civilian immunity, which is the paramount requirement of the *jus in bello* prong of the ethics of war. But Orwell's disparagement of all attempts at constraining and civilizing war as "humbug" suggests a more radical defense: one based on a rejection of *jus in bello* as a whole. That is how Air Marshal Sir Robert Saundby, second-in-command to Arthur Harris, defended the destruction of Dresden and, by implication, the entire bombing campaign:

> It is not so much this or the other means of making war that is immoral or inhumane. What is immoral is war itself. Once full-scale war has broken out it can never be humanized or civilized, and if one side attempted to do so it would be most likely to be defeated. So long as we resort to war to settle differences between nations, so long will we have to endure the horrors, barbarities and excesses that war brings with it. That, to me, is the lesson of Dresden.[9]

This is an instance of the "war is hell" doctrine, originally propounded by General Sherman as the justification of his rampage through Georgia and the shelling, forced evacuation, and burning of Atlanta. It takes on board the *jus ad bellum* prong of the ethics of war, while dropping its other prong, *jus in bello*. "War is cruelty, and you cannot refine it," Sherman wrote in a letter to the mayor of Atlanta who was pleading with him to spare the city. "You might as well appeal against the thunder-storm as against these terrible hardships of war." War is started by human choice, but once started, it cannot be controlled or restrained until it runs its course. Therefore, the only moral issue raised by a war is who is responsible for starting it. Those responsible for starting a war are responsible for whatever is done in its course by *both* belligerent parties. "… Those who brought war into our country deserve all the curses and maledictions a people can pour out. I know I had no hand in making this war …"[10] The responsibility for the mayhem and destruction Sherman's actions visited on Southern civilians is to be laid at the door of their own government.

Sherman does not support this extraordinary claim by any argument. As it stands, it is certainly not compelling, nor even plausible. Just why should we see the breaking out of a war as a matter of human choice and responsibility, and at the same time consider what all those who fight in it do in a completely different light, akin to blows inflicted by a thunderstorm? Just why should we embrace the first prong of the ethics of war, and at the same time dispense with the second?

Interestingly enough, Sherman was not utterly oblivious to the moral requirements of *jus in bello*. In another letter on the same subject, written two days earlier, he had offered a very different justification for the forced removal of the citizens of Atlanta: "God will judge us in due time, and he will pronounce whether it be more humane to fight with a town full of women and the families of a brave people at our back or to remove them in time to places of safety among their own friends and people."[11] In saying this, Sherman is conceding what his "war is hell" view denies: that what we do in war, too, is a matter of our own choice and responsibility; that *jus in bello*, too, is morally binding; and that every one of those who do the fighting can and will be subject to moral judgment for his own choices and actions on the battlefield.[12] This was true of Sherman and is no less true of Robert Saundby and everyone else who played a part in the bombing of German cities and towns in World War II.

Payback

A very different way of defending the bombing is to portray it as payback for what the German air force had done to British cities and towns. This defense has three versions. It might be argued that the bombing was justified as vengeance, that it was justified as belligerent reprisal, or that it was justified as retaliation demanded by British public opinion and required for maintaining its morale. The common core in these three lines of argument is the notion of payback: the idea of harm or injury inflicted in response to harm or injury undeservedly suffered. They differ with regard to the point of paying back for the wrong suffered: such payback may be considered morally appropriate in itself, because deserved and just, or instrumentally, on account of its good consequences of one kind or another.

All three versions are predicated upon the claim that the German air force was the first deliberately to attack British civilians, and that the RAF took to bombing German cities and towns in response. This was indeed the message British propaganda was sending to the public at home and abroad, including the German civilian population that was being bombed. Yet this is very much a moot point.[13] Since I am discussing an issue in applied moral philosophy rather than in history, I will assume, for the sake of argument, that the German air force was indeed the first to engage in such attacks. Could what the RAF did to German cities and towns, then, be defended by saying that the Germans were only paid back in their own currency?

Many reject the very idea of vengeance. Some do so for religious reasons, trusting God to see to it that their tormentors, should they remain unrepentant, receive their just deserts. Some accept Socrates' view that "one ought not to return a wrong or an injury to any person, whatever the provocation is."[14] Others hold that "to strike back and to strike first are two very different things, morally speaking, irrespective of the results they may produce or be intended to produce."[15] I, too, believe that, on certain conditions, vengeance is deserved, just, and therefore morally permissible.

For an act of vengeance to be morally permissible, it must satisfy three conditions: it must be proportionate in severity to the wrong suffered; it must be inflicted on the wrongdoer, not on someone else in some way related to the wrongdoer—the wrongdoer's family, or friends, or compatriots; and it must be exacted in the absence of an impartial authority that could provide redress.

The bombing of German cities and towns has sometimes been portrayed as vengeance richly deserved by the German bombing of British cities and towns. During an air-raid on London, Harris remarked: "Well, they are sowing the wind, and they will reap the whirlwind."[16] On 14 July 1941, Churchill announced: "... We will mete out to the Germans the measure, and more than the measure, that they have meted out to us."[17] Vengeance was a recurring theme in the British press throughout the campaign. Thus John Gordon, editor of the *Sunday Express*, wrote in 1942: "Germany, the originator of war by air terror, is now finding that terror recoiling upon herself with an intensity that even Hitler in his most sadistic dreams never thought possible."[18] These quotations indicate one reason why a justification of the bombing as vengeance does not succeed. Justified vengeance cannot amount to a "whirlwind" in response to a wind sown, cannot mete out "more than the measure" of the wrong suffered, cannot realize, let alone go beyond, the "most sadistic dreams." It must be proportionate. In terms of the numbers of civilians killed, the RAF and USAAF went ten times beyond what the German air force *and* the attacks by the V-1 and V-2 missiles had done.

This lack of all proportion would be enough to condemn the bombing of German cities and towns, when construed as vengeance. But the bombing also failed to satisfy the second condition of morally permissible vengeance: that of being inflicted on the wrongdoer, rather than someone innocent of the wrong, but related in some way to the wrongdoer. For those killed or maimed were neither the crew of the German aircraft that had bombed Britain, nor those higher up in the chain of command and responsibility—their military superiors or political masters. They were common civilians.

In saying this, I am assuming the modern view of moral responsibility as pertaining to individuals and their free and informed choice and action. This view does not rule out all talk of collective responsibility. But the only type of such responsibility the modern view allows for is collective responsibility that is ultimately related to some morally significant act or omission of the individual. To be sure, one can assume a premodern notion of collective responsibility independent of individual choice and based on an ascribed, rather than a chosen, identity, such as nationality or race. That, indeed, is how the Nazis looked at these matters in some contexts. So did Churchill and Harris, at least as far as the Germans were concerned. Neither had much use for the distinction between the Nazi leaders and the German military, on the one hand, and German civilians, on the other. As Stephen A. Garrett tells us, neither did the majority of the British press:

> [It] had played an important part in circulating German atrocity stories in the first war and was generally noted for its unabashed jingoism. ... The majority gave more or less unqualified support to the bombing of Germany. The *Sunday Dispatch* was typical with its comment that "it is right that the German population should 'smell death at close quarters.' Now they are getting the stench of it." Still another outsized headline screamed "NO PITY! NO MERCY!" ... Especially virulent in their support for the area offensive were the Beaverbrook newspapers, for which a typical headline was, "Why all this bosh about being gentle with the Germans after we have beaten them when ALL GERMANS ARE GUILTY!"[19]

If we are not ready to revert to this premodern notion of collective responsibility, then the justification of the bombing as vengeance must be rejected.

Any attempt at justifying the bombing as belligerent reprisal fails for the same reasons. Belligerent reprisal is an act of war. It is a response to a violation of *jus in bello* perpetrated by the enemy, constitutes a violation of *jus in bello,* and is carried out with the aim of forcing the enemy to revert to fighting in accordance with *jus in bello.* A reprisal is often bound up with the hazard of causing the enemy to commit further violations of *jus in bello* in response, rather than desist from them. Nevertheless, the aim of reprisals is to break off the chain of such violations; they are meant to enforce the laws of war. If a reprisal is to be morally justified, it must stand a decent chance of attaining this aim. It must also satisfy the requirement of proportion. The killing and destruction caused by the bombing of German cities and towns by the Allies was out of all proportion to the killing and destruction caused by the bombing of British cities and towns by the German air force. Furthermore, innocent people—whether civilians or prisoners of war—must not be harmed by way of reprisal, even if that is precisely what the enemy has done. As Michael Walzer explains, "with regard to the most important of the rules of war [such as civilian immunity], the violation of the rules for the sake of law enforcement is ruled out. The doctrine of reprisal ... refers only to the lesser parts of the war convention, where the rights of the innocent are not at stake."[20] Yet, that is exactly what the Allied terror bombing was: a systematic, large-scale violation, over more than three years, of the centerpiece of *jus in bello*—the principle of civilian immunity.

Finally, could the bombing be defended as payback demanded by British public opinion? Even if one believes that the satisfaction of vindictive feelings in a community is, in itself, a good thing, one cannot seriously claim that it is good to such a degree that it justifies the killing and maiming of large numbers of innocent civilians as a means of achieving it. Could the killing of German civilians be defended as a demand of the British public that had to be met in order to maintain *its* morale? Here the moral argument presupposes a positive answer to a factual question: did the morale of British civilian population really need to be sustained in this way? It seems it did not: Gallup opinion surveys made in the course of war never showed more than half of the respondents voicing approval of retaliation by bombing German civilians.[21] If a vast majority had done so, that might have been an indication (but not a definite proof) of a significant connection between the bombing and British civilian morale. But the fact that not even a simple majority ever did approve of the bombing of civilians does show that their morale was not conditional on the deliberate bombing of German civilian population centers.

Supreme Emergency

The principle of civilian immunity, which was systematically violated by the bombing, is the centerpiece of the *jus in bello* prong of just war theory. Yet there is also a way of defending the bombing in terms of this theory. A highly influential statement of the theory, Michael Walzer's book *Just and Unjust Wars*, offers a partial defense of the bombing campaign, presenting it as a case of "supreme emergency." This is best understood against the background of Walzer's account of the "problem of dirty hands," as the former is but an extreme case of the latter.

We sometimes face a moral conflict: a situation where different moral considerations pull us in opposite directions, and we can act as required by one only at the price of going against the other. Some such conflicts are not very difficult to resolve, as one moral consideration can have more weight than the other, whether in general or at least in the particular case. When resolved accordingly, such conflict does not leave us with a sense of unease or guilt. But sometimes the conflict is deep and vexing: it presents us with a moral dilemma, defined by Walzer as "a situation where [one] must choose between two courses of action both of which it would be wrong for him to undertake."[22] We face such a dilemma whenever we can prevent something extremely bad from happening only by breaking a stringent moral rule. People in all walks of life may have to deal with such a predicament, but those in politics are particularly likely to have to do so.

As thinkers such as Machiavelli, Weber, and Sartre have pointed out, one cannot govern "innocently"—at least not successfully and not for long. Walzer concurs, and adds that we would not want to be governed by those whose primary concern is to keep their hands "clean" by strict adherence to moral rules, rather than to safeguard and promote the common good. In politics, "sometimes it is right to try to succeed, and then it must also be right to get one's hands dirty. But one's hands get dirty from doing what it is wrong to do. And how can it be wrong to do what is right? Or, how can we get our hands dirty by doing what we ought to do?"[23] This looks paradoxical, but Walzer embraces the apparent paradox: a political leader facing such a quandary should indeed break the moral rule in order to prevent a development that would be extremely detrimental to the community. His action will be wrong, in that it will be a breach of a stringent moral rule, and it will also be right, in that it will stave off the threat to the community. Furthermore, it will be right all things considered. It will leave him with dirty hands and a sense of guilt, yet he ought to do it; if he does not, he will fail to live up to the duties of his office.[24]

Quandaries of this sort are particularly dramatic in wartime. Such was the predicament Britain seemed to be facing in early 1942. The government feared an impending defeat; it also feared that there was nothing its military could do about it, at least as long as they were fighting "clean." Moreover, Britain's defeat was not going to be yet another defeat of a country by another, entailing such things as loss of some territory, war reparations, political concessions, and the like. Britain was perceived as the only remaining obstacle to the subjugation of most of Europe by the Nazis. And the rule of the Nazis over most of Europe would mean genocide of at least one people, expulsion of a number of others from their lands, and something very much like enslavement for still others. In Walzer's words, "Nazism was an ultimate threat to everything decent in our lives, an ideology and a practice of domination so murderous, so degrading even to those who might survive, that the consequences of its final victory were literally beyond calculation, immeasurably awful." It was "evil objectified in the world ... in a form so potent and apparent that there could never have been anything to do but fight against it."[25] Thus, Britain was thought to be facing what Walzer (borrowing the term from Churchill) calls "supreme emergency": an (a) imminent threat of (b) something utterly unthinkable from a moral point of view, a moral catastrophe. In such an emergency, and in such an emergency only, one may act in breach of such a basic and weighty moral principle as that of civilian immunity, if that is the only way one can hope to prevent the catastrophe. Accordingly, Churchill's government decided that Britain would no longer fight "clean," and unleashed its air force on the civilian population of Germany. The onslaught continued almost to the last days of the war. Most of that killing and destruction cannot be defended by this line of argument, since it soon became obvious that Germany was not going to win the war. But in its first stage, in Walzer's judgment, the terror bombing of Germany was morally justified (albeit a crime as well). It was morally justified as the only possible response to the supreme emergency Britain was facing in the first half of 1942.[26]

Some might reject the supreme emergency position on civilian immunity in war. Its rejection would be based on the view that the prohibition of the intentional killing of innocent people is absolute, leaving room for no exceptions, whatever the price of upholding it might be. In response to the supreme emergency argument, adherents of this view will affirm "a willingness to undergo tyrannous domination rather than be ready to carry out vast massacres," indeed, "a willingness to accept anything, even martyrdom, rather than do wrong."[27] I do not share this view. I believe that civilian immunity is an extremely weighty, but not an absolute, moral rule. If the cost of abiding by it were to be a moral catastrophe of the sort that Nazi rule over most of Europe would have meant, I feel that we would no longer be bound by it. What is at issue here, then, is whether the empirical part of the supreme emergency defense of the terror bombing campaign is sound. We need not question the nature and moral implications of the danger that the bombing was supposed to stave off. What we need to do is ask two factual questions: was the danger imminent, and were there good grounds for believing that the bombing would indeed eliminate it?

Although the slide toward what Churchill described as "an absolutely devastating, exterminating attack by very heavy bombers ... upon the Nazi homeland"[28] began as early as mid-1940, the time span I am concerned with can be demarcated quite precisely. It begins on 14 February 1942, when Bomber Command was ordered to concentrate on terror bombing, and ends with the 16 April 1945 RAF Air Staff directive to stop it. Was the danger of German victory imminent at any point within this period? Here, it seems to me, one could argue for three different assessments. According to the first, Britain was, indeed, facing the prospect of defeat after the rout of its expeditionary force at Dunkirk and the capitulation of France. The German air force was seeking to achieve dominance in the air, which was a precondition for the invasion of the country by German ground forces. The Battle of Britain, which lasted from July to October 1940, was supposed to secure this dominance, but it was the RAF that prevailed. As a consequence, Germany had to shelve its invasion plans. On this assessment, the danger of imminent German victory over Britain lasted for several months in mid-1940. On another assessment, although

Germany had to give up its plans of invading Britain for the time being, it still stood a good chance of winning the war on the continent and subsequently bringing Britain under heel. Hitler decided to deal with the Soviet Union first and settle accounts with Britain afterwards. He launched the Russian campaign, which was initially highly successful. But by December 1941, the German army was stopped at the gates of Moscow, and the entire campaign stalled. Another momentous event in the same month was Pearl Harbor, which brought the US into the war. That put paid to any chance of Germany winning the war.[29] On yet another assessment, at that time, Germany still stood some chance of winning. But after its defeats at El Alamein in November 1942 and at Stalingrad in February 1943, it was clear that it no longer had any such chance.

Those who adopt the first or the second assessment must conclude that at the time British political and military leaders decided that the RAF was to concentrate on terror bombing, the country was no longer facing an imminent threat of German victory and that, accordingly, the bombing campaign was never justified as a response to a supreme emergency. Those who find the third assessment of war prospects plausible will say that Britain was, indeed, facing the danger of defeat and subjugation by Nazi Germany at the time its leaders decided to launch the campaign of terror bombing and that, in its first year, the campaign was a response to a supreme emergency, although that was no longer the case in subsequent years. But they can claim that the campaign was a *morally justified* response to a supreme emergency only if an additional condition was satisfied: if those who made the decision had good reasons to believe that the bombing would achieve its aim of undermining the morale of the German people and forcing its leadership to halt the war and accept unconditional surrender.

On the face of it, it is not clear just how demanding this condition is. When facing a supreme emergency, just how confident must we be that violating a stringent moral rule, such as that of civilian immunity, will, in fact, achieve the aim, while nothing else we might do will? It could be argued that when *in extremis*, we cannot apply stringent epistemic standards in deciding how to cope; if we cannot really know what will work, we must take our chances with what might. This is Walzer's view: "There is no option; the risk otherwise is too great."[30] Under the circumstances, British political and military leaders had to "wager" the "determinate crime" of terror bombing against the "immeasurable evil" that was otherwise in store for Britain and most of Europe. It might be objected that Walzer's position highlights the enormity of the threat, while failing to give due weight to the enormity of the means proposed for fending off the threat—the enormity of terror bombing, of deliberately killing and maiming large numbers of innocent people. When that is taken into account, the conclusion should rather be that even *in extremis,* if mass killing of innocent civilians is to be justified, the reasons for believing that it will work and that nothing else will must be very good indeed.

This objection has considerable force. Therefore, I tend to adopt the latter, more demanding position. The supreme emergency justification of the terror bombing of German cities and towns, then, might apply at best to the first year of the bombing, and would prove convincing only if those responsible for the campaign had very good reasons to believe that it would succeed on its own terms—that it would undermine the morale of the civilian population of Germany and eventually force its leaders to halt the war and accept unconditional surrender. This condition is also the condition on which the last line of justification to be considered here—the consequentialist one—would depend.

The Balance of Consequences

In just war theory, civilian immunity is a matter of civilians' rights and justice mandating respect of those rights. Accordingly, civilian immunity is considered an extremely weighty moral rule; breaching it might be justified, if ever, only in cases where not doing so would mean failing to prevent some *moral* catastrophe. This rule is also enjoined by the other major approach to the morality of war—consequentialism. In consequentialist ethics of war, however, civilian immunity is not understood as a matter of justice and rights, but rather as a rule whose adoption has better consequences overall than the adoption of any alternative rule or of no rule at all. Respecting civilian immunity is the best way of reducing the killing and destruction of war. A rule that is justified because it is useful binds only insofar as it is useful. That means that in consequentialist ethics of war, civilian immunity has considerably less weight than it does in just war theory. It is justified because it reduces killing and destruction and accordingly binds only insofar as it does so. In cases where it does not—where it is only by attacking civilians that the best outcome will be achieved—civilian immunity has to give way.

Given that in World War II the best outcome overall was for the Axis powers to be defeated by the Allies, does that war present us with such a case? In an important statement of the consequentialist conception of *jus in bello,* Richard B. Brandt writes that

> widespread civilian bombing might be defended by arguing that a significant deterioration in civilian morale could bring an end to a war by producing internal revolution. Our principle does not exclude

the possibility of such reasoning, in the presence of serious evidence about civilian morale, when the stakes of victory are high. But we know enough about how bombing affects civilian morale to know that such bombing could be justified only rarely, if at all.[31]

Did British political and military leaders have serious evidence that theirs was one of those rare cases when bombing enemy civilians would undermine their morale and make them force their leaders to call a halt to the war or, alternatively, rise up and replace their leaders with another, peace-minded lot? To understand the assessments British leaders made and the decisions they took, we need to recall a view about air force strategy developed in the 1920s by two air warfare theorists, Basil H. Liddell Hart and Giulio Douhet. Both were concerned that the next major war should avoid trench warfare, which made for a prolonged deadlock rather than quick victory and involved unacceptably high casualties, and both argued that air force offered a promising alternative. There was no need to try to destroy an enemy's armed forces, when his will to fight could be broken at its source, in the rear, by concentrated air force attacks on civilian population centers that dislocate normal life and undermine civilian morale. "If we can demoralize one section of the nation," Liddell Hart wrote, "the collapse of its will to resist compels the surrender of the whole."[32] This strategy was only seemingly brutal, since "a swift and sudden blow of this nature inflicts a total of injury far less than when spread over a number of years," as it used to be in "the cannon-fodder wars of the past."[33] Douhet adopted the same approach:

> Take the center of a large city and imagine what would happen among the civilian population during a single attack by a single bombing unit. ... Its impact upon the people would be terrible. ... What could happen to a single city in a single day could also happen to ten, twenty, fifty cities. And, since news travels fast ... what, I ask you, would be the effect upon civilians of other cities, not yet stricken but equally subject to bombing attacks? What civil or military authority could keep order, public services functioning, and production going on under such a threat? ... A complete breakdown of the social structure cannot but take place in a country subjected to this kind of merciless pounding from the air. The time would soon come when, to put an end to horror and suffering, the people themselves, driven by the instinct of self-preservation, would rise up and demand an end to the war—this before their army and navy had time to mobilize at all![34]

Douhet's answer to those who believe that civilians should not be deliberately attacked in war was the same as Liddell Hart's. "Mercifully, the decision will be quick in this kind of war, since the decisive blows will be directed at civilians, that element ... least able to sustain them," and so much less blood will be shed overall.³⁵

This view of air force strategy gained important followers in Britain between the world wars. It exerted considerable influence on the nature and structure of the RAF Bomber Command and the understanding of its role in future wars.³⁶ It came into its own on 14 February 1942, when Bomber Command was issued a new directive, which determined that the "primary object" of its bombing raids should be German civilians. Its operations "should now be focussed on the morale of the enemy civil population and in particular, of the industrial workers." A list of German cities to be "destroyed" was provided. The next day, this was followed by a minute from Chief of the Air Staff, Sir Charles Portal, meant to rule out any misunderstanding: "Ref the new bombing directive: I suppose it is clear that the aiming points are to be the built-up areas, *not*, for instance, the dockyards or aircraft factories ... This must be made quite clear if it is not already understood."³⁷

Over more than three years, almost to the last day of the war, the RAF, later joined by the USAAF, did its best to carry out these instructions. It killed some 600,000 German civilians, seriously injured 800,000 more, made millions homeless, and devastated many German cities and towns. Yet it did not achieve the aim it had set out to achieve: it did not break the morale of the German people and force its leadership to surrender.

This might be thought puzzling, but can be explained if we take into account that—contrary to the implicit assumption of the architects of the bombing campaign—morale is not of a piece. Throughout the war years, Germany was covered by a web of informants of the Security Service (*Sicherheitsdienst*), the SS intelligence branch. They were closely following attitudes and concerns of the population as expressed in people's comments and actions, and sending regular reports to a string of party and government offices.³⁸ These reports made use of a distinction between two layers of morale: mood (*Stimmung*) and conduct (*Haltung*). The picture that emerges is one of a gap between the two. The former sank; the latter held up.

Obviously, the bombing could not fail to affect the *mood* of the people. One cannot remain of good cheer when one's spouse and children have been killed, one's home has been destroyed, and one's city is being reduced to rubble. The trust in the *Führer*, other leading figures of the regime, and the Nazi party, and the faith in eventual victory, were undermined. But at the same time, the message of dehumanization and extermination conveyed by the bombing (as well as the demand for unconditional surrender and various proposals for "punishing" Germany after the war) tended to strengthen, rather than weaken, the will to hold out.

Furthermore, as Olaf Groehler writes, the authorities responded to the crisis with "a long-term program of social bribery, population transfers, and demagogic measures meant to preserve stability in the big cities," which had considerable success.[39] On top of all that, there was the drive to survive, which, in the words of Hans Mommsen, "enabled the individual to achieve immense physical feats, and the community to show a never to be repeated solidarity and willingness to help."[40] Thus, as far as the *conduct* of the civilian population was concerned, the overall effect of the terror bombing was the opposite of what it was supposed to be:

> The population affected by the bombing war responded with discipline and determination and acquitted itself with willingness to help and solidarity to a degree that surprised the authorities. "In their outward and inner comportment most people present a sight that until a short time ago one would not have thought possible," reported the public prosecutor in Darmstadt at the beginning of 1944; "the Germans are in the process of becoming a true national community."[41]

A telling indication of this development was a fact highlighted by Hans Rumpf. Normally, soldiers on the battlefield are held up as the example of courage, determination, and devotion to duty for civilians to admire and seek to emulate. However, "towards the end of the war it was the other way round: the Wehrmacht orders of the day now held up the civilian population, who still defied the bombing terror, as the shining example for the soldiers."[42]

The other side of the coin was that there was no sensible alternative to continuing to do one's job and at least passively complying with state policies. After all, Nazi Germany was a totalitarian state. The population was closely monitored by a web of government and party officials and informants. Draconian penalties, including that of death, were meted out for a wide range of offenses against the war effort itself or the morale required for that effort.[43]

This is not a matter of hindsight, but rather something the architects of the terror bombing campaign could and should have known. They had no good reason to believe that the bombing would achieve its objective. Indeed, they had no reason at all to believe that. As the campaign unfolded, they had no serious evidence it was succeeding. Indeed, they had no evidence at all. Nor did they try to produce convincing arguments and solid evidence. Much thinking went into dealing with the technical questions: what should be the proportion between explosive and incendiary ordnance, how to produce firestorms in cities, which cities were most likely to be thoroughly burnt down, etc.[44] But apparently noone ever gave any sustained thought to the question of *just how* an assault on the morale of German civilian population would produce policy or regime change in Germany. A minute by Lord Cherwell, Churchill's principal advisor on scientific matters, sent to Churchill on 30 March 1942, provides a telling example:

> In 1938 over 22 million Germans lived in 58 towns of over 100,000 inhabitants, which, with modern equipment, should be easy to find and hit. Our forecast output of heavy bombers ... between now and the middle of 1943 is about 10,000. If even half the total load of 10,000 bombers were dropped on the built-up areas of these 58 German towns the great majority of their inhabitants (about one-third of the German population) would be turned out of house and home.
>
> Investigation seems to show that having one's house demolished is most damaging to morale. People seem to mind it more than having their friends or even relatives killed. ... There seems little doubt that this would break the spirit of the people.[45]

Lord Cherwell saw no need to explain just how a people whose spirit had been broken was to proceed to force the hand of the Nazi leaders to halt the war or, alternatively, to overthrow them and put a peace-minded government in their place.

Not only did the British political and military leaders have no reason to believe that the terror bombing campaign would succeed; they had several good reasons to believe that it would not. The lesson to be drawn from the bombing of British cities and towns by the German air force and V-1 and V-2 missiles was that, after an initial shock, bombing does not break, but rather stiffens, the will of the civilian population to hold out. The intelligence concerning the way German civilians were bearing up under the bombs, gathered from a range of sources, was in line with the British experience.[46] Finally, sheer common sense could have told them that a population ruled by the Nazis and policed by the Gestapo was not in a position to change government policy or replace the government with one that would surrender.

Thus, the consequentialist justification of the terror bombing also fails. By the same token, Walzer's supreme emergency argument also fails, since its second factual premise is false.

Conclusion

In this chapter, I have revisited the moral issue raised by the terror bombing of Germany's cities and towns in World War II. I have discussed the main ways in which the bombing campaign has been or might be morally defended: as a way of ensuring a more equitable distribution of inevitable suffering and loss brought about by war; with reference to the complicity of the victims; in terms of the "war is hell" doctrine; as retaliation or reprisal; as a violation of *jus in bello* that was permitted and indeed enjoined by a "supreme emergency"; as a means justified by the aim it was to achieve. I have argued that all these attempts at justification fail. If my arguments are sound, the bombing campaign was an unmitigated atrocity.

Beyond that, it was a campaign of state terrorism—perhaps the longest such campaign in wartime, and the deadliest in terms of the number of victims. In terms of the spirit if not the letter of international law at the time, it was a war crime of immense proportions that deeply compromised "the good war" the Allies were prosecuting. Viewed historically, it was a crucial stage in a process of ever more comprehensive and systematic victimization of enemy civilians as a supplement to, or even a substitute for, fighting enemy soldiers. This process had begun in earnest with the British naval blockade of Germany in World War I and was soon to lead to the conventional and then nuclear terror bombing of Japanese cities, and beyond.

Notes

A shorter version of this chapter was first published in German as "Das Bombardement deutscher Städte im Zweiten Weltkrieg. Eine moralische Frage," *Deutsche Zeitschrift für Philosophie*, vol. 56 (2008): 585–598. Copyright © Akademie Verlag, Berlin. Reprinted with permission.

1. For the sake of brevity, I will focus on the RAF bombing campaign. The terror bombing of German cities was designed by the British political and military leadership; it was started, and for the most part implemented, by the RAF. The USAAF initially focused on military targets and joined the RAF in deliberate attacks on German civilians only at a later stage. My discussion applies to its part in the terror bombing as well. Moreover, some of the things I say about the bombing of Germany apply, *mutatis mutandis*, to the USAAF terror bombing, conventional and nuclear, of Japan's cities.

    Earlier substantial discussions of the morality of the bombing include John C. Ford, S.J., "The Morality of Obliteration Bombing," *Theological Studies*, vol. 5 (1944) (an abridged version is reprinted in Richard A. Wasserstrom, ed., *War and Morality* (Belmont, CA: Wadsworth Publishing Co., 1970)); Stephen A. Garrett, *Ethics and Airpower in World War II: The British Bombing of German Cities* (New York: St. Martin's Press, 1993), chs. 5–7; A.C. Grayling, *Among the Dead Cities: Was the Allied Bombing of Civilians in WWII a Necessity or a Crime?* (London: Bloomsbury, 2006), chs. 6–8; Lothar Fritze, *Die Moral des Bombenterrors. Alliierte Flächenbombardements im Zweiten Weltkrieg* (München: Olzog Verlag, 2007), chs. 9, 11, 19–20, 23.

2. On the history, grounds, scope, and stringency of this principle, see Colm McKeogh, *Innocent Civilians: The Morality of Killing in War* (Basingstoke and New York: Palgrave, 2002); Igor Primoratz, ed., *Civilian Immunity in War* (Oxford: Oxford University Press, 2007).
3. Vera Brittain, *Humiliation with Honour* (London: Andrew Dakers Ltd., 1942), 89.
4. Sonia Orwell and Ian Angus, eds., *The Collected Essays, Journalism and Letters of George Orwell* (London: Secker & Warburg, 1968), vol. 3: 151–152; see also 181–183.
5. Hans Magnus Enzensberger, *Civil War*, trans. Piers Spence and Martin Chalmers (London: Granta Books, 1994), 50.
6. Ibid., 51.
7. The best they ever did in such elections was 37 percent of the votes (July 1932); in the last free elections (November 1932), they got 32 percent. When Hitler ran for president in March and again in April 1932, he came second on both occasions, receiving 30 and 36 percent of the votes, respectively.
8. William L. Shirer, *The Rise and Fall of the Third Reich* (London: Secker & Warburg, 1960), 184.
9. Sir Robert Saundby, "Foreword," to David Irving, *The Destruction of Dresden* (New York: Holt, Rinehart and Winston, 1963), 6.
10. Letter to James M. Calhoun and others of 12 September 1864, in William Tecumseh Sherman, *Memoirs* (New York: The Library of America, s.a.), 601.
11. Letter to General J.B. Hood of 10 September 1864, ibid., 595.
12. For an analysis of several versions of the "war is hell" view, see Daniel A. Dombrowski, "What Does 'War Is Hell' Mean?," *The International Journal of Applied Philosophy*, vol. 1 (1983).
13. See e.g., Horst Boog, "Der Strategische Bombenkrieg der Alliierten gegen Deutschland 1939–1945. Ein Überblick," in *Alliierter Bombenkrieg. Das Beispiel Dresden*, eds. Lothar Fritze and Thomas Widera (Göttingen: V&R Unipress, 2005), 18–27; Hans Rumpf, *The Bombing of Germany*, trans. Edward Fitzgerald (London: Frederick Muller, 1963), ch. 2. Rumpf quotes several British authors—both defenders of the bombing, such as J.M. Spaight (*Bombing Vindicated*, 1944) and its critics, such as F.J.P. Veale (*Advance to Barbarism*, 1948), B.H. Liddell Hart (*The Revolution in Warfare*, 1946), and J.F.C. Fuller (*The Second World War 1939–1945*, 1948)—in support of his conclusion that "in addition to the burden she justly carries, Germany does not carry the further heavy burden of responsibility for the unleashing of total, unrestricted air warfare" (Rumpf, 27).
14. Plato, *Crito*, 49c, trans. Hugh Tredennick.
15. K.G. Armstrong, "The Retributivist Hits Back," *Mind*, vol. 70 (1961): 489.
16. Quoted in Garrett, *Ethics and Airpower in World War II*, 192.
17. *The War Speeches of the Rt Hon Winston S. Churchill*, compiled by Charles Eade (London: Cassel & Co., 1952), vol. 2: 25.
18. Quoted in Brittain, *Humiliation with Honour*, 92.
19. Garrett, *Ethics and Airpower in World War II*, 103. See also chapter 8 in this volume.
20. Michael Walzer, *Just and Unjust Wars: A Moral Argument with Historical Illustrations*, 3rd ed. (New York: Basic Books, 2000), 215.

21. Garrett, *Ethics and Airpower in World War II*, 192.
22. Michael Walzer, "Political Action: The Problem of Dirty Hands," *Philosophy and Public Affairs*, vol. 2 (1972/73): 160.
23. Ibid., 164.
24. The idea of "dirty hands" is very much contested. For a good sample of arguments for and against, see Stephen de Wijze, "Dirty Hands: Doing Wrong to Do Right," and Kai Nielsen, "There is No Dilemma of Dirty Hands," both in Igor Primoratz, ed., *Politics and Morality* (Basingstoke and New York: Palgrave Macmillan, 2007).
25. Walzer, *Just and Unjust Wars*, 253.
26. Walzer's account of "supreme emergency" is actually less straightforward and more permissive than my summary suggests. He goes on to consider a similar threat to a single country and argues that the argument would still apply. Eventually, he says that "the survival and freedom of political communities" are "the highest values of international society" (Walzer, 254). It turns out that he operates with two different conceptions of supreme emergency. It is one thing to meet the fate the Nazis had in store for peoples they considered racially inferior, and another to have one's political community dismantled. By moving back and forth between these two types of supreme emergency under the ambiguous heading of threat to "the survival and freedom of a political community," Walzer is inviting us to extend to the latter the moral response appropriate to the former. The invitation should be declined. While extermination or "ethnic cleansing" of a people from its land does qualify as a moral catastrophe, its loss of independence is, at most, a political one. If a political community to be dismantled lacks moral legitimacy, its demise might actually be a change for the better, morally speaking. Even if a political community does have moral legitimacy, it is difficult to see how a threat to its "survival and freedom" amounts to "an ultimate threat to everything decent in our lives." Therefore, it is also difficult to see how its military could be justified in waging war on enemy civilians in order to defend it.

    For a critique of Walzer's "supreme emergency" position and its application to the terror bombing of German cities and towns along different lines, see Stephen E. Lammers, "Area Bombing in World War II: The Argument of Michael Walzer," *The Journal of Religious Ethics*, vol. 11 (1983); Kenneth L. Brown, "'Supreme Emergency': A Critique of Michael Walzer's Moral Justification for Allied Obliteration Bombing in World War II," *Manchester College Bulletin of the Peace Studies Institute*, vol. 13 (1983).
27. John Finnis, *Moral Absolutes: Tradition, Revision, and Truth* (Washington, DC: The Catholic University of America Press, 1991), 22.
28. Minute to Minister of War Production, 8 July 1940, quoted in Winston S. Churchill, *The Second World War*, vol. II (London: Cassell & Co., 1949), 567.
29. Churchill, for one, thought so at the time: "Now at this very moment I knew the United States was in the war … So we had won after all! … Once again in our long Island history we should emerge … safe and victorious. … Hitler's fate was sealed. Mussolini's fate was sealed. As for the Japanese, they would be ground to powder. … There was no more doubt about the end" (Winston S. Churchill, *The Second World War*, vol. III (London: Cassell & Co., 1950), 539–540).

30. Walzer, *Just and Unjust Wars*, 259–260.
31. R.B. Brandt, "Utilitarianism and the Rules of War," *Philosophy and Public Affairs*, vol. 1 (1971/72): 159.
32. B.H. Liddell Hart, *Paris or the Future of War* (London: Kegan Paul, Trench, Trubner & Co., 1925), 27.
33. Ibid., 50. Later, however, Liddell Hart became opposed to this method of warfare. In June 1942, after the raids on Cologne, he wrote: "It will be ironical if the defenders of civilisation depend for victory upon the most barbaric, and unskilled, way of winning a war that the modern world has seen" (quoted in Brian Bond, *Liddell Hart: A Study of His Military Thought* (London: Gregg Revivals and King's College London, 1991), 145).
34. Giulio Douhet, *The Command of the Air*, trans. Dino Ferrari (New York: Coward-McCann, 1942), 58.
35. Ibid., 61.
36. See Bond, *Liddell Hart*, 43.
37. Sir Charles Webster and Noble Frankland, *The Strategic Air Offensive against Germany 1939–1945*, vol. I (London: HMSO, 1961), 323–324. On the wider context, see Sven Lindqvist, *A History of Bombing*, trans. Linda Haverty Rugg (London: Granta Books, 2001).
38. For a selection of these reports, see Heinz Boberach, ed., *Meldungen aus dem Reich. Auswahl aus den geheimen Lageberichten des Sicherheitsdienstes der SS 1939–1944* (Neuwied and Berlin: Luchterhand, 1965).
39. Olaf Groehler, *Bombenkrieg gegen Deutschland* (Berlin: Akademie-Verlag, 1990), 295–296.
40. Hans Mommsen, "Wie die Bomben Hitler halfen," in *Als Feuer vom Himmel fiel. Der Bombenkrieg in Deutschland*, eds. Stephan Burgdorf and Christian Habbe (München: Deutsche Verlags-Anstalt, 2003), 115.
41. Ibid., 117.
42. Rumpf, *The Bombing of Germany*, 206.
43. See Jörg Friedrich, *The Fire: The Bombing of Germany 1940–1945*, trans. Allison Brown (New York: Columbia University Press, 2006), 396–400.
44. See ibid., 8–18, 91–101.
45. Quoted in Webster and Frankland, *The Strategic Air Offensive against Germany 1939–1945*, vol. I, 331–332.
46. See Garrett, *Ethics and Airpower in World War II*, 164–169.

CHAPTER 6

Four Types of Mass Murderer
Stalin, Hitler, Churchill, Truman
Douglas P. Lackey

The provocative description of these four men as "mass murderers" might be taken as an attempt to show that they were all equally evil. But it is not my purpose to show that Truman was morally on a par with Stalin or that Churchill was morally the same as Hitler. In fact, I do not believe such things. Neither is it my purpose to set up scales to determine which of these four is the worst of the murderers. In the case of Hitler and Stalin, this would involve comparing the number of people killed in Hitler's wars and genocides with the number of people killed in Stalin's famines and purges. Such judgments would require demographic skills that I do not possess. What I hope to demonstrate is that there are different types of mass murder and different types of mass murderers, and that there is a small but diverse set of rationales those who hold power invoke to justify killing large groups of innocent people. Stalin and Hitler and Churchill and Truman were all evil, but they were evil in different ways.

That the four are properly described as "mass murderers" I have no doubt. They each made choices that produced the deaths of a great many innocent people, choices that they knew would produce such results. Other non-deadly choices were available; they were not pressured by external forces or by competing moral norms into the lethal choices they made. Despite Truman's inferiority complex, Churchill's megalomania, Stalin's paranoia, and Hitler's pathological capacity for hatred, none of them was mentally ill. The excuses of ignorance, necessity, coercion, or insanity, are not available. Neither is the justification of self-defense.

True, none of them ever killed anybody with his own hands. But when they gave the orders that ultimately produced mass death, they had every expectation that those orders would be carried out. Furthermore, if a subordinate refused to carry out a deadly order, they were committed to finding others who would do the job. Murderers need not be killers, if they can get others to kill for them.

The cases of mass killing I shall discuss, the ones, among others, that implicate Stalin and Hitler and Churchill and Truman as mass murderers, are the Ukrainian famine of 1932–33, the Jewish Holocaust of 1941–45, the bombing of Dresden in February 1945, and the bombing of Hiroshima in August 1945. Estimates of the number of victims in these tragedies differ, but there is no doubt that in the Ukrainian famine and the Holocaust, millions of people died, and in the bombings of Dresden and Hiroshima, tens of thousands of people died. But, as I explained, I am focusing on the quality of evil done rather than the quantity of evil unleashed. So I suggest, as a thought experiment, that we consider, of all those who died in these four atrocities, just one victim from each: one Ukrainian, one Jew, one German, one Japanese.

Consider the wife of a farmer from Vinnytsa province in the Ukraine who starved to death in the winter of 1932–33. What was Stalin's relation to her death? Consider an elderly Polish Jew gassed at Auschwitz in the fall of 1943. What was Hitler's relation to his terrible end? Consider a young German refugee burned to death at Dresden the night of 13 February 1945: how did Churchill's policy choices relate to her catastrophe? Consider a Japanese child incinerated as he walked to school in Hiroshima that morning of 6 August 1945. How do Truman's choices relate to that child? What could each of these leaders say to their victims? What different types of moral and human relationships bind oppressors and victims together in life and death?

The Famine

In the minds of many people who lived outside the former USSR, the story of the Ukrainian famine of 1932–33 is a story of poor weather followed by a poor harvest followed by starvation: too little food, too many mouths to feed, and government help arriving too late. But this famine, like most famines, originated in politics. Bad decisions, not bad weather, were the origin of the catastrophe, and the government as much caused the disaster as failed to cure it.[1]

After Stalin consolidated his power in 1929, he was committed to Lenin's idea that the creation of a new socialist state required the reorganization of Soviet agriculture. For centuries, farming in Russia and the Ukraine had been feudal. With the emancipation of the serfs in 1860, it began to be bourgeois, and the bourgeois trend toward small private farms was ironically accelerated by the flight of many large landowners after the Bolshevik revolution in 1917. Now agriculture was to become socialist. To achieve socialized agriculture, in Stalin's terms, two things were required:

(1) the abolition of the private farm, via the combination of private holdings into large collectives; (2) the abolition of markets for agricultural products.

The creation of the collective farms or kolkhozes was the bloody work of 1930–32. Naturally, the peasants who had prospered under the various post-emancipation regimes objected to the abolition of their family farms. Viewed now as obstacles of progress, the top-layer farmers soon found themselves classified as kulaks or "rich peasants,"[2] where "rich" meant something like "owning more than one cow." Kulaks so defined were subdivided by the authorities into three groups: (1) those to be shot, (2) those to be transported to collective labor camps in Siberia, and (3) those to be forcibly relocated on collective farms. Public support for these brutal policies was generated and sustained by Soviet propaganda that described the kulaks as enemies of society, parasites on the social organism, disease germs within it, and doomed opponents of historical progress.

Soviet propaganda conveyed the impression that the kulaks were a powerful organized group determined to subvert the building of socialism. In fact, the kulaks had never, even at the beginning of the collectivization process, formed an organized political group in opposition to the regime. Unlike the White opponents of the Bolsheviks in 1919–20, the kulaks had no territory, no army, no foreign support, and no capacity to wage war. Their protests were purely local and invariably ineffective. By the end of 1932, eighty percent of Soviet agriculture had been collectivized, tens of thousands of kulaks had been shot, hundreds of thousands more had been transported, and the remainder were surrounded by a population encouraged to view them as enemies. We can conclude, not by direct evidence, but by reasonable inference, that Stalin knew by 1932 that the kulaks were no threat to his agricultural policy.

Phase two of the new Soviet agriculture entailed replacing markets with production quotas. The ideological bases for this move deserve to be laid out. The land and its products under socialism were viewed as the common property of the Soviet people, to be used for the common benefit of present and future generations. Grain was therefore neither the property of a private landowner nor the possession of farmers who had labored to produce it. In discussions of agricultural policy, a particular effort was made to portray the new form of economic organization as a cooperative interchange between the peasant class and the industrial working class, with the farmers supplying grain to the workers, and the workers, in return, supplying the farmers with steel plows, tractors, combines, and electricity—often from massive hydroelectric projects. It was expected that the use of tractors and other machines on large plots of land would substantially increase both total grain yield and the per hour productivity of each agricultural worker. Such was the message of Eisenstein's brilliant and humorous 1929 film devoted to the new agriculture, *Old and New*.

It is obvious in retrospect that the move to publicly owned collectives and to a command economy in agricultural products could not produce the results that were hoped of it. But in assessing the choices of 1932, it must be acknowledged that it was not obvious how poor the results would be. The move from family farms to "agribusiness" has been the long-term story of US agriculture in the twentieth century, and large-scale US farming methods, by many standards, are the most productive in the world. The notion that rural backwardness could be cured by hydroelectric power was as much a part of the US New Deal as the Soviet five year plans, and the idea that the mechanization of work would usher in an age of leisure and plenty for both rural and urban workers was present not just in the writings of Lenin and the Bolsheviks, but also in anti-Leninists, such as Bertrand Russell.[3] Optimism as regards collectivization was misguided, but not insane.

The theory of collectivization, however, will not tell you, in any particular case, what a production target should be. The Soviets felt by 1932 that they had installed a superior system of agricultural organization, much better than the pre-collectivization system of 1929. Thus, the production targets for 1932, assuredly approved by Stalin, were set substantially above the figures for the 1929 harvest. But, in fact, agricultural productivity since 1929 had gone into a steep decline because (a) many of the most productive farmers, as evidenced by their modest wealth accumulations in the 1920s, had been shot or deported, (b) the radical reorganization of production entailed temporary inefficiencies caused by unexpected bottlenecks and miscellaneous confusion, (c) the tractors and other mechanical support required for increased production had failed to arrive or broke down shortly after arrival, and (d) the lack of personal compensation for hard work, Soviet praise for the Heroes of Labor notwithstanding, produced the usual inefficiency of alienated toil. With productivity in steep decline, the 1932 agricultural target was in fact fantastic. This could have been known before the harvest was in, and it was certainly known soon thereafter.

The Soviets nonetheless proceeded to requisition grain at gunpoint according to the 1932 targets. Needless to report, the targets could not be met, but what grain could be found was taken from the farmers. The result was simple and dreadful; the farmers were left with no grain for themselves, and no food to get through the winter and early spring. For millennia, farmers had kept enough of their product to feed themselves and sold the surplus (if any) to the cities. In this case, the cities had grain for free, the farmers had nothing. They began to starve.

Early reports of starvation could have produced an end to requisitions. They did not, and requisitions, or at least demands for grain, continued through the winter. Since the demanded quota assumed the grain existed, failure to produce the grain was considered proof that the farmers, or at least the kulak farmers, were hiding grain. If grain was hidden, the farmers could not be starving, and there was no need for emergency aid. The farmers could not demonstrate that they were not hiding food, as proof that it was not hidden in one place produced only the assured judgment that it was hidden some place else.

The official position of the government was that the farmers were hoarding grain. Consequently, in early 1933, it could not be admitted that the farmers were starving. The provinces were sealed off; those who spoke of starvation were promptly arrested. Foreign nations could not contribute food; the grain in the cities could not be returned to the provinces; city folk who provided handouts to the desperate peasants staggering in from the countryside were subject to arrest. By the spring of 1933, the livestock had been killed and eaten; the ponds fished out; the bark eaten off of the trees. Hundreds of villages became graveyards. In the Vinnytsa province in the Ukraine, a farmer and his wife slowly starved to death, dying in their home, surrounded by the bodies of their children.

What was Stalin's relation to that woman's death? To begin, we can infer that Stalin did not want that woman to die. In his mind, she could not be an enemy of the regime, because the enemies of the regime, he thought, were kulaks who were hoarding grain. It follows that those who starved could not have been kulaks. Nor could Stalin have viewed her death as a necessary sacrifice in the move to collectivization. There is nothing in the logic of collectivization that says that some should die so that others may prosper. It was, as the preceding sketch indicates, a win-win plan in which everyone was supposed to come out ahead, even in the short run.

It might be argued that Stalin wanted the death of this woman because killing her was one way to display the power of his regime. But this analysis cannot be correct, because the regime, early and late, never acknowledged that there had been a famine. If you are going to impress people with your qualities as a killer, you must let it be known that there are people you have killed. Furthermore, if you want to demonstrate your power, starving people to death is a poor way to go about it. With a famine, it usually appears to outsiders that natural causes, not brutal human power, have produced the deaths.

It is possible that Stalin, early and late, did not believe the reports of starvation. The arguments for socialized agriculture were not insane, and if you believed in socialized agriculture, you believed that productivity would be higher in 1932 than it was in 1929. On this basis, Stalin could plausibly think, at least for a while, that there was more than enough grain for everyone. But as the terrible months of early 1933 proceeded, it was apparent to many people in high positions that the farmers had been left with nothing to eat. People very close to Stalin and involved in agricultural policy, such as Nikita Khrushchev, later, much later, admitted that they knew that people were "dying in large numbers."[4] Some reports of starvation must have been communicated to Stalin, if for no other reason than to inform the leader of what was being said. If he continued to believe, by February 1933, that there was no famine, his belief constituted a pathological rejection of evidence. We do know Stalin had trouble assimilating bad news: witness his refusal to believe, for two long weeks in June 1941, that Germany had invaded Russia. If he could deny reality in 1941, he could have denied it in 1933.

I do not intend by introducing the word "pathological" to provide Stalin with an excuse for persisting in the belief that there was no famine. When political leaders make decisions with immense consequences, it is necessary, morally necessary, for them to consider "What if I am wrong, and what are the consequences if I am wrong?" In this case, the consequence of being wrong was mass starvation. Given that fact, it was murderously reckless for Stalin not to investigate the effects of imposing the quota he himself had set.

But there is a far more probable story, which is that Stalin initially disbelieved the reports of starvation, but, by early 1933, had come to realize that they were true. Stalin then had to choose between (a) acknowledging that the production targets were too high, and returning some portion of the harvest to the farmers, or (b) refusing to acknowledge that the targets were too high, and letting the farmers starve. He chose (b). If so, Stalin was not a person who refused to take steps to discover that he was wrong. Rather, he was a person who discovered that he was wrong, but refused to admit it to others. Instead of conceding that the production quota was too high, he blamed the failure to meet the quota on the hapless kulaks, who (the propaganda proclaimed) were sabotaging the system. And this, I have argued, he knew they did not have the power to do.

What sort of motive might Stalin have for continuing to insist that there was no famine? If the production quota for 1932 was wrong, then the ability of the regime and its leader to set agricultural quotas was called into question. But if the regime could not set proper production quotas in agriculture, could it be trusted to set quotas in steel, or coal, or any other vital area of production? To concede a problem with production quotas was to concede a basic problem with socialism itself, at least if one equated socialism with the abolition of markets. By refusing to admit a problem with the production quota, Stalin was protecting socialism from the critics who said that efficient matches of production and consumption could only be set by market means. But what was the point of protecting this part of socialism from criticism if the famine had already demonstrated that the abolition of markets had deep problems? If we assume that Stalin knew about the famine and let the farmers starve in order to preserve the reputation of socialism, then we have a case of someone who would kill for an idea, and kill for an idea he already knew was false. If the woman from Vinnytsa could have asked the Great Leader why she was starving when the cities had more than enough grain, Stalin would have answered, "You are dying to preserve the idea that production improves with the abolition of markets." The woman could respond with justice, "My death is proof that this is not true."

So of the Ukrainians and others we are considering, as they starved in the winter of 1932–33, it can be affirmed first and foremost that Stalin caused their deaths by approving an absurd production quota. Then, he either believed, against all evidence, that they were not starving, or he believed that they were starving and did nothing about it. He came to the Ukrainians and took their food. Then he sealed them off, refused to hear their cries for help, prevented anyone else from feeding them, and afterwards denied that they had died. They had done nothing to deserve this fate. Even by Stalin's standards, they were not enemies of the state. They did not stand in the way of progress. They were conscripted soldiers whose lives were squandered through the incredible blunders of an incompetent general pursuing a dubious cause.[5]

The Jewish Holocaust[6]

Stalin hated the kulaks, but he had no reason to hate the farmers who starved in the famine. If he could have arranged matters differently, abolishing markets and collectivizing plots of land without starving the farmers, he would have preferred to do so. This is not the case with Hitler and the Jews. Hitler's hatred of the Jews was not a sham designed to attract anti-Semitic followers for the purpose of gaining political power. Indeed, at crucial points in Hitler's career, his anti-Semitism cost him power and political support. In early 1933, the German bourgeoisie supported Hitler for Chancellor despite his anti-Semitism, not because of it, because they viewed him as the best bet to defeat the Bolsheviks. In 1943 and 1944, trains that could have been used to transport vital troops and supplies to the Eastern front were diverted into the campaign to exterminate the Jews. Despite these political and military costs, Hitler never hesitated in his anti-Semitism. For him, hatred of Jews was not a tactic, but a mode of being.[7]

The particular causes of Hitler's anti-Semitic feelings remain a subject of conjecture,[8] but whatever the causes were, they were not special. Anti-Semitic feelings of similar character and intensity were shared by a great many in the surrounding culture.[9] But Hitler was unusual in providing a written summary of his views on "the Jewish problem." The anti-Semitic arguments of *Mein Kampf*, although not original, are worth cataloguing as specimens of Hitler's intellectual pathology.[10]

First, Hitler argued, in standard pseudo-Darwinian style, that human races are in a struggle for survival against each other, that Germanic races are in competition with Semitic races, and in particular that Aryans are in competition with Jews, who collaborate worldwide against Aryan interests through the control of banks, media, the arts, and so forth. It follows from the competitive model that every gain for the Jews is a loss for the Aryans, which makes steps by Aryans against Jews acts of preemptive self-defense.

Second, Hitler held that the Jews were responsible for various crimes in recent history. The surrender of the German military forces to the Allies in 1918, in Hitler's reckoning, was not a necessary step resulting from defeat on the battlefield, but a betrayal of the German people by the Social Democratic party, which in Hitler's mind was in the hands of the Jews. Likewise, Hitler fantasized that the Bolshevik party was in the hands of the Jews, that the crimes of the Bolsheviks were the crimes of Jews, and that the threat of Bolshevism was a Jewish threat. If "the Jews" are responsible for past crimes against Germans, then actions by Germans against Jews are just punishments inflicted on the guilty, assuming that all Jews are guilty for what any Jew does.

Third, Hitler assumed that when Jews perpetrated these and other alleged crimes, they did so because they were Jews; that is, being Jewish implies a hereditary disposition toward evil acts. It follows that even if a Jew has done nothing wrong, he cannot be trusted because he will be inclined to do something wrong in the future. And if he does not do anything wrong in the future, still his children and his children's children will have this tendency to evil.

In sum, the Jews have done evil and will continue to do evil to the Aryan *Volk*. The only way to stop this from happening is either to quarantine the Jews or eliminate them from the world. Quarantine was the tactic of the racial legislation of 1935–39; it provoked resistance and occasional deadly anti-Aryan violence. (I am describing matters here from the *Führer's* point of view.) The alternative and permanent solution was the elimination of the Jewish people. The mental road to this second solution was paved by ferocious anti-Semitic rhetoric, in *Mein Kampf* and in Streicher's pornographic pamphlets, portraying Jews as parasites, vermin, viruses, bacteria, and other disease-causing organisms, living in filth and polluting the body of the *Reich*. Elimination of the vermin was a matter of public health.

I have described at painful length these facts about Hitler's emotions and beliefs to distinguish the situation of the Jews under Hitler from the situation of the Ukrainians under Stalin. Stalin did not want the Ukrainians dead; Hitler wanted the Jews dead. The deaths of the Ukrainians were an unintended consequence of an absurd policy; the death of the Jews was the intended goal of a policy that was rational relative to its objectives. If Stalin had believed that the collectivization of agriculture could have been better facilitated with a lower production target, he would have chosen it. But the extermination of the Jews was not a side effect of Nazi efforts toward some other goal. It was the goal itself, inexorably pursued.

It does not help our understanding of this catastrophe to describe *all* of Hitler's beliefs as "irrational" or "crazy." One must locate the point where his thought processes went from mildly pseudo-scientific to utterly evil. The doctrine of the importance of race and inevitable conflicts between races was a doctrine endorsed by many nineteenth and early twentieth century social scientists, not all of them Nazis and not all of them anti-Semitic. The idea that "inferior" specimens of humanity should be prevented from reproducing and "bred out" of the world was the basis of policy in several counties, including the United States, where thousands of mentally challenged women were involuntarily sterilized in the years prior to World War II. The idea that the Bolshevik revolution was a Jewish plot was affirmed in the early 1920s in speeches by none other than Winston Churchill.[11] But only the Nazis inferred from these empirically shaky premises the necessity, the need, the acceptability or even the slightest desirability of extermination. Where Nazi policy passed over from mediocre social science and madcap history into irrational pathology was in the move from bad premises to murderous conclusions, an invalid inference facilitated by intense hatred focused on a particular race existing independently of any particular beliefs.

I speak here of "Nazi policy," a phrase that does not name responsible individuals. There is a controversy, now a bit stale, about whether the policy of extermination was Hitler's idea, or whether it was Himmler's, carried out largely beyond Hitler's notice.[12] The idea of the death camps, the selection of the methods of extermination, and the details of transportation—all these I take to be the work of Himmler and the SS. But Himmler was acting to implement an idea of extermination evident in *Mein Kampf,* and it is inconceivable that Hitler did not approve these choices and their timing. Hitler did not conceive of the Nazi party and the *Reich* as something greater than himself; it was his creation and his tool, subject to his personal rule: witness his decapitation of the SA leadership in 1934, and his stupendously incompetent micromanagement of the *Wehrmacht* after 1941. I believe that every initiative could have been stopped by Hitler. A clear "Not now, the war comes first" from Hitler and the program of extermination would have been stopped.

I proceed therefore to my imagined meeting between Hitler and the elderly Polish Jew who dies at Auschwitz. The Jew discovers that he is soon to die, and demands of the *Führer*, "Why, why are you doing this to me?" Hitler replies, "You are a member an accursed race and the world is a better place if you do not exist." "But what have I done to you?" says the Jew, "in my entire life I have committed no crime." Hitler replies, "You stabbed Germany in the back in 1918, and because of this millions of brave German men died for nothing." "I was not in Berlin in 1918," says the Jew, "I was in Poland, praying that Russia would lose to Germany." "You Jews spawned the evil of Bolshevism," Hitler proceeds. The Jew replies, "I am a Hassid and we do not profess dialectical materialism, if you know what that is." "You harbor criminal tendencies which you will pass on to your children," Hitler proceeds. "I am too old to have children and you know it," says the Jew. "There is one last thing," says Hitler, "you are a Jew, and that alone suffices." "You hate me regardless of any facts," says the Jew. "How can you hate what you do not know?"

By the end of this dialogue, we have uncovered a hatred based on no reasons at all, a self-sustaining emotion unsupported even by fantasized facts. Such a hatred creates a preference—the eradication of its object—but the satisfaction of this preference does not enhance any recognizable human interest in the person who harbors it. It is as if Hitler had a preference that Neptune be colored red. The sudden satisfaction of this preference via some eruption on Neptune might produce momentary exultation, but it would not make Hitler's life go better. Since the preference for the extermination of the Jews does not point to any interest, the hatred and actions based on it are completely irrational. But they are not irrational in any sense that provides an excuse of insanity. Hitler had not lost the power of cognition, or his ability to choose the means that would indeed produce the ends that his hatreds dictated to him. True, Hitler did not choose to have this hatred of the Jews, but most feelings that people have are not feelings that they have chosen to have. What they retain is the ability to choose what they do, despite their feelings. In this, Hitler had no less free will than anyone else.

I return again to my theme that for the Nazis, killing was not a means but an end. In his public speeches, between outbursts of emotion against the Jews and the Bolsheviks, Hitler projected a positive ideal: the redemption of Germany, the unification of *das Volk*, the establishment of a thousand-year *Reich*, the creation of a better world. How, we ask the *Führer*, is the extermination of the Jews going to produce this better world? "Isn't it obvious?" says the *Führer*, "the new world will have the feature of being free of Jews." Means and ends, cause and effect, have fused together in a spinning circle of hate. Millions died to consummate a tautology.

Dresden

The standard view of the Dresden bombing is that this was a necessary act in a just war. That the war against Hitler was a just war I shall not dispute. That the bombing was necessary, that it was a step toward Nazi surrender, that it had any positive effects at all—this I will dispute.

The British bombing campaign against Germany commenced in late 1941, with daylight raids on *bona fide* military targets, especially the submarine bases the destruction of which was essential to winning the battle of the Atlantic. The British soon discovered that such raids were costly and fairly ineffective. German military targets were well camouflaged. When located, they were difficult to damage and easy to repair. Daylight raiding opened up bombers to concentrated anti-aircraft fire and deadly fighter attacks, against which British bombers carried few guns. Rates of attrition were high, and it was soon apparent that the British Bomber Command had to choose between (a) continued daylight raids and high losses, (b) foregoing raids altogether except for exceptionally favorable cases, (c) shifting over to tactical support for British air and sea operations, or (d) shifting over to bombing raids at night. Choice (a) was unacceptable from the military point of view. Choice (b) was unacceptable from the diplomatic point of view, as Stalin had to be persuaded that Britain was doing its fair share in the war against the common enemy. Choice (c) was unacceptable to those who sought a distinctive role for the air forces in combat, that is, unacceptable to the airmen themselves. Bomber Command and Churchill opted for choice (d). It was *something*, and less costly than a second front.[13]

But if you bomb at night, you cannot see particular targets and you must bomb "areas" instead. And the only areas that it was plausible to bomb were cities. Such raids violated the written and unwritten conventions regarding bombardment, but these were consciously brushed aside.[14] But a case might be made in 1942 (indeed, was made, by Lord Cherwell, the Scientific Adviser to the Prime Minister) that the outcome of the war was in doubt, and that against a monstrous opponent monstrous means were necessary.[15] If you blow up Germany bit by bit, Cherwell wrote to Churchill on 30 March 1942,[16] then either there will be nothing left or the residue will surrender. Churchill accepted the argument, and appointed

Arthur Harris, a vociferous advocate of area bombing, to head Bomber Command. "The destruction of factories could be regarded as a bonus," Harris later explained. "The aiming points were usually right in the center of the town."[17] Throughout 1942, enormous resources were diverted to the development of Bomber Command. By 1943, whole cities like Hamburg were being destroyed in 1,000 plane area bombings that discarded any pretence of conscious direction against military targets.

Even in 1943, the rationale that area bombing would produce German surrender was strained. Cherwell's idea was that such bombing would destroy vital German military assets and undermine German civilian morale. But the German industrial machine was so prodigious that it was still turning out civilian radios late into 1943; and, at no point in the war could it be demonstrated that German ground troops anywhere had run out of supplies or fuel because of British area bombing. (Ball bearings and fuel were in short supply, but as a result of daylight raids by the US Eighth Air Force.) As for civilian morale, the British knew best that area bombing does not undermine morale. German bombing had not destroyed *their* morale during the Blitz. If anything, the bombing would drive anti-Nazi Germans into Hitler's arms, just as the Blitz forced the British Left to bury the hatchet with Churchill. Besides, the attitudes of German civilians could have little effect in a country run by Nazis and policed by the Gestapo.

Whatever arguments, limited, inadequate, morally shallow, could be produced for area bombing in 1943, they had completely evaporated by February 1945. By 1945, it could not be argued that area bombing was needed *in lieu* of a second front, as D-Day was long past. By 1945, it could not be argued that area bombing was needed to save needed planes, as there was an oversupply of planes of all kinds. By 1945, it could not be argued that area bombing was necessary to destroy German military assets, as those assets could be more effectively destroyed by US bombers in daylight raids conducted under the protection of long-range P-51 fighters. By 1945, it could not be argued that the outcome of the war was in doubt, as the Bulge had already collapsed and Germany was nearing defeat.[18] Nothing good could come of a raid on a city like Dresden, a cultural center of no industrial or military importance, crammed with refugees fleeing (with good reason) before the Red Army advancing from the East. Yet on the night of February 13 and early morning February 14, the RAF dropped 650,000 thermite bombs on Dresden, and set the city on fire. Tens of thousands burned to death; ten of thousands more suffocated in basements and shelters from lack of oxygen. The next day, US bombers dropped tons of high explosives on the city center, and US fighters strafed crowds fleeing to the countryside.

I turn now to Churchill's role in the Dresden atrocity. I have already noted that Churchill had endorsed the general idea of area bombing, accepting the arguments of Lord Cherwell and rejecting the views of Henry Tizard, Solly Zukerman, and other prominent science advisers who doubted that area bombing could break German morale. By late 1944, the old controversy about "precision bombing" versus "area bombing" broke out again, with Charles Portal, Chief of Air Staff, arguing that Bomber Command should concentrate on German oil refineries and Air Marshal Harris supporting continued raids on German cities. Harris wrote to Portal on 1 November 1944, that "in the past eighteen months, Bomber Command has virtually destroyed forty-five of the sixty leading German cities ... Are we going to abandon this vast task?"[19] Portal replied, "I have, I must confess, wondered at times whether the magnetism of the remaining German cities has not in the past tended as much to deflect our bombers from their primary objects as the tactical or weather difficulties [in attacking oil refineries] which you describe ..."[20]

Harris never hesitated in ordering city raids. "I was against putting everything into oil," he later wrote. "It was using a sledgehammer to crack a nut." He threatened to resign, and Portal gave in, at least to the extent of listing as targets: "Berlin, Dresden, Chemnitz, or any other cities where a severe blitz will ... hamper the movement of troops from the west." This idea of bombardment to harass German troops in the East was conveyed to Churchill via Sir Archibald Sinclair, Secretary of State for Air. From the Prime Minister, Sinclair received this prompt and stunning reply (26 January 1945):

> I did not ask you about plans for harrying the German retreat from Breslau. On the contrary, I asked whether Berlin, and no doubt other large cities in East Germany, should not now be considered especially attractive targets. I am glad that this is "under examination." Pray tell me tomorrow what is to be done.[21]

This memorandum, the military historian Alexander McKee writes, "sealed the fate of Dresden."[22] It supports Harris's contention in his memoirs that the choice of Dresden as a target came directly from "higher quarters."[23] But why did Churchill side with Harris's city raids, and not with Portal's oil attacks or Sinclair's troop bombardments? If Harry Truman, whose leadership was not particularly respected (at least at first), could strike Kyoto off the list of bombing targets in Japan, on the grounds that Kyoto was an artistic and religious center, certainly Churchill, whose leadership *was* respected, could have struck Dresden off the list of targets, for similar reasons. But he did not. Why?

The reason could not have been that Churchill thought future good would come from the raid. Indeed, soon after the Dresden raid produced an outcry in Parliament, Churchill penned a self-serving and self-revealing memo that raids of this sort went against British interests (28 March 1945):

> It seems to me that the moment has come when the question of the area bombing of cities simply for the sake of increasing the terror, though under other pretexts, should be reviewed. Otherwise we shall come into control of an utterly ruined land. We shall not, for instance, be able to get housing materials out of Germany for our own needs because some temporary provision would have to be made for the Germans themselves.[24]

But the production of future good is not the sole rational basis for action. There is also the rationale of retribution, which looks to the past. The Germans had bombed the British, so it was just retribution for the British to bomb the Germans. The Blitz had hardly been a matter of a few British people sleeping some nights in the Underground. Fifty thousand British civilians had been killed in the Blitz; tens of thousands more had been maimed. The anger, intense and deep, of the British public demanded that those who caused this suffering be themselves made to suffer in kind. The Germans destroyed Rotterdam, so the Allies could destroy Hamburg. The Germans destroyed Coventry, so the Allies could destroy Lübeck. The German bombed London, so the Allies could bomb Berlin. In the eyes of many British and Americans, the destruction of German cities was just punishment for crimes committed. When Hans Rumpf's study of the effects of Allied bombing was published in the US in 1965, the publisher added in a prefatory note:

> This book must be read with care. In the course of his study of aerial bombardment during World War II, Hans Rumpf has described in detail the horror and suffering that visited German civilians and German cities under Allied bombing attacks. But he has devoted no more than passing comment to the equally terrifying experiences inflicted by German air attacks on the people of London, Rotterdam, and Coventry.[25]

"They bombed Manchester, so we can bomb Dresden." Was there a thought like this in Churchill's mind, when he told Sinclair that "large cities in East Germany should be considered attractive targets?" One might argue that Churchill, distracted by his preparations for the Yalta Conference (4–11 February 1945), was attending to the pressing diplomatic issues and hardly had retribution in mind when he penned the memo that condemned Dresden. But the focus of the Yalta conference was the territorial arrangement of Europe after the surrender of Germany, which implies that participants in the Yalta conference thought of Germany as already defeated. If you think of your enemy as defeated, is not your next thought going to be how the enemy is to be punished?

If Churchill was thinking about punishing Germany, what might he have thought about an appropriate form of punishment? It is interesting that throughout the war, whenever measures against Germany were considered that ran up against the laws of war, the British under Churchill adhered to legal restrictions, except in such cases where they had already been broken by the Germans. The British had poison gas that Churchill considered using on German troops, but he chose not to. The British had anthrax bombs that Churchill considered dropping on Berlin, but he chose not to. The Germans, after all, had not used poison gas or anthrax against the British. But the Germans *had* set London afire on Christmas eve in 1940, and this seems to have dissolved any qualms about British fire raids on German cities.[26] In 1944, the bombing of Britain had recommenced with the advent of unmanned V-1 bombers and 1945 brought the V-2. For Churchill, it was an eye for an eye. As he remarked in the radio broadcast of 9 February 1941, "All through these dark months the enemy has had the power to drop three or four tons of bombs on us for every ton we could send to Germany in return."[27] The metaphor of payback appears in a speech on 22 June 1941: "Here in London, and throughout the cities of our island, and in Ireland, there are seen the marks of devastation. They are being repaid, and presently they will be more than repaid."[28]

Now there is in this Deuteronomic reasoning about bombing an obvious crudity of thought: the rule of an eye for an eye is being applied not to a particular wrongdoer and his particular victim, but to "the British" and "the Germans," collective entities of a philosophically suspicious sort. But Churchill was never scrupulous in distinguishing "the German people" as a moral agent from individual Germans as moral agents. As the author of a book entitled *A History of English Speaking Peoples*, he was comfortable thinking in collectivist terms.[29] Before the House of Commons, on 7 May 1941, he remarks, "The German name and the German race have become and are becoming more universally and more intensely hated than any name or any race of which history bears record."[30] A later speech describes "Hun raiders," led by "clanking, heel clicking, dandified Prussian officers."[31]

But the bombs at Dresden fell on particular people, including a young farm girl who came into Dresden by train from Breslau after widespread reports of rape by Red Army troops. As she died of asphyxiation in the Dresden train station shelter, one could imagine Churchill explaining to her the rationale of her death. "You must die," he might begin, "so that Stalin will be impressed with my power and I will have bargaining chips at the conference table." "The conference ended four days ago," the girl could say, "it's a little late for that." "My friend Lord Cherwell has spoken highly," Churchill continues, "of the psychological effects of 'de-housing' the German population." "I have already been 'de-housed' by the Red Army," the girl could say. "Spare yourself the effort of de-housing me a second time." "You must die because you German people have hit London with V-1s, and the Germans must suffer for what they have done." "I attacked nothing," the girl says, "I only tended cows. As for 'my people,' I am half Polish. I never believed in *das Volk*. But apparently you do."

Hiroshima

As with Dresden, some part of the motivation for the bombing of Hiroshima was revenge. It was not just a matter of getting back at the Japanese for the sneak attack on Pearl Harbor. In February 1945, Americans learned for the first time of the atrocious treatment of their prisoners of war by Japanese military forces in Bataan and elsewhere. In March of 1945, US marines suffered tens of thousands of casualties in the assault on Iwo Jima; thousands more died in the ensuing attack on Okinawa. When fire raids over Tokyo killed tens of thousands of civilians in March and May of 1945, few US citizens felt sympathy for the Japanese victims on the ground.

But in all the discussions of the first use of the atomic bomb, the focus was not on exacting revenge, but on how to use the weapon to end the war.[32] The basic idea was that the atomic bomb, a new and different weapon of war, would produce a "shock" that might induce surrender. The alternative, so the discussion went, was to invade Japan, an operation sure to produce a high number of military and civilian casualties.

Truman asked the Interim Committee, formed to advise the President about the bomb, to estimate the number of people that would die in an atomic attack on a Japanese city. He was told to expect 10,000 to 20,000 deaths. He asked his military experts to estimate the number people who would die in a ground invasion of Japan. He was told to expect 100,000 to 200,000 deaths. From this point on in Truman's thinking, arithmetic took over: it was better to kill 10,000 than to kill 100,000; therefore, it was good moral mathematics to drop the bomb on Hiroshima. We have direct and indirect evidence that Truman engaged in these morbid calculations. When it became known that over 100,000 people died in the bombing of Hiroshima, Truman began to say to interviewers that "he had been told" (by whom?) that "a million" lives would be lost in the invasion of Japan,[33] a figure that had no basis in reality, but which served to keep the hypothetical invasion death count higher than the actual bombing death count.

It was perhaps the simplicity of the arithmetic comparison that prompted Truman to tell *Life* magazine, by way of celebrating the tenth anniversary of the bombing in 1955, that he never lost a night's sleep over the destruction of Hiroshima. The president never felt that the bombing was wrong; never felt that the bombing needed to be excused. Human life has value; a net saving of 90,000 lives justified the attack. "My object," he explained to Senator Richard Russell the day after the bombing, "was to save as many American lives as possible but I also have a human feeling for the men and women of Japan."[34] So Truman thought, but he did not think enough.

To begin, if one is going to justify a decision of this gravity by comparing numbers, one must make sure that the numbers are right. The figure of 10,000 deaths Oppenheimer and the Interim Committee provided Truman was absurdly low: incorrect by a factor of ten. The bomb was commonly described by those in the know in early 1945 as a weapon that could "wipe out" an entire city in a single blow, which would imply "wiping out" most of the people that lived within the city. If the bomb was as terrible as everyone was saying it was, Truman should have wondered why the projected casualty figures were so low and raised questions that would have produced better estimates. Similarly, the estimate of 100,000 deaths to be expected in a land invasion was open to question. That estimate was derived by assuming that the Japanese would fight for the home islands the way they had fought for Iwo Jima and Okinawa, but the Japanese had fought on to the death at Iwo Jima and Okinawa out for loyalty to the Emperor, who had not yet decided to surrender to the US. If the Emperor and his Council surrendered in the face of an invasion, or in the immediate wake of one, resistance on the ground would drop to zero. It does no good to object that Truman did not know whether the invasion would induce such a surrender. Truman did not know that the bombing would induce surrender either. In the absence of surrender after a land invasion, the killing would have gone on. In the absence of surrender after Hiroshima and Nagasaki, the bombings, atomic or conventional, would have gone on. The casualty estimate for "continued bombing" would have converged with the casualty estimate for "continued invasion."

Next, Truman should have considered not just the numbers of the dead, but who the dead were. Those who would die in the invasion of Japan would be mainly soldiers, intentionally killed in the course of battle; those who would die in the bombing of a city would be mainly civilians, intentionally killed for the purpose of inducing surrender. Intentionally killing soldiers is morally permissible in pursuit of victory in a just war; intentionally killing civilians is plainly murderous, as the Allies insisted whenever the Nazis did it.[35] The fact that the US had been engaged in intentionally killing civilians in large numbers in Japan starting in January 1945 is irrelevant; murder does not become more permissible as it becomes more frequent. Besides, the earlier terror bombings did not happen on Truman's watch; he was under no obligation to continue what had been done before.

Next, in considering the bombing choice, Truman should have devoted more attention to alternative uses of the atomic bomb. True, the Interim Committee told him that they could see no alternative to using the bomb against a city, as a "demonstration bombing" might fizzle, as Oppenheimer said, "like a firecracker over a desert." But the same scientists who were saying in August 1945 that the bomb would be unimpressive unless dropped over a city were saying, in July 1945, that the explosion of the first atomic bomb over the sands of New Mexico was the most awe-inspiring event they had ever seen. If the bomb over New Mexico could make Oppenheimer exclaim, as he reported in his memoirs, "I am Shiva, destroyer of worlds," why would not the Emperor of Japan say the same thing, if the bomb were exploded over some uninhabited island in the Sea of Japan?

The choice to use the bomb was portrayed by Truman as a choice between "bombing or invasion." In fact, there was no such choice, as there was no possibility of a land invasion of Japan before late October 1945. The president could not legitimately think, "if I do not bomb in August, I must invade in October," as the bombing could have been deferred for three months without precluding the possibility of invasion. In October of 1945, with the invasion ready, the president might perhaps think, "either bomb now or invade now," but he faced no such dilemma in August 1945.

I say, "the president might *perhaps* think, either bomb or invade." If he did so think, his thinking was mistaken indeed. In fact, neither the bombing nor the invasion was necessary in any moral sense. From 1931 to 1944, the Japanese had done atrocious damage to the world. But by August of 1945, Japan was a defeated power, unable to do much harm to anyone. The invasion of Japan would have caused great harm to the Japanese. The atomic bombing of Japan did cause great harm. What is the point, what is the necessity, of causing such great harms if not to prevent further harms on a similar scale? It might be argued that Japan was starving US prisoners of war, and that hastening the end of the war saved their lives. But the number of American POWs saved by bombing was tiny compared to the tens of thousands that died at Hiroshima. And the lives of the American POWs interned at Hiroshima, several dozen at least, ended when the atomic bomb fell on their heads.

Why did Truman insist on thinking that his only choice was "bombing or invasion?" True, the invasion would have involved many killings. Perhaps, the bombing might have involved fewer killings than the invasion, but those killings, killings of the innocent, would be murders. To say that the bombing is justified because it involves fewer killings is like saying that because I did not kill my entire philosophy class this morning, I am entitled to murder my chairman this afternoon. What morality demands is not that we do fewer murders, but that we do none at all.

Truman could have avoided murder, but he did not. The thinking behind his decision to drop the bomb on Hiroshima, with its false dichotomies and spurious necessities, was superficial, indicative of a morally mediocre man who did not grasp the ethically superior alternatives made possible by the great power that had fallen into his hands. What is appalling is not that Truman was a utilitarian, but that he was an inept utilitarian. Within hours of Hiroshima, Truman was trying to conceal from the world his lack of justification for the bombing. "The world now knows," Truman told the American people in his radio address of August 6, "that the first atomic bomb was dropped on Hiroshima, a military base." This sentence, elided from the text of the address reprinted in David McCullough's admiring biography of Truman,[36] inaugurates the tradition among US presidents of covering up the Hiroshima crime and prevaricating about all things nuclear. Sometimes one can grasp the character of an event by the degree to which people are prepared to lie about it. Certainly a small child, one of thousands walking to school in Hiroshima at 8:15 a.m. on 6 August 1945, might have said to Truman, had he not been blinded, mutilated, or blown to ashes, that his house, his street, his school, and his city, were *not* a military base.

A Final Thought Experiment

I have presented four political leaders, four historical episodes, and four victims. All of the victims were treated murderously, but treated murderously for different reasons. To explore further the differences in these supposed rationales, I supply one final thought experiment. Imagine, reader, that you are yourself each of the four victims, that you can look your killers in the eye and hear what they have to say.

The first killer says to you, "I do not think you have done anything wrong, and I bear no personal animosity toward you. It is just that your life has gotten in the way of the plan, or rather that your life has gotten in the way of respect for the plan. Though I like you personally, I am committed to the preserving respect for the plan; therefore, regretfully, I arrange your death."

The second killer says to you, "When I see something I hate, I want to remove it from the world, and among the things I hate are people like you. When I was young and wandering through Vienna, when I saw Jews, indeed, as I wrote in my book, when I smelled Jews like you, I felt an immediate visceral disgust, an instinctive repulsion. Now I have power, and I destroy what disgusts me. If anything repelled you as much as Jews repel me, you would want to destroy it, too."

The third killer says to you, "I am in grief because some distant cousins of mine, decent English speaking people, were killed by distant cousins of yours, who like you speak German. Because I am in grief I am entitled to retribution, and since I cannot find those who killed my cousins, I choose to kill you instead. It does not matter that you are not the murderer, what matters is that you happen to speak the same language and live within the same borders, and this transfers my righteous indignation from the killers to you."

The fourth killer says, "I am engaged in a calculation of how to save the greatest number of lives. The calculation has a number of steps, and almost every step contains an error that a small child could discover, but my mind is such that I am incapable of discovering my mistakes. My conclusion is that if I do not kill you, I will kill a great many other people. Why I must kill the others is not exactly clear, but I choose to kill you rather than choosing to kill them."

It is, I think, natural to react to the four killers in four different ways, to think that to die one way is worse than to die another way. But finding arguments to justify these natural reactions is difficult. Are the men who kill you regretfully, like Stalin and Truman, treating you better or worse than the men who kill you with exultation or at least some sense of satisfaction, like Hitler and Churchill? Are the men who murder you intending to produce a better future, like Hitler and Truman, treating you with more or less respect than those who murder you believing that your death does not improve the world, like Stalin and Churchill? Are those who murder you falsely thinking that you are a terrible antagonist treating you with more or less respect than those who murder you falsely thinking your existence is a trivial obstacle? Is the man who kills you in the grip of a foul emotion, like Hitler, treating you better or worse than a man who murders you in the grip of a foul calculation, like Truman? Are those who kill you on the basis of bankrupt collectivist concepts, like Hitler and Churchill, treating you better or worse than Stalin or Truman, who kill you on the basis of bogus scientific estimates? The proceedings of the Nuremberg trials run to dozens of volumes. Addressing these questions would take hundreds of volumes. No verdict beyond mass murder is suggested here. But it is a dismal observation about our species that we have produced, not only so many murderers, but also so many different kinds of them.

Notes

First published as: Douglas Lackey, "Four Types of Mass Murderer: Stalin, Hitler, Churchill, Truman," in *Moral Philosophy and the Holocaust*, eds. Eve Garrard and Geoffrey Scarre (Aldershot: Ashgate Publishing, 2003), 117–137. Copyright © Ashgate Publishing. Reprinted with permission.

1. For accounts of the Ukrainian famine and the policy decisions that led to it see R.W. Davies, *The Socialist Offensive: The Collectivization of Soviet Agriculture 1929–1930* (Cambridge, MA: Harvard University Press, 1980); Herbert Ellison, "The Decision to Collectivize Agriculture," in *Russian Economic Development from Peter the Great to Stalin*, ed. William Blackwell (New York: New Viewpoints, 1974); Dana Dalrymple, "The Soviet Famine of 1932–34," *Soviet Studies*, vol. 15 (1964), and Robert Conquest, *The Harvest of Sorrow* (New York: Oxford University Press, 1986). The number of people who died in the famine is a matter of controversy, and the totals given by Conquest are perhaps double the most reasonable estimates; cf. Barbara Anderson and Brian Silver, "Demographic Analysis and Population Catastrophes in the USSR," *Slavic Review*, vol. 44 (1985). Nothing in the present chapter, however, hinges on the precise number of people who died in this famine.
2. In 1940, Stalin arranged to have John Ford's film "The Grapes of Wrath" shown to Russian peasants to demonstrate the advantages of Soviet agriculture over US farming. The screenings were stopped when the peasants declared that Ford's Okies were rich because "they have a truck."
3. See Bertrand Russell, *Principles of Social Reconstruction* (London: Allen & Unwin, 1916).
4. Nikita Khrushchev, *Khrushchev Remembers*, trans. and ed. Strobe Talbott (Boston: Little Brown, 1970), 120.
5. For a terrifying example of the capacity of history to repeat itself see Jasper Becker, *Hungry Ghosts: Mao's Secret Famine* (New York: Free Press, 1966). *Pace* Marx, this second time around was not a farce, but utter tragedy.
6. The discussion presumes a general familiarity with the facts of the Jewish Holocaust. One early guide that remains one of the best general accounts is Raul Hillberg, *The Destruction of the European Jews* (Chicago: Quadrangle Books, 1961). See also Lucy S. Dawidowicz, *The War Against the Jews 1933–1945* (New York: Holt, Rinehart & Winston, 1975).
7. For biographies of Hitler see Alan Bullock, *Hitler: A Study in Tyranny* (New York: Harper & Row, 1952); Joachim Fest, *Hitler: A Biography* (New York: Harcourt Brace Jovanovich, 1974); Ian Kershaw, *Hitler*, vol. I: *Hubris* (London: Allen Lane, 1998; vol. II: *Nemesis*, London: Allen Lane, 2000).

8. The best psychiatric (not psychoanalytic) study of Hitler is perhaps Fritz Redlich, *Hitler: Diagnosis of a Destructive Prophet* (New York: Oxford University Press, 1998).
9. For a study of the particular culture of Hitler's youth, see Brigitte Hamann, *Hitler's Vienna: A Dictator's Apprenticeship* (New York: Oxford University Press, 1999).
10. Adolf Hitler, *Mein Kampf*, trans. Ralph Mannheim (Boston: Houghton Mifflin, 1943).
11. "[The Bolsheviks] believe in the international Soviet of the Russian and Polish Jew." Robert Rhodes James, ed., *Winston Churchill: His Complete Speeches* (London: Chelsea House Publishers, 1974), vol. III: 291.
12. The controversy commences with David Irving's *Hitler's War* (New York: Viking, 1977), and the subsequent furor and literature surrounding this book including Lucy S. Dawidowicz, *The Holocaust and the Historians* (Cambridge, MA: Harvard University Press, 1981).
13. The official history of British decision making in the bombing campaign against Germany is Sir Charles Webster and Noble Frankland, *The Strategic Air Offensive Against Germany, 1939–1945* (London: HMSO, 1961). Good general accounts include Anthony Verrier, *The Bomber Offensive* (New York: Macmillan, 1969), and Max Hastings, *Bomber Command* (New York: Dial Press, 1979).
14. The argument that "area bombing" is a euphemism for mass murder was pressed by Dr. George Bell, Bishop of Chichester. Of Bell, the historians Peter Calvocoressi and Guy Wint write: "For keeping these Christian ideas before men's minds in spite of the clatter of arms the Bishop of Chichester was not elevated to the highest Christian office in England when the see of Canterbury, for which many inside the Church and out had considered him pre-eminently qualified, fell vacant at the end of 1944" (*Total War* (New York: Pantheon Books, 1972), 490). For Bell's speeches see George Bell, *The Church and Humanity* (London: Longmans, 1946).
15. Even as sensitive a critic as Michael Walzer, in *Just and Unjust Wars: A Moral Argument with Historical Illustrations* (3rd ed., New York: Basic Books, 2000), succumbs to the excuse of "supreme emergency," a phrase he introduces specifically for the crisis years of World War II. Given that morality often requires individuals to give up their lives, one wonders why Walzer rejects the idea that morality might require giving up the life of a nation-state.
16. Cherwell wrote, in part, "in 1938 over 22 million Germans lived in fifty-eight towns of over 100,000 inhabitants, which, with modern equipment, should be easy to find and hit … If even half the total load of 10,000 bombers were dropped on the built up areas of these fifty-eight German towns the great majority of the present inhabitants (about one third of the German population) would be turned out of house and home …" (quoted in Hastings, *Bomber Command*, 141). Cherwell neglects to say openly that some Germans might die in the process of being "turned out," but we can presume that Churchill was capable of drawing the inference.
17. Hastings, *Bomber Command*, 146. In public announcements, there was little hint that the policy had changed. Churchill always referred to hits on German dwellings as "near misses" (*Winston Churchill: His Complete Speeches*, vol. VI: 6589).

18. Apologists for Churchill sometimes argue that the Prime Minister authorized the bombing of Dresden in fulfillment of an agreement made at Yalta to assist the Russian advance into Germany. "The Russian purpose, explained at Yalta eight days earlier, was achieved: refugees on the roads, fleeing westwards from the firestorm, disrupted the movement of German reinforcements seeking to pass through the city to the front further east" (Martin Gilbert, *Churchill: A Life* (New York: Henry Holt & Co., 1991), 824). The idea that German armored columns could be slowed down by ragtag stragglers from Dresden is ludicrous as is the suggestion that Churchill, who for two years after the invasion of Russia had delayed opening a second front in Europe, was worried about Russian troop losses on the way to Berlin. In fact, the existence of "troops moving east" toward Dresden cannot be verified. The "Russian request" story is also part of the official history of the US Army Air Force in World War II: "It was this blow [the Dresden bombing] that set off the controversy about terror bombing already described. The Secretary of War had to be apprised of Dresden's importance as a transportation center and the Russian request for its neutralization" (Wesley Frank Craven and James Lea Cate, *The Army Air Forces in World War II* (Chicago: University of Chicago Press, 1950), vol. 3: 731).
19. Hastings, *Bomber Command*, 385.
20. Ibid., 386. Harris's rhetoric about not abandoning "this vast task" bears an eerie resemblance to the language in Himmler's 1943 plea to commandants at Auschwitz to finish the job, however difficult.
21. Quoted Alexander McKee, *Dresden 1945: The Devil's Tinderbox* (New York: E.P. Dutton, 1982), 102.
22. Ibid.
23. Arthur Harris, *Bomber Offensive* (London: Collins, 1947).
24. Hastings, *Bomber Command*, 401.
25. Preface to Hans Rumpf, *The Bombing of Germany*, trans. Edward Fitzgerald (New York: Holt, Reinhart, Winston, 1965). Rumpf's pathbreaking study was originally published in 1961.
26. Churchill was once asked in the House of Commons whether attacks on Berlin and Rome were "reprisals" for attacks on London. Churchill replied, "There is not much to be gained from putting questions of this kind" (*Winston Churchill: His Complete Speeches*, vol. VI: 6254).
27. Ibid., 6344.
28. Ibid., 6423.
29. Churchill's speeches throughout his lifetime abound with collectivist metaphors, e.g.: "The Slav and the Teuton are quite different kinds of metal ..." (22 February 1919, in *Winston Churchill: His Complete Speeches*, vol. III: 2672).
30. Ibid., vol. VI: 6392.
31. Ibid., 6429 (22 June 1941).
32. For the decision-making leading to Hiroshima see Richard Hewlett and Oscar Anderson, *A History of the Atomic Energy Commission*, vol. I.: *A New World* (University Park, PA: State University of Pennsylvania Press, 1962); H. Feis, *The Atomic Bomb and the End of World War II* (Princeton: Princeton University Press, 1966); Gar Alperovitz, *Atomic Diplomacy, Hiroshima and Potsdam* (New York: Simon and Schuster, 1965); Gregg Herken, *The Winning Weapon* (New York: Knopf, 1980).

These books are listed in increasing order of moral condemnation of the Hiroshima decision.
33. Rufus E. Miles, "The Strange Myth of a Million Lives Saved," *International Security*, vol. 10 (1985): 121–140.
34. David McCullough, *Truman* (New York: Simon & Schuster, 1992), 458.
35. Cf. Churchill: 12 June 1941, "The ruins of Warsaw, of Rotterdam, of Belgrade are monuments which will long recall to future generations the outrage of unopposed air-bombing applied with scientific cruelty to helpless populations" (*Winston Churchill: His Complete Speeches*, vol. VI: 6423). Perhaps one argument against bombing Dresden and Hiroshima is that the earlier Nazi atrocities are no longer recalled, having been eclipsed in scale by Allied attacks.
36. McCullough, *Truman*, 455. The full text is given in Barton Jay Bernstein, ed., *The Truman Administration* (New York: Harper and Row, 1966). The official text of the quote says "Hiroshima, an important military base," but in the actual broadcast, as heard on the recording, Truman omits the word "important." Perhaps the President was too embarrassed by the magnitude of this whopper to follow his own script.

CHAPTER 7

Was It Genocidal?
Eric Markusen and David Kopf

> Whoever fights monsters should see to it
> that in the process he does not become a monster.
> And when you look into an abyss, the abyss also looks into you.
>
> —Friedrich Nietzsche (1886)[1]

Was the Twentieth Century the Most Murderous?

Our basic answer to this question is "yes." In an early chapter of our study *The Holocaust and Strategic Bombing*, we reviewed the work of Pitirim Sorokin, Gil Elliot, and William Eckhardt, all of whom undertook detailed study of the toll of collective violence during the twentieth century in comparison with prior centuries and concluded that the twentieth century was the worst.

Why was this century so violent? A combination of ancient psychological capacities, combined with modern bureaucratic and technological developments, helps account for the fact that organized killing has been so common and massive during the past hundred years or so. The phenomenon of dehumanization, promoted by religious and political ideologies and facilitated by rhetoric, undoubtedly operated throughout history as a means by which killing of others was justified and made psychologically easier. Likewise, the healing-killing paradox is by no means a modern development. Killing others in order to save one's own group, and having such killing justified by religious and political leaders, are as old as civilization.

Although bureaucracy did not originate during the twentieth century, it certainly did become the predominant form of large-scale social organization. Most, indeed virtually all, of the wars and genocides during that century relied heavily upon bureaucracy in order to plan and implement policies and operations, including the deliberate slaughter of enemies. Such features of bureaucracy as hierarchical structure, division of labor, organizational loyalty, and amoral rationality all have made it easier for the large numbers of people needed for mass killing projects to make their contributions, whether as accomplices or as perpetrators. We also note Israel W. Charny's conclusion, based on a careful study of many cases of genocidal killing, that the vast majority of men and women who contribute to such killing are psychologically normal, rather than being sadists or psychopaths.[2] Charny's conclusion has been corroborated by other scholars.[3] Bureaucracy plays an important role in enabling such "normal" individuals to participate in mass killing projects by routinizing obedience, diminishing the sense of personal responsibility, and impeding concerns with moral and human implications.

Like bureaucracy, science and technology did not originate during the twentieth century, but in no prior century have they possessed such prestige and influence. One of the most striking features of the twentieth century was the increased capacity for destruction and killing. Another crucial feature was the ability to kill large numbers of people from ever greater distances, a development that significantly enhances the ability to dehumanize the victims. Both features are direct results of advances in science and the application of technology. Moreover, in our age of science and technology, scientific (and pseudo-scientific) rationalization of governmental policies is a ubiquitous practice. Policies involving mass killing are no exception.

* * *

What is the Relationship Between Genocide and Total War?

There are several important connections and commonalities between genocide and total war. One connection on which there is considerable consensus is that war in general, and total war in particular, creates psychological, social, and political conditions conducive to genocidal killing. It does so in a number of ways: by exacerbating fears and anxieties that can be directed against a scapegoat group, either within the society or in an enemy society; by reducing democratic checks and balances or reinforcing totalitarian tendencies; by utilizing trained and often brutalized professional killers in the military to hunt down and slaughter internal and external enemies; by increasing the vulnerability of the victims in a variety of ways; and by creating a climate of psychological numbing and desensitization among members of the society that is engaged in the genocidal killing.

A fundamental similarity stems from the fact that both genocide and total war employ massacre of large numbers of innocent, helpless non-combatants as a means of obtaining their objectives. There is a growing trend toward increased vulnerability of civilians in modern war; while civilian deaths constituted only about 5 percent of the total death toll in World War I, they constituted as much as 66 percent in World War II, and reached the 70 and 80 percent level in wars of the 1970s and 1980s. Moreover, the crime of genocide, as defined by the United Nations Genocide Convention, is not necessarily excluded from war crimes and crimes against humanity. All three categories of crime under international law prohibit the indiscriminate slaughter of civilians.

Yet another commonality between genocide and total war is the fact that most modern genocides and wars are conducted by nation-states (or collectivities aspiring to become nation-states) and are rationalized as being necessary for the enhancement, protection, or restoration of national security. Also, both genocide and total war thrive in a totalitarian political environment. Put conversely, both forms of governmental mass killing are less likely to be employed by democracies than by totalitarian regimes. Finally, a number of psychological, organizational, and scientific-technical processes and factors facilitate both genocide and total war.

Was Strategic Bombing Genocidal?

> Stench everywhere: piles of human bone remnants at the furnace. Here is the antidote to qualms about strategic bombing.
>
> —Bruce Hopper (after visiting Buchenwald in 1945)[4]

> ... In principle, the extermination camps where the Nazis incinerated over six million helpless Jews were no different from the urban crematoriums our air force improvised in its attacks by napalm bombs on Tokyo ... Our aims were different, but our methods were those of mankind's worst enemy.
>
> —Lewis Mumford (1959)[5]

Leo Kuper, one of the world's foremost genocide scholars, has asserted that the term "genocide" should "be applied to the atomic bombing of the Japanese cities of Hiroshima and Nagasaki by the USA and to the pattern bombing by the Allies of such cities as Hamburg and Dresden."[6] More recently, Kuper wrote, "I should have added the firebombing of Tokyo."[7] Kuper is not the only scholar to label strategic bombing, of which the atomic bombings of Hiroshima and Nagasaki were the apex, as genocidal. In an article accusing both Japan and the United States of committing war crimes during World War II, Shigetoshi Iwamatsu called the atomic bombs "genocide weapons" and claimed that "the devastation [they caused] might be termed genocide."[8] Even Jack Nusan Porter, who compiled a catalogue of misapplications of the term "genocide," labeled the atomic bombings an example of "questionable genocide" in the same article in which he decried the inappropriate application of the term.[9]

Other scholars—including Irving Louis Horowitz, Israel W. Charny, and R.J. Rummel—have demonstrated inconsistency in their writings on the question of whether genocide and warfare in general should be regarded as convergent or as mutually exclusive and, by extension, whether acts of war like strategic bombing may fit within definitions of "genocide" and "genocidal."[10]

Still other scholars have strongly disagreed with the premise that war and genocide may overlap, and that strategic bombing was genocidal. Thus, in their important textbook on genocide, Chalk and Jonassohn wrote: "our definition of genocide also excludes civilians of aerial bombardment in belligerent states."[11] And Helen Fein, one of the leading genocide scholars, has clearly stated her disagreement with those "genocide-labelers" who regard the atomic bombings as genocidal: "To equate Hiroshima and Auschwitz belies the distinctive ends and design of each plan and their distinctive effects."[12]

In order to answer the question of whether strategic bombing was genocidal, we employ two approaches. First, we summarize differences and similarities between the two cases of mass killing. Since there is widespread consensus that the Holocaust did in fact constitute an extreme case of genocide, finding that strategic bombing had important features in common with the Holocaust would lend support to those who argue, as Kuper has done, that strategic bombing was in fact genocidal.[13] The second approach assesses the extent to which strategic bombing meets the criteria for genocide as specified by the closest approximation to a universally accepted definition—the United Nations Genocide Convention. For this purpose, we will rely on the criteria derived from the Genocide Convention by Helen Fein for her comparative study of the US war in Vietnam and the Soviet war in Afghanistan. (Fein concluded that the Vietnam war was not genocidal, but that the Afghanistan war was.)

The Holocaust and Strategic Bombing: Differences and Similarities

We shall first highlight a number of important differences and similarities between the Holocaust and strategic bombing, and then consider whether strategic bombing met Fein's criteria for designating these actions as genocide. Finally, we shall state our answer to the question: Was strategic bombing genocidal?

One very important difference between the two cases concerns the degree of risk to which the agents were exposed. The SS and auxiliary troops that staffed the *Einsatzgruppen* and the death camps incurred very little personal risk. They were heavily armed, and their victims, with very few exceptions, were completely defenseless. Compared with service on either the Eastern or Western fronts, where soldiers engaged in armed combat with the enemy, the death camps were an oasis of security for the Nazis stationed at them. In strong contrast, the Allied bomber crews were frequently at extreme personal risk due to German and Japanese anti-aircraft artillery and planes. The casualty rates for British and US heavy-bomber crews were extremely high. Even the very process of taking off and flying complex machines loaded with tons of incendiary and high explosive bombs was inherently risky. Accidents on takeoff, in flight, and on landing claimed hundreds of Allied lives.

A second difference involves the goal of the mass killing. In the case of bombing, mass killing is widely seen as a means to an end, i.e., surrender, rather than an end in itself, as many regard the Nazi attempt to exterminate the Jews of Europe. While we largely agree with this assessment, we suggest that closer analysis may narrow the differences somewhat. We return to this point below.

A third difference concerns the nature of the victims. The Jews and other victims of Nazi genocide were almost entirely unarmed civilian members of minority groups who had done nothing to threaten German national interests and warrant reprisals, much less warrant being slaughtered. In contrast, the majority of the victims of Allied strategic bombing were civilian citizens of enemy nations that had committed acts of aggression against Great Britain and the United States. Unlike the Jews, the German and Japanese citizens had heavily armed protectors manning anti-aircraft and other defenses and governmentally organized rescue and relief operations designed to reduce the risk and suffering as much as possible.

There are also three important similarities between the Holocaust and strategic bombing. Perhaps the most important for the purposes of this study is the fact that both projects entailed the slaughter of masses of helpless, innocent civilians. Few, if any, would contest the assertion that the victims of the Holocaust were innocent and, in virtually all cases, helpless. Many were killed abruptly and by complete surprise, with no chance to escape or resist. Others were forced into ghettos, where extended periods of hunger and disease weakened them physically and mentally prior to their being rounded up and transported to death camps. Those who managed to escape found themselves in a harsh environment of anti-Semitism and were at constant risk of being turned over to authorities by local people motivated by fear, greed, or hatred. While the victims of strategic bombing were not nearly as defenseless as were the victims of the Holocaust, even flak, fighter planes, and fire departments were unable to spare tens of thousands of inhabitants of cities such as Hamburg, Dresden, and Tokyo from airborne destruction. A family cowering in its basement in a German or Japanese city under massive incendiary attack was no more able to escape or defend itself than its counterpart confined in a Polish ghetto. By the same token, just as most of the victims of the Holocaust were killed indiscriminately because they were members of a group deemed undesirable or threatening to the Nazis rather than for what they had done or not done as individuals, so were many of the victims of strategic bombing. Large numbers of these victims were disabled or elderly; many were women and children—all killed anonymously and indiscriminately simply because they happened to live in areas targeted for annihilation.

Second, both killing projects were authorized by the highest national leaders, rationalized as being in the service of vital national interests, and implemented by duly authorized agents of their respective governments. Third, neither project would have been possible without the contributions of psychologically normal individuals, many of whom were highly educated, scientifically accomplished, and culturally refined.

These points do not exhaust relevant differences and similarities between the Holocaust and strategic bombing. A further important difference involves the nature of the political systems of the nations involved. Germany, of course, was a totalitarian nation with a dictatorial leader, a secret police network dedicated to ruthlessly suppressing any dissent within the *Reich,* and a Ministry of Propaganda that tightly controlled the information to which Germans and others under German domination were exposed. In contrast to Nazi Germany, Great Britain, the United States, and other nations that contributed to the strategic bombing campaigns were democracies with freely elected leaders, civil liberties, and a free press. It is important to note, however, that under the pressures of total war, those elected leaders and their delegates made important decisions in secret, many civil liberties were curtailed, and censorship and propaganda permeated the media. Engaging in total war tends to narrow the differences between totalitarian and democratic political systems.[14]

Also, the postwar fate of key policymakers in the Holocaust differed greatly from that of comparable figures in the British and US bombing campaigns. The Nazis were appropriately vilified after the war by world opinion, and several dozen of their leaders were brought to trial as perpetrators of terrible war crimes and crimes against humanity. In contrast, the men responsible for strategic bombing, particularly in the United States, fared much better. The postwar fate of Curtis LeMay, under whose leadership much of the destruction of Japan had taken place, provides a good example. LeMay went from World War II to become Chief of Staff of the United States Air Force and an early commander-in-chief of the Strategic Air Command, the branch of the US Air Force equipped with nuclear weapons.[15]

Rather than expressing doubt or shame over the atomic bombings, President Harry Truman proudly proclaimed to a group of sailors shortly after Hiroshima and Nagasaki had been destroyed: "This is the greatest thing in history."[16] In contrast to many ordinary Germans who felt a profound sense of shame for what their nation had done to so many millions of innocent people, the American public expressed little shame for what the United States had done when it dropped the atomic bombs on Japan. At the time of the bombings, according to historian Paul Boyer, the American public was "overwhelmingly favorable" in its response to news of the Hiroshima attack. Indeed, Boyer has pointed out that public opinion polls at the time indicated that 85 percent of respondents approved of the atomic attacks.[17]

Other similarities between the Holocaust and strategic bombing include the incremental nature of each project; the fact that both were facilitated by similar psychological, organizational, and scientific-technical processes; and the fact that both represented gross violations of international law.

The Holocaust did not begin as an outright extermination program, but rather as a campaign of random violence, social and economic harassment, and legal discrimination designed to coerce the Jews into emigrating from the German *Reich*. Only after this policy proved unfeasible, and only after *ad hoc,* trial and error development of mass killing techniques had occurred, did the goal evolve to become genocide. Both the United States and Great Britain began the war with a firm commitment to avoid bombing population centers and killing civilians, but during the war this resolve progressively eroded until the point was reached where both nations carefully designed their aerial attacks to inflict maximal damage to enemy cities and their inhabitants.

Comparative analysis discloses six facilitating factors operating in both cases of mass killing, though the specific manifestations and the relative contributions varied in each case. Thus, in the Holocaust, ideological dehumanization of victims played a crucial role in contributing to the willingness and ability of members of the German nation to engage in the mass killing of Jews. The official government ideology declared the

Jews to be members of an inferior race to whom customary moral and empathic concerns did not apply. In the US bombing campaign, ideological dehumanization of the Asiatic Japanese was far more extensive than that of the European Germans, and a number of scholars have argued that this difference played an important, though not exclusive, role in the willingness to engage in area incendiary bombing in Japan—but not in Germany.

The healing-killing paradox played an important role in the Holocaust in a number of ways. At the political level, the official ideology identified the Jews as a mortal threat to the "Aryan" Germans and declared the elimination of the Jews to be an important contribution to the vitality of the *Reich*. This political legitimation of the "Final Solution" was incorporated into the mentalities of the Nazi perpetrators and their accomplices, thus making it psychologically easier to engage in behavior their Christian heritage and cultural tradition regarded as atrocious.

The importance of the healing-killing paradox in facilitating the Holocaust calls into question the conventional notion that, unlike the mass bombing campaigns, in which slaughter was a means to the end of unconditional surrender that would end the war, the Nazi killing was purely and simply an end in itself. A closer examination suggests that for some Nazis and their accomplices, exterminating Jews was regarded as being in the service of a greater good—for example, eliminating the risk of race pollution; destroying the threat of communism, which the Jews were alleged to promote; or reducing the danger of partisan resistance (which was a rationale for involving the *Wehrmacht* in anti-Jewish actions in Russia). In all these cases, killing functioned as a means to an end. To say that killing Jews was a means to an end, however, does not presume that the end was valid or justified, but it does remind us that relatively few of the perpetrators and accomplices of the Holocaust were sadists who killed simply for the sake of killing, and that the majority were "ordinary" men and women who regarded themselves as "good" people doing the necessary "dirty work" in the service of their nation.[18]

With respect to strategic bombing, the healing-killing paradox operated among three groups of people who contributed to the mass bombing campaigns: prewar air power theorists, wartime bombing policymakers, and scientists involved with the atomic bomb project. It did so by making a difficult, controversial decision—the slaughter of enemy civilians—more emotionally and morally palatable.

Two organizational facilitating factors—bureaucratic compartmentalization and organizational loyalty—played important roles in the Holocaust. In the Holocaust, many so-called "desk murderers" were needed to locate, collect, and transport the millions of victims to the hidden sites where the actual killing took place. Compartmentalization enabled them to make their contributions by muting their awareness of the end results of their labors. Loyalty to organizations with interests in the killing project was also found to play a role in key individuals such as Adolf Eichmann as well as in many others whose career advancement was promoted by their service to the "Final Solution."

Evidence of both bureaucratic compartmentalization of knowledge and tasks, and organizational loyalty, was also found in the mass bombing campaigns. With respect to the former factor, top-level decision-makers were organizationally and geographically removed from the results of their decisions, and crew members were at times deliberately misled regarding the actual nature of their targets. With respect to the latter factor, an intense inter-service rivalry between the air forces and the older branches of the military was noted in both the British and the US cases. The autobiographies of Harris and LeMay are replete with statements of their need to prove the unique worth of their service against the competing claims of rivals in the army and navy. In both the British and the US cases, mass bombing during the war was seen by the airmen as a means by which the postwar preeminence of their service might be assured. Not only did this yearning for organizational advancement facilitate the dismissal or distortion of moral concerns, but it also led the air leaders of both nations to engage in deliberate deceit about the true nature of the bombing war.

In both the Holocaust and strategic bombing, scientific rationalization helped legitimate the adoption of policies that entailed mass killing. Thus, members of several academic disciplines in Nazi Germany, including physics and medicine, provided allegedly scientific justification for racist anti-Jewish measures. Scientific rationalization also played an important role in promoting the adoption of mass bombing. Policymakers tended to ignore scientific findings with which they disagreed and to uncritically accept those supporting their preferences. Again, science was manipulated for the purpose of rationalizing a controversial policy. Finally, technical distancing eased the psychological burdens on both Nazi killers and bomber crews by imposing physical distance between killer and victim and by rendering the victims anonymous.

A final, and crucial, similarity is that both the Holocaust and strategic bombing violated international law. Specifically, both projects featured actions constituting war crimes (which include "murder, ill-treatment or deportation to slave labor or for any other purpose of civilian population of or in occupied territory") and crimes against humanity (which include "murder, extermination, enslavement, deportation and other inhumane acts committed against any civilian population, before or during the war").[19]

That the Holocaust violated such laws is well known, and was extensively and indisputably documented during the Nuremberg trials. However, our allegation that the Allies did so in their mass bombardment of German and Japanese cities, which appear on face value to clearly fit within the definitions given previously, needs further discussion. Why, it might be asked, was not strategic bombing included among the offenses for which German leaders were charged at Nuremberg? After all, the Germans killed thousands of civilians with their bombardment of Coventry, Rotterdam, and London, and with their indiscriminate attacks with V-1 buzz bombs and V-2 ballistic missiles. Nor was strategic bombing cited at the International Military Tribunal-Far East, in which Japanese military and political leaders were charged with war crimes and crimes against humanity—despite the fact that the Japanese employed aerial bombardment against crowded cities in their aggression against China.

The reason for such apparent illogic is given quite bluntly by Telford Taylor, who served as a US prosecutor at the first trial in Nuremberg and then as chief prosecutor at the twelve subsequent war crimes trials. In a book on the relevance of the Nuremberg principles to the US war in Vietnam, Taylor wrote that "aerial bombardment had been used so extensively and ruthlessly on the Allies as well as the Axis side that neither at Nuremberg nor at Tokyo was the issue made a part of the trials."[20] More recently, in his memoirs of the trials, Taylor wrote that the German bombing "paled by comparison" to that conducted by Great Britain and the United States against Germany and Japan.[21] In other words, the victorious Allies chose not to focus on the criminal nature of aerial bombardment of civilians, because to have done so would have probably aided the attorneys for the German and Japanese defendants, to say nothing of directing attention to the fact that they, themselves, had wrought vastly greater aerial carnage than their fascist enemies.

Some authorities have acknowledged the atrocious and criminal nature of strategic bombing, particularly in the form of the atomic bombs. For example, President Truman's wartime chief of staff, Admiral William Leahy, wrote in his postwar memoirs: "In being the first to use it [the atomic bomb], we had adopted an ethical standard common to the barbarians of the Dark Ages."[22] Similarly, in the postwar Tokyo war crimes trial, in which the United States and ten other nations found Japanese political and military leaders guilty of war crimes and crimes against humanity, one of the justices, in a dissenting opinion, called the dropping of the atomic bombs "the only near approach to the directives ... of the Nazi leaders during the second world war."[23] Michael Walzer, in his widely cited book on ethics and warfare, asserted that had the Japanese destroyed a US city with an atomic bomb, "the action would clearly have been a crime, one more for Truman's list" in the war crimes trials.[24] Finally, Helen Fein, in a discussion of why she does not accept the label of "genocide" for the atomic bombings, acknowledges that, on the basis of her reading of relevant international law, she does view them as constituting a war crime.[25]

Did Strategic Bombing Meet the Criteria for Genocide?

Our second approach to answering the question of whether strategic bombing was genocidal is to apply the criteria derived by Fein in order to discriminate between the crime of genocide and other international crimes to the case of strategic bombing.

On the basis of the United Nations Genocide Convention, Fein identified five criteria that spell out "necessary and sufficient conditions to impute genocide." The criteria are the following:

1. There is a sustained attack, or continuity of attacks, by the perpetrator to physically destroy group members.
2. The perpetrator is a collective or organized actor or a commander of organized actors.
3. Victims are selected because they are members of a collectivity.
4. The victims are defenseless or are killed regardless of whether they surrendered or resisted.
5. The destruction of group members is undertaken with intent to kill and murder is sanctioned by the perpetrators.[26]

With respect to the first criterion, there can be little doubt that the strategic bombing campaigns, particularly during their incendiary phases, constituted a series of sustained, continuous attacks that physically destroyed hundreds of thousands of members of the German and Japanese national groups. It has been estimated that "approximately 600,000 German civilians lost their lives to Allied bombing."[27] In Japan, American bombers "burned out 180 square miles of sixty-seven cities, killed more than 300,000 people, and wounded another 400,000."[28] The atomic bombs had the additional dimension of killing people years after their direct exposure, due in large part to the delayed effects of radiation. Psychiatrist Robert Jay Lifton, who conducted the first in-depth interview study of Hiroshima survivors, observed that the bomb evoked for them "a special terror, *an image of a weapon which not only instantly kills and destroys on a colossal scale but also leaves behind in the bodies of those exposed to it deadly influences which may emerge at any time and strike down their victims.*"[29] Thus, the initial death toll from the atomic bombing of Nagasaki was approximately 70,000; within five years, an additional 70,000 had died, many, no doubt, due to radiation.[30]

It should be noted that Fein's criterion does not require that the entire group be destroyed, nor that there be specific intent to destroy it in its entirety. Indeed, the Genocide Convention specifically included intent to destroy designated groups "in whole *or in part*" under its jurisdiction (emphasis added).[31] Thus, genocide scholar Uriel Tal has written: "According to the Genocide Convention an act of annihilation is termed genocide even if it is not directed at or carried out on an entire group; the concept of genocide can apply also to the intention of exterminating parts of a group, because of their membership in it."[32]

Fein's second criterion specifies that the perpetrator be "a collective or organized actor or a commander of organized actors." Like the Holocaust and most other cases of genocide in the modern era, the bombing raids were authorized by national governments and carried out by officials of the governments—in other words, by "collective," "organized" actors. The fact that the killing policies, in both cases, were legitimated at the highest levels of government helped secure the cooperation of the large numbers of ordinary citizens and soldiers who were needed to implement them.

Her third criterion stipulates that the "victims are selected because they were members of a collectivity." Although the Genocide Convention excludes political groups from among those, such as racial and ethnic groups, under its protection, many scholars have criticized this provision and in their own definitions have included political groups. It is noteworthy that Fein, who is well known for her commitment to very careful use of the term "genocide," does not limit the coverage of this criterion only to the groups originally specified in the Genocide Convention. Moreover, the Genocide Convention does, according to some scholars, permit some latitude in interpretation in its listing of protected groups by stating that "genocide means any of the following acts committed with intent to destroy, in whole or in part, a national, ethnical, racial or religious group, *as such*" (emphasis added).[33] Regarding this rather ambiguous phrase, Leo Kuper has written: "I prefer to interpret the phrase to mean 'using the national or racial origin, or religious belief, as the criterion for selecting the individuals killed'."[34]

The collectivity to which the victims of bombing belonged was an enemy nation, rather than a religious or racial group as was the case with the majority of victims of Nazi genocide. As members of a national group, the vast majority of Germans and Japanese who died in the incendiary and atomic attacks were targeted in an anonymous, impersonal manner. They were killed, not because of what they had done as individuals, but simply because of their national origin and the fact that they lived and worked in target zones. By its very nature, mass bombing, particularly by incendiary and atomic bombs, is indiscriminate. As R.J. Rummel—a scholar who shifted from an initial conviction that genocide and war are mutually exclusive categories to the belief that certain kinds of mass killing during war do constitute a form of genocidal violence—has written, "deliberately targeting civilians with explosive and incendiary bombs simply because they happen to be under the command and control of an enemy Power is no better than lining them up and machine gunning them, a clear atrocity."[35]

The fourth criterion requires that the victims are either defenseless "or are killed regardless of whether they surrendered or resisted." Clearly, the vast majority of the civilian victims of strategic bombing were personally defenseless. While it is true that efforts were made by their governments to provide protection in the form of active defenses and bomb shelters, the high death tolls attest to the inadequacy of those defenses. Indeed, the Allies deliberately tried to degrade rescue and recovery efforts in a variety of ways, including the use of delayed-action bombs. Moreover, in certain bombing attacks, such as the combined British and US attack against Dresden and the US atomic bombings of Japan, enemy defenses were very inadequate. The individual civilian cowering in a shelter was completely powerless. Most civilian victims, furthermore, were indeed "killed regardless of whether they surrendered or resisted." Their national leaders did have the capacity to surrender and thereby end the bombing, but the individual citizens of the totalitarian states had virtually no influence over their leaders. Nor could they, as individuals, surrender to or resist their killers, who attacked from high in the air.

Fein's final criterion requires that the destruction be done "with intent to kill" and that the killing was "sanctioned by the perpetrators." The issue of intent is complex and problematic. As Leo Kuper has observed, the Genocide Convention did not specify objective criteria for determining intent, and the resulting ambiguity has created "a ready basis for the denial of guilt."[36] However, Fein has provided valuable guidance in her discussion of the intent issue, where she emphasizes that the essence of intent is "evidence of repetition of destruction either in design or as a foreseeable outcome."[37]

We suggest that strategic bombing—particularly the incendiary bombing of large areas of cities crowded with defenseless civilians—manifested a clear intent to destroy masses of human beings and, by doing so, demoralize the survivors into reducing their contributions to the war effort and perhaps even pressing their leaders to surrender. Euphemistic expressions such as "dehousing" notwithstanding, the fire raids were planned carefully to take advantage of weather conditions, highly flammable buildings, and calculated disruption of rescue efforts to wreak maximal damage by deliberately creating firestorms in densely populated residential and industrial areas of cities. To use Fein's words, the firebombing "manifested repetition of destruction" as a "foreseeable outcome" designed to produce "foreseeable results," namely, vast areas of densely populated cities turned into ash. After each raid, the results were carefully photographed and the areas that had been incinerated were marked on maps to help plan future raids to fill in the gaps.[38]

The second component of this criterion, that the "murder" must be "sanctioned by the perpetrators," is also met by the strategic bombing campaigns. For this criterion to be met, the destruction must not be an aberration or an exception, but an integral element of official policy. Nor must the actual implementers of the policy be punished for their roles. In her comparative analysis of the US war in Vietnam and the Soviet war in Afghanistan, Fein found the fact that US soldiers who participated in the My Lai massacre were brought to trial and Soviet perpetrators of massacres were not to be an important factor in her conclusion that the US war was not genocidal, but the Soviet war was.[39] The decisions to engage in area bombing were made by legitimate authorities and approved by government leaders in both the United States and Great Britain, which is to say they were "sanctioned" at high levels. The military officers and enlisted men in the European and Pacific theaters who did the operational planning for the incendiary attacks on cities and who serviced and flew the planes were in no way punished during or after the war for their contributions. On the contrary, many, particularly on the US side, were promoted into higher rank and greater responsibility in the postwar US Air Force.

Our Answer to the Question

Having reviewed important differences and similarities between the Holocaust, as a quintessential example of genocide, and strategic bombing, we now must state our answer to the question: was strategic bombing genocidal? Put bluntly, our answer is: yes, it was. Before discussing our rationale for reaching this answer, however, we would like to address several points that bear upon the question itself.

First, why is the question worth asking? Why do we regard it as an important question? We realize that even posing it will offend many people who believe in the moral rightness of the World War II bombing campaigns, particularly those veterans who still carry scars, both physical and mental, and who cherish the memories of compatriots who gave their lives to a cause in which they deeply believed. And even suggesting that another case of mass killing may have something in common with the

Holocaust will offend those who believe that the Holocaust was a singular, *sui generis* event in history. We are acutely aware that we ask this question and give our answer from the sheltered ivory tower of academia, looking back with hindsight on decisions and events made decades ago under conditions of threat and uncertainty.

Possible reasons for investigating whether the term "genocide" is applicable to strategic bombing, or any other case of mass killing for that matter, include a desire to lay a basis for legal proceedings against the perpetrators, or to make a case that the surviving victims deserve some form of compensation or reparation. These, however, are not our reasons.[40]

We feel the question is worth asking for a number of other reasons. The first and most fundamental reason is simply that governmental mass killing has been and continues to be a threat to the survival of millions of human beings. Yet our understanding of this threat is still rudimentary, and our efforts—as individual scholars, as citizens of powerful nations, and as a world community—to contain, prevent, and resist it are grossly inadequate. In view of the magnitude of the problem and the inadequacy of our understanding of it, we feel strongly that a wide spectrum of inquiries and analyses, no matter how iconoclastic or provocative, is not only justified, but urgently needed. The fact that some of the leading nations of the world continue to base their national security on what has appropriately been described as a policy of retaliatory genocide with nuclear weapons and that other dangerous trends portend future outbreaks of genocidal killing, makes creative study of collective violence even more necessary.[41] Our primary reason and goal, in short, is to learn from the past in order to understand and prevent genocidal killing in the future.

Another reason for posing the question of whether strategic bombing was genocidal is that the question bears directly on the ongoing controversy over the relationship between genocide and war, on both the conceptual and operational levels. A positive answer would lend support to those, such as Leo Kuper, who have argued that the strategic bombing, and the atomic bombings in particular, were genocidal. It would also lend support to the arguments that war and genocide are not necessarily mutually exclusive, that the line between war and genocide may be narrow and blurred, and that warfare itself can be genocidal. A related implication of a positive finding is that the popular conception of genocide, which, for a number of reasons, is closely associated with the specific case of the Holocaust, might be broadened to encompass a wider range of events, thereby raising awareness of the magnitude and seriousness of the problem of genocidal killing. A finding that there were no important parallels and commonalities between the Holocaust and the atomic bombings—or that differences between them were more significant than any similarities—would reinforce the alternative viewpoint, that war and genocide are indeed distinct, discrete, separate phenomena.

There are risks involved in answering this question. One is the probability of offending many people by staining the memory of the courageous aircrews and by insulting the feelings of Holocaust survivors and scholars. Another risk, and one that we have not taken lightly, is that the term "genocide" itself may become weakened if we broaden its scope to include additional cases of deliberate mass killing. As Helen Fein has written, "we study, work, and act in a public arena in which the term 'genocide' has been so debased by semantic stretch that its use stirs suspicion."[42] And we agree with Hugo Adam Bedau that "genocide is not just another crime, not even another 'war crime' or 'crime against humanity.' For many it is the ultimate crime."[43] However, it is necessary to acknowledge and understand the extent to which practices of war, both in the past and potentially in the future, fit within what Charny has called "the universe of genocide."[44]

Having made these points, we turn now to our rationale for claiming that the strategic bombing campaigns deserve to be labeled as "genocidal." Our first reason is that, as we sifted through the welter of definitions and controversies over just what genocide is, we reached the conclusion that its essence lies in the deliberate, calculated slaughter of masses of defenseless, innocent human beings on the basis of their membership in a group, rather than because of what they as individuals did or did not do. As Fein has correctly pointed out, the motives for genocidal killing vary widely from case to case, as do the methods of killing and the proportion of the victim group that is extirpated. But one thing that all cases of genocide and genocidal killing have in common is that large numbers of people are destroyed in a purposeful manner. We would add that genocide is usually a crime committed by and for governments and that the killing can either be direct and immediate, as was the case with gas chambers and mass shooting, or indirect and delayed, as is the case with socially created famine. With these features in mind, and in view of the realities of strategic bombing—particularly incendiary and atomic bombing—we suggest that strategic bombing was genocidal.

Our second reason for reaching this decision is that strategic bombing, in our opinion, clearly fits the criteria specified by Fein for discriminating between war crimes and the crime of genocide. In other words, the same criteria that led her to conclude that the US war in Vietnam was not genocidal and that the Soviet war in Afghanistan was genocidal have led us to conclude that Allied strategic bombing was genocidal.

In closing, we would make the following points. If, in fact, strategic bombing warrants being labeled as "genocidal," then thinking about genocide, both by the general public and the scholarly community, needs to be expanded to include a wider range of cases than many have been willing to consider. Such expanded thinking must contend with the premise that the capacity for genocidal killing is not limited to obvious monsters such as Joseph Stalin, Adolf Hitler, Idi Amin, and Pol Pot, but is widely shared. We must face the fact that religious conviction, advanced education, and scientific expertise do not automatically confer immunity from the capacity to become implicated in a genocidal project; nor does the fact that one is a loving spouse and parent. Psychologically normal, "good" people can and have participated in demonic projects. Not only totalitarian regimes, but also democracies have been willing to directly engage in genocidal killing, to support client states that engage in it, and to make the preparations for it.

Notes

This is an edited and slightly abridged version of chapter 11 in Eric Markusen and David Kopf, *The Holocaust and Strategic Bombing: Genocide and Total War in the Twentieth Century* (Boulder: Westview Press, 1995), 242–258. Reprinted with permission.

1. Quoted in Daniel Ellsberg, "The Responsibility of Officials in a Criminal War," in *Papers on the War* (New York: Simon & Schuster, 1972), 277. (The book from which the Nietzsche quote was taken, *Beyond Good and Evil: Prelude to a Philosophy of the Future*, originally was published in 1886. The passage quoted is on p. 89 of the New York, 1966 Vintage Books edition, trans. and ed. Walter Kaufmann.)
2. Israel W. Charny, "Genocide and Mass Destruction: Doing Harm to Others as a Missing Dimesion in Psychopathology," *Psychiatry*, vol. 49 (1986): 144–157.
3. For examples, see Henry V. Dicks, *Licensed Mass Murder: A Socio-Psychological Study of Some SS Killers* (London: Heinemann, 1972); John P. Sabini and Maury Silver, "Destroying the Innocent with a Clear Conscience: A Sociopsychology of the Holocaust," in *Survivors, Victims, and Perpetrators*, ed. Joel E. Dimsdale (Washington, DC: Hemisphere, 1980), 329–358; Raul Hilberg, *Perpetrators, Victims, Bystanders* (New York: Harper Perennial, 1993).
4. Quoted in Conrad C. Crane, *Bombs, Cities, and Civilians: American Airpower Strategy in World War II* (Lawrence, KS: University Press of Kansas, 1993), 144.
5. Lewis Mumford, "The Morals of Extermination," *The Atlantic*, October 1959: 39.
6. Leo Kuper, *Genocide: Its Political Use in the Twentieth Century* (New Haven, CT: Yale University Press, 1981), 46.
7. Leo Kuper, "Theoretical Issues Relating to Genocide: Uses and Abuses," in *Genocide: Conceptual and Historical Dimensions*, ed. George L. Andreopolous (Philadelphia: University of Pennsylvania Press, 1994), 35.
8. Shigetoshi Iwamatsu, "A Perspective on the War Crimes," *Bulletin of the Atomic Scientists*, February 1982: 32, 35.

9. Jack Nusan Porter, "What Is Genocide? Notes Toward a Definition," in *Genocide and Human Rights: A Global Anthology*, ed. Jack Nusan Porter (Washington, DC: University Press of America, 1982), 16.
10. See *The Holocaust and Strategic Bombing*, ch. 4.
11. Frank Chalk and Kurt Jonassohn, *The History and Sociology of Genocide: Analyses and Case Studies* (New Haven: Yale University Press, 1990), 24.
12. Helen Fein, "Genocide, Terror, Life Integrity, and War Crimes: The Case for Discrimination," in Andreopolous, *Genocide*, 104. Fein's wording is rather peculiar. We know of no one who has *equated* strategic bombing with the Holocaust. The comparative approach we have utilized in *The Holocaust and Strategic Bombing* involves identifying differences, as well as similarities, between cases or phenomena. For two cases of mass killing to fit within the concept of "genocide," or "genocidal," they need not be equal, but they would need to have crucial features in common.
13. The consensus on the Holocaust as an extreme example of genocide unfortunately is not universal, as evidenced by the current prominence of scholars who deny that there was a Holocaust and by public opinion polls indicating that as many as one in five US citizens express doubt that it actually occurred. For an excellent discussion of Holocaust deniers, see Deborah Lipstadt, *Denying the Holocaust: The Growing Assault on Truth and Memory* (New York: The Free Press, 1993). On the Roper Poll results, see Anonymous, "1 out of 5 in New Survey Express Some Doubt About the Holocaust," *New York Times*, 20 April 1993: A8.
14. See, for example, Marjorie Farrar, "World War II as Total War," in *War: A Historical, Political, and Social Study*, ed. L.L. Farrar (Santa Barbara, CA: ABC-Clio, 1978), 171–179.
15. Ironically, in 1964, LeMay was awarded the highest honor that a foreigner can receive from the Japanese government—the First Class Order of the Grand Cordon of the Rising Sun. Unfortunately, the Japanese writer who mentions this in his book does not explain the rationale behind the award. (See Hoito Edoin, *The Night Tokyo Burned* (New York: St. Martin's Press, 1987), 238.)
16. Quoted in Michael Sherry, *The Rise of American Air Power: The Creation of Armageddon* (New York and London: Yale University Press, 1987), 349.
17. Paul Boyer, "The Cloud Over the Culture: How Americans Imagined the Bomb They Dropped," *The New Republic*, 12 August 1985: 26–27. The passage of time has not appreciably weakened the approval, as shown by a poll conducted in late 1991 that indicated that only 16 percent of US citizens felt that their government should make an apology to Japan for the bombings. (Steven Weisman, "Japanese Think They Owe Apology and Are Owed One on War, Poll Shows," *The New York Times*, 8 December 1991: A26.)
18. Kuper, *Genocide*, 19.
19. Everett C. Hughes, "Good People and Dirty Work," *Social Problems*, vol. 10 (1962): 3–11. Both war crimes and crimes against humanity also constitute violations of what Michael Walzer has called "the war convention," that is, "the set of articulated norms, customs, professional codes, legal precepts, religious and philosophical principles, and reciprocal arrangements that shape our judgements of military conduct." An important tenet of the war convention,

and of the religious tradition of "just war," is the principle of "noncombatant immunity": adversaries must make all possible efforts to discriminate between soldiers and civilians and to spare the latter from direct attack (Michael Walzer, *Just and Unjust Wars: A Moral Argument with Historical Illustrations* (3rd ed., New York: Basic Books, 2000), 44).
20. Telford Taylor, *Nuremberg and Vietnam: An American Tragedy* (New York: Quadrangle Books, 1970), 89.
21. Quoted in "Misjudgment at Nuremberg," a review essay by Istvan Deak of Taylor's *The Anatomy of the Nuremberg Trials: A Personal Memoir* (New York: Knopf, 1993), in *The New York Review of Books,* October 7, 1993, 50.
22. Quoted in Ronald Schaffer, *Wings of Judgment: American Bombing in World War II* (New York and Oxford: Oxford University Press, 1985), 164.
23. Quoted in Richard Minear, *Victor's Justice: The Tokyo War Crimes Trial* (Princeton, NJ: Princeton University Press, 1971), 100–101.
24. Walzer, *Just and Unjust Wars,* 264.
25. Fein, "Genocide, Terror, Life Integrity, and War Crimes," 105.
26. Helen Fein, "Discriminating Genocide from War Crimes: Vietnam and Afghanistan Reexamined," paper prepared for the First Raphael Lemkin Symposium on Genocide, Yale University Law School, February 1991, 19–22. The criteria are also listed in Fein, "Genocide, Terror, Life Integrity, and War Crimes," 97.
27. Stephen A. Garrett, "The Bombing Campaign: The RAF," chapter 1 in this book.
28. Crane, *Bombs, Cities, and Civilians,* 140. Though Crane does not say so explicitly, presumably this figure excludes the victims of the atomic bombs.
29. Robert Jay Lifton, *Death in Life: Survivors of Hiroshima* (New York: Random House, 1967), 57.
30. Richard Rhodes, *The Making of the Atomic Bomb* (New York: Simon & Schuster, 1986), 740.
31. Quoted in Kuper, *Genocide,* 19.
32. Uriel Tal, "On the Study of the Holocaust and Genocide," *Yad Vashem Studies,* vol. 13 (1979): 18.
33. Quoted in Kuper, *Genocide,* 19.
34. Leo Kuper, *The Prevention of Genocide* (New Haven, CT: Yale University Press, 1985), 14.
35. R.J. Rummel, "Power Kills; Absolute Power Kills Absolutely," *Internet on the Holocaust and Genocide,* no. 38, June 1992: 10.
36. Kuper, *Genocide,* 33.
37. Fein, "Genocide, Terror, Life Integrity, and War Crimes," 97.
38. In his valuable critique of the British bombing of German cities, Stephen A. Garrett notes that apologists for the area offensive often defend it by citing the "principle of double effect," which states that under certain circumstances it is morally acceptable to harm non-combatants. One of the criteria for the principle of double effect to apply is that the destruction of civilians must be a reluctantly tolerated side effect rather than a deliberate goal or a means to a goal. Garrett concludes that "the principle of double effect hardly can be offered as a defense of the area offensive simply because the evil side-effect in this case (the random killing of non-combatants) was not an unintended or

regrettable consequence of a legitimate military action but was instead one of the main points of the strategy" (Garrett, *Ethics and Airpower in World War II: The British Bombing of German Cities* (New York: St. Martin's Press, 1993), 143). The same could be said for the US area offensive against Japan.
39. Fein, "Discriminating Genocide from War Crimes," 65.
40. We thank Daniel Ellsberg for suggesting these points in a personal communication.
41. Daniel Ellsberg, personal communication. Ellsberg was intimately involved in the development of US nuclear weapons policies, serving on a Joint Staff Study Group on Survivability of National Command and Control of Nuclear Weapons in 1960, on a Defense Department Task Force on Limited War Research and Development in 1961, and as a member of two high-level working groups reporting to the Executive Committee of the National Security Council during the Cuban Missile Crisis of 1962, among other relevant positions.
42. Fein, "Genocide, Terror, Life Integrity, and War Crimes," 95.
43. Hugo Adam Bedau, "Genocide in Vietnam?" in *Philosophy, Morality, and International Affairs*, eds. Virginia Held et al. (New York: Oxford University Press, 1974), 8.
44. Israel W. Charny, "Toward a Generic Definition of Genocide," in Andreopolous, *Genocide*, 70.

PART III
THE DEBATES

CHAPTER 8

The British Debate

Mark Connelly

The British put more effort into the strategic air campaign than any other nation, and in the process created a controversy that has haunted them down to the present. Exploring the British wartime debate over the bombing campaign reveals the way in which information was shaped and deployed to create ambiguities about the role of Bomber Command, particularly in the middle years of the war. Wishing to chastise Nazi Germany and yet at the same time wanting to appear in the moral ascendancy created tensions and disputes that were debated in both the popular and highbrow media. Encouraged by the British media's ambiguous interpretation of Bomber Command's strategy, the British were led to believe that the campaign was the just scourge of all Germans, the terrible and terrifying retribution of the righteous against the wicked; a view that was then confused by the official insistence that British bombing sought only to hit vital war industries and other targets essential to the Nazi economy. While the vast majority of the British people supported this campaign either actively or through silent acquiescence, some questioned it, and the strategy became a subject of controversy in a few small, elite circles, that was expressed publicly. Wrapped in ambiguities and deliberately marginalized for wider reasons of *realpolitik* at the end of the war, the British bombing campaign is still largely misunderstood by the vast majority of the British people, as well as by two much smaller groups, one claiming that the British need to face up to their complicity in an atrocity, while the other fiercely defending the strategy.

In the 1930s, the role of air power dominated British thinking about future conflict. Few Britons could escape the debates concerning the potency of the bomber and its seeming ability to evade all forms of defense. Within the RAF, formed as an independent force as early as 1918, bomber strategists dominated. Led by their first commander-in-chief, Lord Trenchard, the RAF's bombing theorists believed that in a future war, self-defending bomber fleets would deliver their loads with pinpoint accuracy on pre-selected targets.

The flip side of this theory was much darker: it was believed that a general attack on an enemy people, especially their working classes who were thought to be more susceptible to demoralization and panic, would bring dramatic results. Problematically, the RAF managed to create a contradictory bombing policy for itself. Seemingly without realizing it, Bomber Command was expected to act as a precision weapon capable of cutting out the enemy's vital economic organs with the subtlety of a well-practiced surgeon using a razor-sharp scalpel, while also containing the ability to destroy vast areas of enemy territory and simultaneously terrify citizens into submission. Already, therefore, there was confusion among the professionals, which spread to the politicians and general public. Was bombing a cudgel or a rapier? It was a confusion that grew with the outbreak of war.[1]

Since 1908, the year in which H.G. Wells published his novel *The War in the Air*, the fear of bombing had found its way into the British psyche. During the Great War, German airships and aircraft turned Wells' science fiction into awful reality, and the vociferous reaction of the British people to this new threat made a deep impression on politicians. Developments in aviation technology coupled with the worsening international scene gave little cheer throughout the nineteen-twenties and nineteen-thirties. The propaganda of the League of Nations Union and the Peace Pledge Union stressed the awesome potential of marauding bombers if unchecked by international agreement. Even more potently in an era of mass communication, the cinema discovered the shock value of bombing and promoted the seemingly limitless ability of air power in the form of feature films and newsreels. In 1935, Alexander Korda's screen adaptation of H.G. Wells' *The Shape of Things to Come* (retitled *Things to Come* for the film) was released. It presented audiences with a chilling vision of a world dominated by aerial warfare. The film depicted the erosion of civilization into an atomized, chaotic tribal society dominated by petty warlords under the pressure of incessant bombing. Two years after Korda's nightmare vision hit the screens, the newsreels illustrated the reality of bombing showing shocked audiences the charred ruins of Guernica. Thus, although officially committed to a policy of disarmament and appeasement, from the mid nineteen-thirties onward, the British government began to rearm. The fragility of European and world peace demanded that more money be spent on the armed forces, and few doubted that air defense was the priority.[2]

Publicly, British politicians made confusing statements about aerial warfare both to their own people and to the international community. Revisions to the Hague Conventions on war drawn up in the twenties made it clear that civilians were not to be targeted, and that legitimate targets were to be avoided if attacking them entailed placing civilians at significant risk. These rules were never fully ratified, but confusion was created by Neville Chamberlain's insistence as Prime Minister that Britain would abide by them provided others followed suit. On many occasions, Chamberlain reiterated his abhorrence of area bombing and his determination that Britain would not resort to this form of warfare. Having staked out a high moral position, Chamberlain bequeathed his successors a moral and military problem.[3]

At the outbreak of war, RAF Bomber Command commenced operations within the constraints laid down by Chamberlain. Events changed rapidly in 1940 after the Nazi assaults on France and the Low Countries, and the evacuation of the British Expeditionary Force from Dunkirk. Facing the threat of invasion, which was followed up with German indiscriminate bombing of British cities, the desire to strike back grew. Bomber Command's ability to retaliate was, however, extremely limited. War conditions ruthlessly exposed the weaknesses in much of the RAF's prewar thinking. Within three months of the outbreak of hostilities, Bomber Command was forced to abandon the concept of the self-defending bomber fleet capable of daylight operations. Further misery came during the winter of 1940–41, when it also became apparent that night bombing with any degree of accuracy was an equally difficult task. Gradually a new policy was developed. Men such as Sir Arthur Harris, who became Commander-in-Chief of Bomber Command in 1942, grasped the problem and turned it on its head. For Harris, the solution was simple. If the RAF could not bomb accurately and safely by day or night, it should concentrate on destroying the central and industrial zones of German cities. It meant the destruction of workers' houses, their places of employment, and their lives. Harris set about making his preferred strategy operable with a ruthless zeal and fixedness of purpose. He accepted the brutal reality of his decision, but his political masters, although they too understood it, were never bold enough to make it clear in public.[4]

Given this lack of transparency, press comment was, unsurprisingly, a mixture of confusion and self-delusion. Inefficient management of the press then served to compound the issue. Realizing that management of public opinion was crucial, the government established a Ministry of Information in 1939, but the new ministry was beset by problems. Unable to achieve a satisfactory working relationship with the services and the media, it found itself the subject of ridicule in the early years of the conflict.[5] The press filled this information gap with much speculation and debate. In the autumn of 1940, a favorite topic was the ranking of targets, and in light of the bombing of London, whether Berlin should be attacked. On one level, there was a thirst for revenge and retaliation, but at the same time there was a desire to retain the moral ascendancy. On 25 September 1940, the *Daily Mail*, the mouthpiece of the lower middle class right-wing, announced British moral superiority: "Berliners are learning that their city is no more immune than is London from large-scale bombing. The one difference is that our airmen select their targets and concentrate on objects of military value. We hope to see Berlin bombed again—repeatedly."[6] A similar ambiguity can be seen in a lead article of the *Daily Sketch*, a paper aimed at the working class, on the same day that warned against relying on the methods of the terrorist as the Germans had done while also arguing that German morale was highly susceptible to bombing. In the first instance it advocated the bombing of German military targets, and concluded: "When this has been fully accomplished we can think again—if it should still be necessary and if he [Hitler] is not already whimpering in fear of the wrath to come."[7] Thus, from an early stage in the war, the British press coverage contained a veiled acceptance of area bombing designed to terrorize and demoralize.

Other papers wished to discern a distinction between militarily worthless reprisal bombings and targets likely to assist in the wider war effort. The *Daily Telegraph*, a conservative, "quality" broadsheet, warned that revenge attacks were "contrary to sound strategy," and that they would deflect from the "main objective, which is to weaken the enemy's power of mischief by attacking his bases and factories."[8] A month later, the point was reiterated when the *Daily Telegraph* wrote that Londoners, "who have endured the frightfulness of persistent indiscriminate bombing night after night, with its wanton slaughter and torture of civilians will see in these effective attacks on the military objectives in Berlin, the most deadly form of counter-stroke."[9]

Given the prewar popular belief that bombing was immediately and intensively destructive and degrading, these assessments stressed that there was very little military value in bombing unless it was carefully directed at the appropriate target. This about-turn was largely dictated by the need to publicly undermine the impact of German bombing, and show the USA, the crucial neutral power, that Britain had a moral superiority and that the RAF had the ability to carry out a strategy of precision night bombing. Whatever the lead article writers might have argued and whatever they thought of the capability of the RAF, there was always the simmering feeling of revenge in the air. A defense of British policy in the *Daily Mail* was rounded off with this rather more ambiguous statement: "The ruined homes and broken lives of Britain will be avenged. When Hitler has spent his fury in his useless effort to bring this country to her knees, the hour for attack will come. Then Britain must launch against Germany the most devastating offensive that has yet been seen."[10] Similarly, the staunchly working class *Daily Mirror* warned that British operations should never be associated with the word "reprisals," but then thundered "in war when you're hit, you hit back. Hit of course. That, dear friends, you must do." The attitude of its lead article was extremely blunt and culminated in a crucial leap of British wartime logic by accepting the idea of unrestricted aggression, and stressing that modern war had destroyed the distinction between civilian and soldier:

> This [the bombing of Berlin] is the only policy. This is the only effective method available to us in self-defence. This is the *offensive* ... Bomb for bomb and the same all round! The only policy.
>
> And the only policy on which our dauntless suffering people *insist*. If the Air Minister doesn't agree with them he must clear out. The air war is no time for lecturers, and gloved persons wishing to live up to a high standard of ancient chivalry. The invention of the bombing plane abolished chivalry for ever. It is now "retaliate or go under."
>
> We are not dedicated to passive and polite martyrdom. We *must* hit back ...
>
> Also the dislocation of German communications and nerve-centres is essentially a "military objective"—if really it is reasonable to go on making this almost obsolete distinction.
>
> A distinction that wears very thin. People are killed, in the devilish war of today, everywhere, anyhow. People killed are, in tens of thousands, useful workers; mainly war workers. They are in the war. Everybody matters. Maybe everybody is a victim.[11]

After the bombing of Bremen in January 1941, the *Daily Express* pointed out that the RAF had hit Bremen's industries, but also crowed that it "lies heaped today with more fire-blackened ruins than the City of London."[12]

The period of September 1939 to February 1941 was crucial in the British bombing war. The reality of war ripped up many of Bomber Command's preconceptions and forced it to reassess its strategy. In turn, the presentation of the bombing war to the British public became a rather confused affair. The main confusion was over the role and effectiveness of Bomber Command. Was it a weapon of mass destruction dedicated to revenging the blitz or was it a weapon capable of precision bombing? At that particular moment it was in fact neither, but few were prepared to admit it.

Partly inspired by the ambiguous media coverage of Bomber Command, some sections of British society were expressing their unease with British bombing policy by 1941. The opponents of the strategy fell into two indistinct and overlapping groups. For some, the problem was first and foremost a moral one, while for others it was essentially a question of military effectiveness. On the question of tactics, the opponents were split between those who advocated bringing the matter to public attention and those who believed in more private approaches to figures of power and influence. A significant moment in the public campaign came in April 1941 when some newspapers threatened that the RAF would flatten Rome if indiscriminate bombing of Athens or Cairo was instigated by the Axis. This had the effect of forcing George Bernard Shaw and the Classicist Gilbert Murray to make a statement. In a letter to *The Times*, which took a largely neutral editorial view on the question of bombing, they made it clear that they were not advocating any sort of armistice, but wanted to question the military effectiveness of night bombing, and used a detailed statistical analysis of the effects of bombing to support their case.[13] A rational argument largely removed from morality was therefore stated, but there can be little doubt that the morality of bombing by night was being impugned.

The *Daily Telegraph* took a keen interest in bombing and became a forum for debate. According to "A Yorkshire Woman," the wide powers of the Gestapo would ensure the obedience of the German people whatever the impact of British bombing.[14] Another letter writer cited British resistance to bombing as proof that a campaign aimed at morale would not work and revealed a degree of moral reservation in the comment, "let us fight in as clean a manner as modern warfare can be fought."[15] Similarly, "Target," in a letter written to the *Spectator*, a highbrow weekly journal, believed that German national characteristics would negate the effect of bombing and came to the conclusion that there was "no justification for the assumption that the enemy's morale will be undermined any more than that of this country."[16] Others found the idea of reprisal and area bombing contrary to British national character. Lord Queensborough, President of the Society of St. George, advocated the bombing of German industry in the August edition of the society's journal, but added that revenge was not true to the spirit of England's patron saint.[17]

Such responses show that British consciences were stirring, including those of the Anglican bench of bishops. Bishop Clifford Woodward of Bristol and Bishop George Bell of Chichester made their views known. Woodward declared his doubts about the morality of night bombing in a public speech in Bristol, and Bell expressed his disquiet in a letter to *The Times*.[18] A few weeks later, the highbrow *Fortnightly Review* reprinted Bell's statement, and the editor invited responses from a number of influential and well-known figures. Bell believed that German civilians were being accidentally killed by a British bombing policy aimed solely at legitimate industrial sites. He therefore advocated a convention between the combatant nations codifying bombing practice, and asked whether daylight attacks would be militarily more effective. The invited respondents then gave their views. One element united virtually all, and that was their amazement at Bell's naivety. Bell was, ironically enough, one of the great believers of Bomber Command's claim to be a precision instrument. His criticism was built on the belief that in daylight, and against areas declared to be legitimate military targets (a move that provided the Germans with the chance to empty them of their non-combatants), the RAF would be able to conduct a brilliant campaign. On exactly how all this was to be achieved the bishop made no comment.[19]

The two most senior figures invited to air their views were the Marquess of Crewe, a respected Liberal politician who had reported on alleged German atrocities in the Great War, and Viscount Sankey, a legal expert and former Lord Chancellor. Neither man made a controversial statement. The Marquess of Crewe simply doubted whether the RAF could do more to avoid civilian casualties, which he deemed to be an accidental by-product of British strategy. Viscount Sankey provided a dense philosophical argument citing both international law and the seventeenth century English philosopher, Thomas Hobbes. He picked his way through Hobbes' theories on man's essential selfishness, the construction of the state and its powers, which were invested in one individual empowered to act in its defense, and came to the safe conclusion that the complex issue of bombing policy was best left to Churchill. Lord Esher, another senior member of the Lords, was equally orthodox but slightly more forthright as he denied the distinction between combatant and non-combatant in modern war. According to the Irish dramatist St. John Ervine, the writings of Hitler, Rauschning, and Clausewitz revealed a great deal about the German national character, and he further claimed that area bombing would reduce the morale of the German people. The novelist, Dorothy L. Sayers, creator of Lord Peter Wimsey, condemned as naive those who advocated approaching Hitler in order to devise a convention, and Henry Nevinson produced much the same point. Another novelist, Storm Jameson, an advocate of internationalism, opined that bombing was not effective, but feared its indiscriminate effects, which would leave Europe's "fields soured, and its energy spent for a generation or more." The most well-constructed dissenting contribution came from Richard Stokes, Labour MP for Ipswich, who believed that night bombing besmirched the British cause: "The guerrillas in their tribal wars have made more sense than the leaders of our civilisation today … Bombing alone will not win the war and more destruction and the spirit of vindictiveness will ultimately get us nowhere. We should set an example to the world, not follow others down the slippery slope of abandoned principles." This was the most interesting piece in the collection, for Stokes was a passionate supporter of the idea of tactical bombing and the righteousness of the British cause. Moreover, he was a veteran of the Great War, winner of the Military Cross and the Croix de Guerre, and therefore no rarefied Bloomsbury philosopher pontificating from an ivory tower.[20]

Stokes followed up this statement in November 1941 by supporting a petition against night bombing, and along with Bell, Shaw, and Vera Brittain, established the Committee for the Abolition of Night Bombing. A month later, Stokes took his battle to the Commons and asked the Secretary of State for Air, Sir Archibald Sinclair, whether the government was afraid to admit that British bombing was aimed at civilians. Sinclair repeated the official line that civilians were killed as an unpleasant side effect of the air campaign against German industry.[21]

Morality and military expediency were clashing more intently than at any time since September 1939. Wishing the Church of England, and the Archbishop of Canterbury, Dr. William Temple, in particular, to take a stronger line, Bell maintained the pressure. In July 1943, he asked Temple to raise the issue of area bombing in the Lords and force a clear response from Bomber Command. Temple dismissed the whole idea and remained silent, but the Archbishop of York, Dr. Cyril Garbett, was prepared to make a public statement, though not of the sort Bell wanted. Expressing his view in a diocesan letter, which then appeared in *The Times,* Garbett stated his understanding that British bombing killed German citizens, but not because they had been deliberately targeted. Life often involved difficult choices, Garbett admitted, and individuals often had to acquiesce in a degree of wrong in order to prevent an even greater evil. "Often in life," he noted, "there is no clear choice between absolute right and wrong."[22] Like Bell, he therefore accepted that the RAF aimed at military objectives, and that in pursuit of this strategy, civilians were unintentionally killed. But, he argued, if the bombing succeeded, it would shorten the war and save thousands of lives. Further, unlike Bell, he turned on those who demanded the suspension of the British bombing campaign, and reminded them that they were probably condemning thousands more British soldiers to death. Finally, he added: "frequently the choice has to be made of the lesser of two evils, and it is a lesser evil to bomb a war-loving Germany than to sacrifice the lives of thousands of our own countrymen who long for peace and to delay delivering millions now held in slavery."[23]

Frustrated at his lack of progress, Bell brought the debate to a head in February 1944 when the RAF's campaign against Berlin was still raging. Addressing the Lords, he attacked Bomber Command's policy as one that shamed the British cause and threatened a wholesale collapse of morality and civilized society. As in his earlier protests, he was at pains to point out that he was not against all bombing and he understood that civilians would be killed, but he believed the current strategy of area bombing was too horrifically random to be accepted:

> I fully realise that in attacks on centres of war industry and transport the killing of civilians when it is the result of *bona fide* military activity is inevitable ... But there must be a fair balance between the means employed and the purpose achieved. To obliterate a whole town because certain portions contain military and industrial establishments is to reject the balance.[24]

Bell's protest has been taken as the cry of decent British people everywhere when they began to realize the implications of British bombing policy. However, this misses the complexity of the response. The "quality" newspapers remarked upon the outburst, in particular the *Daily Telegraph*, but the popular dailies were not at all interested. Analyzing his position closely, the lead article of the *Daily Telegraph* took on Bell and found his argument wanting. His attitude was condemned as naive, and the shadow of appeasement was raised. He was placed in the same category as the so-called "Guilty Men" who led Britain into the mire of war, and was reminded that those who had tried to reason with the Nazis had got nowhere. At the same time, the article denied British bombing policy was dedicated to revenge and pointless destruction. "It is an indispensable prelude to a peace which shall be more than a mere armistice."[25]

A few days after Bell aired his reasoned concerns, a reader wrote to the *Daily Telegraph* pointing out her admiration for his moral courage and asking why the other bishops had remained silent, expressing no view one way or the other, and thus either ignored or forgot the contributions of Garbett and Woodward.[26] Around the same time, Vera Brittain's pamphlet *Seeds of Chaos: What Mass Bombing Really Means* was published for the Bombing Restriction Campaign. The Quaker T. Corder Catchpool formed the committee in 1941 with the intention of raising public awareness of Britain's bombing campaign and putting pressure on the government to modify Bomber Command's strategy. Brittain used the pamphlet, the latest in a series produced by the committee, to carefully dissect the claims of Bomber Command, the government, and the Air Ministry.[27] Rather than lay immediate claim to the moral high ground, Brittain used the calm argument of military effectiveness. She claimed that bombing was not achieving its objectives and was therefore inexcusable, as it was not a wickedness accepted in order to prevent a further wickedness, but, because ineffective, a wickedness in itself. Turning to the press, she berated it for taking such a glib and bloodthirsty attitude to the whole campaign and claimed it was making people tolerant of all kinds of appalling transgressions. She concluded by speculating on the wealth of further problems the campaign might be stoking up, such as postwar resentment in Germany. Just how many people ever came across this work and its accompanying titles is a debatable point. They certainly did not provoke much comment from the popular press or on the newsreels.

Others, unconnected with the Bombing Restriction Committee, took the opportunity to publish anti-bombing pamphlets. The Duke of Bedford's *Wholesale Bombing* was published in the spring of 1944. It implied that the German blitz on Britain was nothing more than retaliation against British bombing of Germany in the early days of the war. He felt that it was difficult to "avoid the conclusion that the British government had the chief share of responsibility for starting the grim contest in night bombing ... [and they] have been mainly responsible for re-starting it in the spring of 1942."[28] Like Brittain, he condemned the attitude of the press and wondered whether it was possible to get sense from "the thick skulls and torpid imaginations of our politicians."[29] However, the Duke of Bedford was hardly likely to influence views as he was far from an impartial observer. He was a friend of the British Union of Fascists' leader Oswald Mosley, had been a Nazi sympathizer, and had come close to internment earlier in the war.[30]

Running alongside these dissenting statements was a vast weight of media material designed to buttress support for the British strategic bombing campaign. The information presented to the British people remained ambiguous throughout the war, as it continued to insist on the legitimacy of British bombing, while also implying that the Germans were getting their just punishment. All reportage was laden with innuendo, which suited a squeamish government perfectly, but sowed the seeds for later misunderstandings of the campaign, and deeply frustrated Sir Arthur Harris, who consistently demanded a frank public statement on the nature of the British strategy.[31]

With British victories extremely thin on the ground between 1941 and 1942, the onus was placed on Bomber Command to deliver good news. In the spring of 1942, the British reached their lowest point in the war with the debacle of the escape of the German warships *Prinz Eugen*, *Gneisenau*, and *Scharnhorst* from French Atlantic-coast harbors to safety in German ports under the noses of the British in what became known as the "Channel Dash," and the collapse of Singapore. The newspapers were filled with a mixture of anger, indignation, and resignation, as was much of the country, and the British people demanded a way of hitting back. The Ministry of Information's Home Intelligence Weekly Report for February 16–23 noted that the public felt that it had been "the blackest week since Dunkirk."[32] However, there was a key difference. Dunkirk produced a sense of solidarity. This time the mood was of recrimination and introspection. For the newspapers and the public, the war now had to be fought by new men with new ideas. In a frenzy of frustration, the popular press bemoaned those who wanted to prosecute the war as a gentleman's game, and not with all the ruthlessness and dedication of the Nazis.

Therefore, when the newly appointed Commander-in-Chief of Bomber Command, Sir Arthur Harris, mounted his first major attack against Lübeck in April 1942, the havoc he wrought on that city gratified the British public. The *Daily Express* displayed aerial photographs of the smouldering ruins and crowed: "This is what happened to the city of Lübeck, where 150,000 Germans live and work, on the night last month when the RAF decided to render an English translation of the word 'blitz.' No city in all Britain ever suffered so much in a single attack."[33] As new Lancaster bombers began to stream off the production line in August 1942, British Movietone quoted Harris: "No part of the Reich is safe."[34]

In May 1942, Harris launched his first 1,000-bomber raid on Cologne and achieved a public relations *coup de théatre*. The *Daily Express* headline read: "The Vengeance Begins!"[35] The newsreels also made much of the attack. Gaumont British reminded its viewers of the just retribution the Germans were receiving; its item was titled "1000. RAF Lets Hitler have it, right on the chin!"

> Do you remember how those jackbooted German troops marched over Cologne Bridge to re-occupy the Rhineland in 1936? That for the world was the rebirth of German lust for bloodshed and conquest. It's poetic justice that it should be Cologne that got the first raid of the Thousand Plan. What's coming to the Nazis in Germany is what they would do to us if they could: and still will, if they can … Never forget—it was Hitler's Germany that started this: we never wanted it: and since our would-be peacemakers, for all their trying, failed to keep the peace, let the men of war get peace back again in the only possible way … the hard way.
>
> Thanks, Bomber Command! You're doing a grand job: this was Cologne, making war with factories: but the RAF has thrown a spanner in the works.[36]

When Hamburg was attacked in July 1943, an awful firestorm was created; British Movietone News reported: "The second largest city of the Reich is being liquidated in a series of record attacks by the RAF."[37] The British press filled the gaps in the official silences with such dramatic statements.

According to this popular press version of events, Britain was absolved from moral obloquy because it had not instigated the campaign. British Movietone newsreel caught this tone perfectly. The Germans were reeling, according to the commentary, and were also regretful. "How he must regret the ruthless attacks he made on Warsaw, Rotterdam, Belgrade, London, Coventry and the rest. The day and night of reckoning is definitely near."

It was not merely the popular media that took such a stance. The *Spectator* invited J.M. Spaight, a civil servant at the Air Ministry, to express his views. He chastised those who wanted to compromise Britain's only powerful weapon:

> We cannot allow the weapon in which we excel to be blunted by people who see only the suffering which bombing and counter-bombing inflict, and, like the Bishop of Chichester and others, urge the abandonment of the night bombing which constitutes the main part of our strategic bombing ... The bombing of factories cannot be stopped because women and children in the vicinity may suffer if they remain in the vicinity. They suffer also under the blockade.[38]

Readers of the right-wing *Daily Telegraph,* a newspaper that followed the debate over bombing closely, expressed similar views. C.D.L. Enoch wrote: "We ought, with utter impunity, to bomb Berlin and bomb it unmercifully."[39] In order to avoid unnecessary bloodshed, the RAF should announce these raids in advance, thus allowing civilian evacuation to take place. "A Medical Psychologist" contradicted other correspondents by stressing the weaknesses in German national character.[40] German morale was extremely susceptible according to this correspondent: "they [the authorities] don't seem to realise that what merely stiffens our backs flattens a German." Seeing this was the case, he advocated "whip[ping] them as they have whipped us."[41] "There must be thousands in this country," wrote B.M. Maynard, "who feel with me that until the people of Germany themselves are made to feel and suffer what they are willing to make others suffer it will be a very long time before we can shatter the prestige which the Nazi regime continues to enjoy."[42] G.L. Braidwood added that "civilian morale is the most important of all strategic objectives in this war and may ultimately be the crucial one ... Berlin and Munich in ruins would shake Nazism more profoundly than the next twelve months' bombing of 'military targets'."[43]

The concept of a war-loving Germany was used as an excuse for the area bombing. It was felt that the accidental deaths of ordinary German civilians might help to chastise a people who had twice in one century brought war to the world. Sir Robert Vansittart, a leading member of the Foreign Office civil service, was a prominent exponent of this view. In broadcasts and in print, Vansittart described the Germans as an inherently aggressive race that deserved to face the full force of Allied power. A vehement opponent of Nazi Germany since the nineteen-thirties, Vansittart drew upon images of Germans familiar from the Great War, and provided an intellectual-philosophical justification of the strategic air campaign.[44] Even those who doubted whether bombing was having any great effect on the outcome of the war thought this "punishment element" justified. According to an article by "XYZ" in the *National Review*, the Germans were suffering the realities of war for the first time for over a century. "All the other wars of aggression which the Germans have waged during the nineteenth and early twentieth centuries have devastated other nations … Now the Germans are having a lesson they have long needed."[45]

Opponents of British bombing policy were often treated very sharply. When Bishop Woodward declared his doubts about the morality of night bombing, the Mayor of Bristol announced his complete disagreement and pointedly told the bishop that civilians should not interfere in military matters. The populist right-wing *Sunday Dispatch* also commented on the bishop's lack of military qualifications: "he suggested that Britain—fighting with her back to the wall against the greatest gangsters in history—should sacrifice the weapon which will most help her to victory. If the battle of the darkness were to stop tonight it would mean that a war of attrition would last years longer."[46] This was indeed a potent argument. Running throughout British life in the nineteen-twenties and nineteen-thirties was the shadow of the Great War, and in particular the memory of the appalling battles of the Somme and Passchendaele. Most Britons held a deep-seated fear of repeating such a struggle, as evidenced by support for the Peace Pledge Union in 1934. Bomber Command was supposed to be the answer; it was meant to reduce Germany to submission without the need for a protracted land campaign.

The *Sunday Dispatch* unequivocally stated its disagreement to the dissenting MP, Richard Stokes, and pronounced a message of retribution and punishment claiming it had the support of the public:

> Those MPs who appear to regard the German civilians as their own constituents can be assured that the British public is not shedding any crocodile tears over the bombing of German cities. … Hundreds of German civilians who exulted in the sufferings of Rotterdam, London, and the English provinces exult no more. They are dead in the ruins of those cities from which their flamboyant columns set out to enslave the peoples of the world … We are in a position, after years of humiliation and suffering, to blast an understanding of the war into the real German mind. That is not a matter for which we should apologise. It is a service to the rest of mankind.[47]

Such views cannot be dismissed lightly, as has often been the case by those anxious to prove that the British were not interested in reprisal raids on

Germany. Winston Churchill himself publicly encouraged a spirit of reprisals and revenge. On 14 July 1941, he reviewed the London fire and civil defenses services in Hyde Park and then attended a luncheon at County Hall. His speech referred to the sufferings inflicted on the British people and those of other nations by the Nazi bombers, and then proclaimed:

> If tonight the people of London were asked to cast their vote as to whether a convention should be entered into to stop the bombing of all cities the overwhelming majority would cry, *"No, we shall mete out to the Germans the measure and more than the measure they have meted out to us."*[48]

As British industry swelled the number of aircraft and ordnance available to Bomber Command, its ability to hit Germany increased enormously, and for a publicity-conscious leader such as Sir Arthur Harris, it was the chance to harness opinion by showing the results of his strategy. The RAF and the press carefully fostered the image of Bomber Command as the cutting edge of modernity and technology, the only force capable of delivering a knockout blow. Harry Watt took precisely this line in his 1941 drama-documentary *Target for Tonight*. The film was greeted with great public acclamation, and a copy was even presented to Stalin in order to show the Soviet people that the British were maintaining an effective second front.[49] As such, Bomber Command became the darling of the British people and was presented as the bearer of the nation's hopes and desires. Perhaps the most striking example of public support for the RAF, and Bomber Command in particular, was the Wings for Victory week in the spring of 1943. Two Lancaster bombers dominated Trafalgar Square, and a Stirling was placed in St. Paul's churchyard. The response of the public was remarkable. Over a million people flooded through Trafalgar Square and then blocked the Strand as they made their way toward St. Paul's Cathedral. The *Daily Express* announced "the Biggest Crowd since the Coronation."[50] Designed as a fundraising event, the organizers were overwhelmed, and the system of collecting money broke down under the strain, leaving many people unable to invest in War Bonds. This event fully reveals the commitment of the British people to the RAF and Bomber Command.

The BBC also achieved one of its greatest successes of the war in a program about Bomber Command, "Cutting the Skipper." On 4 September 1943, Wynford Vaughan Thomas accompanied the crew of Lancaster in a raid on Berlin. The recording revealed the *sangfroid* of the crew, and their dedicated determination shone through. Vaughan Thomas described vividly the defensive and offensive fire that swathed Berlin: "That's the city itself. And there in the heart of the glow there goes a red flash—the biggest we've yet seen ... it's pretty obvious as we're coming in now through the searchlight cones that it's going to be hell over the city itself."[51] All the time during the recording, the drone of the Lancaster engines shuddered in the background along with the odd dull thud of flak and bombs.

Investigated by a BBC survey, it was found that listening figures were "exceptionally large for an isolated feature programme."[52] The appreciation index was 92, which had been equalled only once before by a program about the Battle of Britain. Listeners were asked whether the live material was worth it considering its technical shortcomings. "95% gave an emphatic affirmative … 80% considered that the additional material made the programme much more interesting."[53]

The most commonly expressed feeling was of admiration for the crew and, not far short of it, admiration for the BBC technicians who accompanied them. It is clear from the report that people were thrilled by the realism and felt they had learned something about the dangers involved in bombing. Many expressed the deep impression the stoic, quiet heroism of the crew made on them. It was noted that very few objected to the recording of a bombing mission. Fewer still expressed sympathy with the Berliners. "Others expressed great satisfaction to have participated in the sensation of dropping a bomb on Berlin." "Retired" called it "a magnificent programme"; "Secretary" considered it "the finest broadcast to date"; and "Civil Servant" said "a most exciting broadcast and one that would stand repeating."[54]

Bomber Command sought out good propaganda continually, and, as noted, Harris was acutely aware of the value of positive publicity. When considering the release of aerial photographs of the Cologne raid, he told his Public Relations Officers to pick good, clear examples. He added in his own inimitable style: "even Service Officers in many cases have not the vaguest idea what they are looking at when viewing an air photograph … one never knows whether they are vertical photographs of air damage or the south end of a bathing beauty looking north!"[55]

An enormous publicity coup was scored with the dams' raid of March 1943. "Huns get a flood blitz / Torrent rages along Ruhr," proclaimed the banner headline in the *Daily Mirror;* while "Floods roar down Ruhr Valley" met the readers of the *Daily Express*.[56] For *The Times*, it was a moment of well-deserved retribution: "Only now are the German people beginning to pay the penalty of their own leaders' crimes—the bombs rained on Warsaw in 1939 without so much as a declaration of war, and in 1940 on the open and defenceless city of Rotterdam."[57] Operation Chastise lived up to its name and achieved legendary status within hours of its completion.

Harris's campaign against Berlin, which raged from the autumn of 1943 through to the spring of 1944, was the culmination of his strategy. The battle received regular press attention as the capital of the Nazi empire was brought under regular and heavy attack, which was regarded as just retribution on the heartland of Nazi Germany. The *Daily Mirror* noted that "in about thirty minutes a load nearly six times as big as the heaviest tonnage ever dropped on London in a night was unleashed."[58] British Movietone also picked up on this statistic and referred to the "heavy saturation bombing of Berlin," and in March 1944, it trumpeted a new record of tonnage dropped in one night.[59] A *Daily Sketch* article referred to "the elimination of the capital of Nazism," and a few weeks later still it succinctly stated that Berlin had suffered "an obliteration attack. Just that."[60] The raids on Mannheim and Ludwigshafen in February 1944 were covered by British Paramount News under the title "How the RAF 'Obliterate,'" and the edition referred to the easily visible water communications, which made both cities perfect targets for the RAF, a "bomber's dream," in fact.[61]

In February 1945, Bomber Command took part in the attack on Dresden. The raid has become synonymous with Harris and all that is thought most reprehensible about British bombing. However, Dresden was not a *cause celebre* at the time. Rather, it was just another raid that gained notoriety after the event thanks to Churchill's sudden attack of conscience and discomfort at some reports in the US press. In Britain, the media coverage provided the public with a familiar diet and contained no perceptible hint of disquiet. The *Daily Express* told its readers that, according to sources in neutral Sweden, the attack on Dresden had "brought confusion to southern Germany comparable only with that in the north after the last big raid on Berlin ... Now the Dresden artery is severed, temporarily at least. Railway stations and yards have been demolished, bridges and viaducts blown up, and factories laid in ruins."[62] The *Daily Sketch* noted that "Dresden, capital of Saxony and key control centre in Germany's defence against Koniev's land forces, less than seventy miles away, was the principal target of two great blows by the RAF on Tuesday night, and by American airmen yesterday."[63] Readers of the *Daily Telegraph* were met by the headline: "Non-Stop Air Blows Aid Both Fronts / 650,000 RAF Fire Bombs on Dresden."[64] The report mentioned German claims that a terror attack had taken place, but this was part of a well-oiled German routine, and it was countered with the fact that "Dresden is desperately needed as a concentration area for troops and administrative services evacuated from elsewhere in the Reich."[65] The newsreels were equally unrepentant. British Paramount News told its viewers that the RAF and American air force had "shattered" Dresden, and added: "Dresden lies on both banks of the River Elbe. A city of great beauty in peacetime is now a mass of ruins, one more sacrifice made by the German people to their insane desire for world domination."[66] On March 5, the *Daily Mail* reported: "Dresden was completely wiped out by the massive Allied air blows on February 14 and 16, said the German Overseas News Agency last night … 'Today we can only speak of what once was Dresden in the past tense.'"⁶⁷ But there was hardly any remorse in the report.

As the allied armies advanced and captured German cities, the newsreels took the chance to look at the devastation caused by bombing. The commentaries contained a reflective element, but it was not one designed to cause angst in Britain. According to British Paramount, the ruins of Cologne were presented as a monument to the righteous anger of the allies.⁶⁸ The significance of Dresden, and the haunting, accusing, sight of Germany's devastated cities, is a postwar imposition on British memory.

Public opinion on bombing itself remained remarkably consistent and provides hints that the British people had a shrewd idea of the implications of the policy pursued in their name, but shied away from them, taking comfort in the ambiguities of the reportage. Tom Harrisson of Mass-Observation noted at the height of the blitz that residents of bombed cities displayed little obvious desire for revenge, but the elapse of time kindled an appetite for retribution.⁶⁹ In May 1941, the *News Chronicle* published a Gallup survey of attitudes toward bombing, which supported Harrisson's understanding. Gallup asked people across the country: "Would you approve if the RAF adopted a policy of bombing the civilian population of Germany?"⁷⁰ The results proved "the people of Britain are in favour of reprisal bombing of Germany," but it was not as clear-cut as that conclusion seemed to suggest. It was found that people living in areas away from the main German attacks, in the rural northwest for example, were far more likely to support the idea of reprisals than Londoners. "It would seem that sentiment in favour of reprisals is almost in inverse ratio to the amount of bombing experienced," the survey concluded.⁷¹ A survey conducted in December 1940 had found a much more even spread across the country, with forty-six per cent saying they approved of reprisals, while forty-eight per cent disapproved and six per cent did not know. The ensuing period had the effect of raising by seven per cent for the whole country those in favor of reprisal bombing.⁷² In revealing that most people did not like the idea of reprisals—most people who had been bombed that is—it made no statement about whether people believed all bombing was wrong or ineffective. Indeed, according to some sources, the public had not rejected the idea of reprisals at all. Two months earlier, Home Intelligence had reported to Churchill that "people will want a lot of convincing that really heavy raids on civilian centres in Germany are not our most efficacious weapon."⁷³

In 1944, the *New Statesman* published Mass-Observation's survey of opinions on British bombing. It found that in London, six out of ten people gave unqualified verbal approval to the raids. Two said they were necessary, but expressed major qualms about their effects on the civilian population of Germany. Only one in ten felt they were too awful to be approved in any way, "though few go so far as wanting them stopped."[74] It was found that very few expressed gloating or vengeful sentiments. Only one in six felt that bombing would end the war, but considerably more believed that it would shorten it "and this is the most usual reason for approval of our raids."[75] The survey was obviously carried out in the knowledge that British bombing was aimed at civilians, for it was noted that "an interesting reflection of the depth of guilt felt about bombing *people* is afforded by the extent to which men and women still manage to believe that we are only bombing military targets."[76] To imply that people were not interested in retribution is wrong, however, for the survey also found that most people wanted Germany to be dismembered and comprehensive war crimes trials to be conducted. Whatever ambiguities surround the public knowledge of, and debate about, British bombing, the overwhelming conclusion is that most people wanted it to continue and believed that it was proving effective in some way.

During the course of World War II, the British public was presented with many different interpretations of the aerial war and fed a diet of truths, half-truths, and outright lies. The attitude of the newspapers varied only slightly; a reader of the broadsheets may have consumed slightly less lurid reportage, but the information and stance was remarkably similar to that of the tabloids. Later, this allowed the British people and politicians to claim ignorance as to the true nature of strategic air campaign. The British people were told Germany was going to be ruined from top to bottom. They knew this was the promise of Bomber Command, and the newspapers and newsreels reminded them of this promise on an almost daily basis. Some managed to convince themselves that it was going to be done by bombing factories alone. Most did not manage this trick and silently accepted the implications of the policy, probably even rejoiced in it. There were opponents of the policy who publicly exposed the ambiguities of its intentions and presentation. Despite all the powers available to the wartime state, these views were never suppressed, but how many people actually came into contact with them is difficult to assess. Readers of the popular press did not have the chance to assess these arguments first hand and would have seen only condemnation of the opponents.

A significant change occurred at the end of the war when the government decided to distance itself from the bomber campaign, and made Harris a scapegoat for agreed wartime policy by implying that he was the sole architect of the strategy. Although later supporters of Harris often believed that the reaction against him was one led by the Labour party, it was started by Churchill after the Dresden raid and emphasized by his omission of Bomber Command from his victory speech.[77] Clement Attlee's Labour government then compounded the issue by omitting Harris from the Victory Honours List, failing to offer him a major award, and by not striking a medal for the strategic air campaign.[78] It led to an official campaign of forgetting, and in turn created a situation in which Harris and Bomber Command became the black sheep of the British popular memory of World War II. Sensitive to Soviet allegations that the Dresden raid was an act of capitalist vengeance and increasingly aware of the power of the Campaign for Nuclear Disarmament, British governments preferred to avoid the issue of the strategic air campaign. It suited the state not to contradict the idea that the flamboyant and headstrong Harris was the instigator of the entire campaign.[79] Bomber Command was then largely left out of the glorious reenactment of World War II in British cinema during the 1950s. With the publication of the official history of the campaign in the 1960s and increased sensitivity over the issue of bombing due to events in Vietnam and a new generation of atomic and nuclear weapons, the role of Harris and Bomber Command became even more questionable, particularly among the center-left.[80] Even decades later passions ran high, as was shown in 1992 by the protests against the erection of a statue to commemorate Harris and his men.[81]

This position is too comfortable, for it allows a neat identification of heroes and villains and ignores the complexities of the wartime situation. Due to this confusing development of the history of Bomber Command's actions, modern popular opinion holds it as a truth that Harris devised and carried out the bombing war according to his own ruthless desires without reference to the British government or people. Television, the great disseminator of history, has buttressed this version and shows little sign of revising it. It is an image born in the truths, half-truths, and collective deceptions forged during the war. The British people lacked the whole story then; they lack it today.[82] The British shied away from what they had taken part in then. Today, they deny they ever suspected the truth, although that was far from the case during the war itself, and Harris still provides the most convenient figure to carry the burden of guilt. It can be claimed that during the war the full truth was never known, but it was guessed and imagined. If it was guessed, why was there not greater protest? Probably because most people were silently content to let it go ahead. After the war, the government confirmed the inner qualms about the campaign. By ignoring Harris and his men, the state ensured a diminished role for Bomber Command in the share of victory. This shunning did not lessen over the years and served merely to strengthen the inner guilt felt by some British people. But rather than admit the anxieties collectively or attempt to explain their wartime actions within their context, many went along with the easy option of blaming Harris. Ironically, when

British populist right-wing newspapers like the *Daily Mail* complain of the debunking of British heroes, the blame lies not with dilettante intellectuals or the "loony left," but with the State itself, starting with a Conservative Prime Minister, Winston Churchill, in the closing stages of the war.

The British state found it politic to blame Harris and eventually took the British people with it. Harris and Bomber Command are still the black sheep of the British popular memory of World War II. This memory relies upon incomplete and inaccurate knowledge. But even those who are trying to rehabilitate the memory use inaccuracies, or have gaps in their knowledge. The most often-heard defense is that the Command never set out to kill German civilians. Clearly, that was not the case. Historians have tried to take a more measured line pointing out that if it was an atrocity, it was an atrocity for which the wartime government must take responsibility.

Notes

1. For details see Uri Bialer, *The Shadow of the Bomber: The Fear of Air Bombardment and British Politics, 1932–1939* (London: Royal Historical Society, 1980); Richard Overy, *Bomber Command, 1939–1945: Reaping the Whirlwind* (London: HarperCollins, 1996).
2. See Jeffrey Richards, *The Age of the Dream Palace: Cinema and Society in Britain 1930–1939* (London: Keegan Paul, 1984); I.F.C. Clarke, *Voices Prophesying War 1763–1984* (Oxford: Oxford University Press, 1992).
3. See Stephen A. Garrett, *Ethics and Airpower in World War II: The British Bombing of German Cities* (New York: St. Martin's Press, 1993), 25–30.
4. For a detailed discussion of Bomber Command policy see Charles Webster and Noble Frankland, *The Strategic Air Campaign Against Germany, 1939–1945*, 4 vols. (London: HMSO, 1961).
5. For the Ministry of Information see Ian McLaine, *Ministry of Morale, Home Front Morale and the Ministry of Information in World War II* (London: Allen & Unwin, 1979). For a wider discussion of Bomber Command and press coverage see Mark Connelly, *Reaching for the Stars: A New History of RAF Bomber Command in World War II* (London: I.B. Tauris, 2000).
6. *Daily Mail*, 25 September 1940.
7. *Daily Sketch*, 25 September 1940.
8. *Daily Telegraph*, 27 August 1940.
9. *Daily Telegraph*, 26 September 1940.
10. *Daily Mail*, 10 September 1940.
11. *Daily Mirror*, 12 September 1940.
12. *Daily Express*, 3 January 1941.
13. *The Times*, 28 April 1941.
14. *Daily Telegraph*, 19 April 1941.
15. *Daily Telegraph*, 16 April 1941.
16. *Spectator*, 3 October 1941.
17. *Sunday Dispatch*, 3 August 1941.

18. *Sunday Dispatch*, 18 May 1941; *The Times*, 21 May 1941.
19. *The Times*, 21 May 1941.
20. *Fortnightly Review*, June 1941, 67–70.
21. Great Britain, *5 Parliamentary Debates* (Commons), 395 (1 December 1943) 338.
22. *The Times*, 25 June 1943.
23. *The Times*, 25 June 1943.
24. Great Britain, *5 Parliamentary Debates* (Lords), 130 (9 February 1944) 736–738.
25. *Daily Telegraph*, 14 February 1944.
26. *Daily Telegraph*, 14 February 1944. The correspondent was Lady Macassey.
27. Vera Brittain, *Seeds of Chaos: What Mass Bombing Really Means* (London: Committee for the Abolition of Night Bombing [a.k.a. Bombing Restriction Committee], 1944).
28. Duke of Bedford, *Wholesale Bombing* (Glasgow: Strickland Press, 1944), 5–6.
29. Ibid., 6.
30. See NA PRO KV2/1367 for examples of wartime security surveillance operations on the Duke of Bedford.
31. See NA PRO AIR 2/7852, Letter from Harris to Sir Charles Portal, 23 December 1943.
32. Quoted in Anthony Aldgate and Jeffrey Richards, *Britain Can Take It! The British Cinema in the Second World War* (Oxford: Basil Blackwell, 1986), 126.
33. *Daily Express*, 25 April 1942.
34. British Movietone News, 13 August 1942.
35. *Daily Express*, 1 June 1942.
36. British Gaumont Newsreel, 6 August 1942.
37. British Movietone Newsreel, 8 June 1942.
38. *Spectator*, 12 September 1941.
39. *Daily Telegraph*, 10 April 1941.
40. *Daily Telegraph*, 10 April 1941.
41. *Daily Telegraph*, 10 April 1941.
42. *Daily Telegraph*, 10 April 1941.
43. *Daily Telegraph*, 10 April 1941.
44. See Garrett, *Ethics and Airpower*, 91–92.
45. *National Review*, January 1944, 11.
46. *Sunday Dispatch*, 18 May 1941.
47. *Sunday Dispatch*, 14 March 1943.
48. The Decca recording of this speech reveals a good deal of table-rapping and noises of assent when this line is delivered (emphasis added). W.S. Churchill, *War Speeches* (London: Cassell, 1952), vol. 2: 25.
49. See Ken Short, "RAF Bomber Command's Target for Tonight (1941)," *Historical Journal of Film, Radio and Television*, vol. 17, No. 2, 1997: 181–218.
50. *Daily Express*, 8 March 1943.
51. BBC Written Archives, File LR/2094.
52. BBC Written Archives, File LR/2094.
53. BBC Written Archives, File LR/2094.
54. BBC Written Archives, File LR/2094.
55. NA PRO AIR 20/4229, memo 28 June 1942.
56. *Daily Mirror*, 18 May 1943; *Daily Express*, 18 May 1943.

57. *The Times*, 18 May 1943.
58. *Daily Mirror*, 17 February 1944.
59. British Movietone News, 29 November 1943, 14 March 1944.
60. *Daily Sketch*, 17 February 1944.
61. British Paramount News, 24 February 1944.
62. *Daily Express*, 14 February 1945.
63. *Daily Sketch*, 14 February 1945.
64. *Daily Telegraph*, 15 February 1945.
65. *Daily Telegraph*, 15 February 1945.
66. British Paramount News, 22 February 1945.
67. *Daily Mail*, 15 March 1945.
68. British Paramount News, 22 March 1945.
69. Tom Harrisson, *Living Through the Blitz* (Harmondsworth: Penguin, 1990), 314–316.
70. *News Chronicle*, 2 May 1941.
71. *News Chronicle*, 2 May 1941.
72. *News Chronicle*, 2 May 1941.
73. Quoted in Michael Balfour, *Propaganda in War, 1939–1945* (London: Routledge & Kegan Paul, 1979), 251.
74. *New Statesman*, XXVII, 677, 12 February 1944.
75. *New Statesman*, XXVII, 677, 12 February 1944.
76. *New Statesman*, XXVII, 677, 12 February 1944.
77. See Connelly, *Reaching for the Stars*, 140–142.
78. See ibid., 141–143.
79. See ibid., 150–152.
80. See ibid., 148–152.
81. See *Sunday Telegraph*, 31 May 1992.
82. In the spring of 1996, the Bomber Command Association told *The Times* of its dismay at the public ignorance of the true facts about Harris and Dresden. Bomber Command Association found that most people still thought the city was bombed on Harris's order alone and were still convinced that everyone knew the end of the war was in sight in February 1945. *The Times*, 6 May 1996.

CHAPTER 9

The German Debate
Lothar Kettenacker

Though the historian cannot escape from the present, it is important for him or her to see things in perspective. When in early 1945 it was all too obvious to the British Cabinet that the Germans had lost the war, Churchill asked the Foreign Office for a paper on their most likely reaction to defeat. This generation of British politicians was, of course, greatly influenced by Germany's irrational denial of what had happened in 1918. Con O'Neill, the most likely author of the subsequent memorandum submitted to the Cabinet, speculated that the defective gene was not National Socialism, but collectivism and militarism, a dangerous mixture of discipline and idealism. "Other forms of totalitarianism equally unpleasant and effective may occur," he wrote, "for these instincts and capacities will remain largely what they are."[1] Soon, the Germans would only remember their victorious battles and war heroes and would strive to regain their lost territories in the East. This is also how the Nazis themselves visualized the future. When faced with his record at the Nuremberg Military Tribunal, Hermann Göring, second in command after Hitler and in charge of the *Luftwaffe*, believed that in fifty or sixty years' time, Germany would be covered with statues in his honor.[2]

For fifty years since the war, the Germans have coped with their past in very different ways. The evils and war crimes of the Nazi regime have dominated public opinion to such an extent that now foreign observers seem to be surprised, some even shocked, at a slight change of track. The German media, which in the past have been in the forefront of re-education, have realized that the time has come to draw attention to the fact that the Germans, too, were victims of the war launched by their government. In some foreign reviews, one could get the impression that it was Günter Grass, in his novel on the sinking of the ship *Wilhelm Gustloff* and the drowning of more than 9,000 passengers—most of them civilian refugees from the East—who had been a trailblazer for a new perspective of the past.[3] After all, three times as many Germans perished while fleeing from the Red Army in the winter of 1944/45 as fell victim to Allied bombing.[4] In his novel, Grass admits that in the past, his generations had shunned an important topic for reasons of political correctness,[5] only to go on to hold the neo-Nazis in such abhorrence that his story has the appearance of a concocted plot. Conscious of his carefully nurtured reputation as the conscience of Germany's leftwing intelligentsia, he saw himself as breaking a taboo. This signal of apparent change was eagerly taken up by foreign critics who would otherwise not be aware of what had been going on in the more mundane German media. German critics of Grass were less impressed. Hubert Spiegel, for instance, pointed out that by now there was no risk in talking about German suffering.[6] A year before the book was published, German television had shown a detailed three-part program on what refugees and expellees had to endure during the last six months of the war. Throughout the 1950s, the Federal Republic had is own Ministry for Refugees, which had launched a multi-volume documentation on the flight and expulsion of millions of Germans from their homesteads in the East.[7] Nor had German literature turned a blind eye to the fate of those Germans.[8] It is true, though, that while refugee organizations still questioned the validity of the Oder-Neiße border, the subject had been a delicate issue generally avoided by mainstream media. However, after this problem had been settled once and for all in 1990,[9] as a precondition of the Four Powers for accepting German unification, no more strings were attached to the memory of the lost territories. The memoirs of great landowners already had paved the way for a new, unprejudiced recollection of Germany's landed gentry in the East, whose last days had so much in common with the US South at the end of the civil war.[10] With the demise of the German Democratic Republic, which had treated the forced exodus from the East as a taboo, this topic had become a perfectly legitimate subject of the media. The only bone of contention left, mainly due to Polish reservations, was the question of a public memorial in Berlin: should it be devoted to the fate of refugees and expellees in general, or to the German refugees and expellees from the East in particular? This question has now been settled in favor of the more comprehensive conception: the center is to document the horrors of expulsion in twentieth-century Europe and beyond.[11]

What has been viewed by foreign observers as an ensemble of remembrances signaling a change of attitude, the fate of the refugees and that of civilian victims of area bombing are in fact two different stories with their own track record in Germany's collective memory. By the 1990s, the latter had been deeply imbued with the general awareness that both indiscriminate bombing and ethnic cleansing had been first practiced by the Nazis. No doubt German unification and the fact that all Germans under fifty had hardly any personal experience of the war eased the path toward answering the call, first made by the late Martin Broszat in the 1980s, to try to understand the Third Reich as part of German history, rather than treat it as an exceptional event and a shadow cast over the Federal Republic.[12]

Once the victors of World War II had reached a final settlement with Germany in September 1990,[13] the equivalent of a peace treaty, the time for stocktaking and sharing—sharing both wealth and memory—seemed to have come for Germany as well. More than ever before, East Germans were perceived as the real losers of a war once started by Germany as a whole. While East Germany suffered the loss of its agrarian hinterland and Soviet occupation for more than 40 years,[14] it was the West that was hardest hit by Allied bombing raids. If the nation was to develop a common historical consciousness, it was important to remember both tragedies in equal measure. It was, after all, hard enough for the East Germans now to be confronted with a common past of singular shamefulness, which their masters had tried to deny in the name of anti-fascism. As a kind of antidote, the colossal devastation and suffering as a result of Hitler's war had to be given due recognition. In other words, the suffering of all Germans caused by the war and its impact on the collective memory must be seen as an inevitable process in the context of growing historical consciousness in the wake of German unification.

The nationwide debate on the bombing war has been triggered off, or so it seems, by two recent publications: Winfried Georg Sebald's *Luftkrieg und Literatur*[15] and Jörg Friedrich's *Der Brand*.[16] Both authors were born in 1944, and thus neither could rely on any personal memories of the bombing war. They were all the more surprised and shocked at what they discovered when they acquainted themselves with the most devastating catastrophe in German history. Why did nobody ever tell them what had really happened? Sebald's analysis of German postwar literature and its inadequate treatment of the country's worst nightmare[17] has received nothing but praise both in Germany and, following its translation, in Britain as well. The reception of Friedrich's book was much more ambiguous. Yet his evocative exposition of the actual devastation of the German cities from the perspective of the victims caused a sensation, went into ten print-runs in the first year, and sold nearly 200,000 copies, unheard of for a German work of historical writing. It was not only reviewed by all the important papers and radio stations, but, because of its vivid and explicit narrative, it was even serialized in the only national tabloid *Bild-Zeitung*. This was too much for some German academic historians, who were irritated by an author with a left-wing reputation who would embrace a topic hitherto considered the domain of the political Right. However, Hans Mommsen defended Friedrich's unblemished record as an historian.[18]

Others, such as Heribert Seifert, adopted a more relaxed stance, and argued that it is precisely because German guilt is no longer being questioned that the horrors suffered by the Germans themselves can now be tackled with less inhibition than in the past, when that could have served the wrong purpose.[19] No doubt, Friedrich has not been intimidated by political correctness. British reviewers, even those who by their admission had not yet read the book, reacted with indignation, even fury, when they realized that Churchill and Air Marshal Sir Arthur Harris had been singled out as the chief perpetrators.[20]

In fact, Friedrich had only been delivering what Sebald had found sadly missing: an emotional break-through. Surveying German postwar literature, Sebald had come to the conclusion "that the images of this horrifying chapter of our history have never really crossed the threshold of national consciousness."[21] In his view, "the darkest aspects of the final act of destruction, as experienced by the great majority of the German population, remained under a kind of taboo like a shameful family secret, a secret that perhaps could not even be privately acknowledged."[22] He wondered why "the guild of German historians, known to be among the most industrious in the world, has not yet, so far as I am aware, produced a comprehensive or even an exploratory study of the subject"[23]—with one exception: Friedrich in chapter eight of his book *Das Gesetz des Krieges*. Friedrich's remarks, Sebald wrote, "have not aroused anything like the interest they deserve."[24] In the meantime, they have, indeed, as though Friedrich had taken these words as an inspiration for his *chef d'oeuvre*.

When Friedrich's book was published in 2002, Sebald was dead and could not give his blessing. I am sure he would not have withheld it in spite of certain linguistic *faux pas*. As a literary critic and writer in his own right, he would have noticed that Friedrich's work was as much a piece of literature, of non-fictional narrative, as of historical research. It is therefore not surprising that writers such as Martin Walser ("epos") and Cora Stephan ("lamentation of the dead") responded more sympathetically to this exposition of horror and devastation than some of Germany's academic historians, who had wished for a more balanced historical analysis.[25] Writing in the *Süddeutsche Zeitung*, Germany's quality paper with the largest print-run, Willi Winkler points out that German historical scholarship, with all its devotion to detail, would never have produced the emotional break-through that Friedrich has achieved in his own unique way.[26] Some journalists realized that in today's society, a sentimental approach is necessary. One of the leading though non-academic German historians, Joachim Fest, has coined a new word: *Vergegenwärtigungsbedürfnis* (the need to make the past present to us).[27] Friedrich, it is argued, has satisfied the public desire to turn the past into an event of the present. It is what Alexander Kluge, writer and film director, meant by saying that Friedrich had turned "history into story." No doubt, the author felt that half a century after the catastrophic event the time had come to confront a new generation of Germans with the "unspeakable" horror that earlier generations had experienced, but were unable to divulge.

However, Friedrich's book also has a central message that is easily overlooked: people can be bombed into submission, but not into rebellion against their leaders. The British advocates of area bombing referred to this strategy as "morale bombing" and argued that incessant bombing would weaken public morale to such an extent that people would rise against the regime and thus shorten the war. Nothing was further from reality, as those who had experienced the reaction of the British people to the Blitz should have known. In his review, Hans Mommsen points out that indiscriminate bombing in fact had the opposite effect, at least up to the summer of 1944: it helped to enhance the reputation of the Nazi Party as the only institution able and prepared to relieve the suffering.[28] He thus comes to the conclusion that this form of warfare had been misguided in that the expenditure in terms of production and loss of life, both of pilots and their victims, was out of all proportion to its contribution toward the expected result of shortening the war. The senselessness of destruction is indeed Friedrich's strongest argument. This argument, however, is not spelled out by the author, but rather conveyed by his unique exposition of the devastating facts.

What then is the secret of Friedrich's success, what is so exceptional about his narrative? The German context with which this chapter mainly deals is, of course, crucial: the Germans' past as the victims of the bombing, the attitudes of German readers today, as well as the way the subject had been dealt with before Friedrich's book was published. Friedrich's unusual approach and language are equally important. His focus is on the victims and he divides his narrative into seven chapters with headings quite unusual for an historical study in Germany (if less so in Britain): *Waffe* (Weapon—targets, types of bombs, radar, the crew), *Strategie* (Strategy—morale bombing), *Land* (Land, the central chapter—actual raids bringing havoc to North, West, South, and East Germany), *Schutz* (Protection—air-raid shelters, home front, care for the "dehoused," evacuees), *Wir* (Us—morale, thoughts of revenge), *Ich* (Myself—sense perception, emotion, experience), and finally *Stein* (Stone—historical monuments, protection of valuable items, fate of libraries). The author does not take sides in the way he describes the work of the pilots or their target, the people on the ground; they are both victims of a kind of *force majeure* that had been unleashed and that exposed the German urban landscape to the fury of war. The emotional intensity is achieved by the clinical, matter-of-fact language of a war correspondent, whose task it is to face up to the most horrid aspects of human suffering and systematic destruction.

Some reviewers have criticized this approach: sketching specific historical events or monuments of a city up to the hour of its visitation by the squadrons of death and destruction. Why should an historian not be allowed to make use of the same means of communication as any tourist guide? The professional historian would say that modern historical scholarship, first developed in Germany in the nineteenth century, should not relapse into storytelling. Clearly this is a mistaken philosophy, the academic ethos taken too far, inasmuch as history is closer to literature than to science and achieves its educational purpose in more than one way. Just one example of Friedrich's storytelling: before Air Marshal Harris sends his bombers to the old Roman city of Mainz, the author vividly describes the town's previous destruction through the Prussian bombardment of 1793 as watched and described by Goethe.[29] So, each city's history is touched upon before the final calamity strikes. In this way, Friedrich creates both a feeling of impending doom and a huge panorama of wanton destruction, as though it had been the intention of the Western Allies (not the Russians) to destroy not only Germany's military potential, but also its cultural prowess. All of Germany's medieval city centers but one (Ratisbon) were wiped out. If an American tourist wants to have an idea of what a German medieval town looked like at the time of Luther, he or she has to cross the border into France (Strasbourg) or the Czech Republic (Prague). Another way of illuminating the madness of war, and of the bombing war in particular, is Friedrich's almost devotional emphasis on the question that constantly occupies Bomber Command: how to increase the efficiency of its deadly cargo, how to make destruction more devastating, more widespread. By following its own logic, the war takes leave of all common sense. Therefore, with all its faults, Friedrich's narrative is a brilliant manifesto against modern war as such rather than a charge brought against the British conduct of the war.

The unexpected reception of *Der Brand* has been compared to the deep impact that the US television movie *Holocaust* had made on its German audience 30 years ago. It was due to this film that the word *Holocaust* entered the German vocabulary, which hitherto had to put up with *Endlösung* (final solution), a term invented by the Nazis. At the time, German academic historians were quite baffled by this unexpected outcome in view of the many documentaries and scholarly studies on the subject.[30] The very same reaction has been registered by some German historians who recall the numerous—though mostly local or technical—studies of the bombing war. They are reluctant to acknowledge that in order to attract the attention and thus to arouse the conscience of modern society, a journalistic approach, with its personal touch, is called for. One cannot escape the feeling that Thomas Mann's unfortunate distinction between German culture and allegedly superficial Western civilization still lingers on, long after its rejection by the author himself.[31] German historians should ask themselves why their British colleagues who specialize in contemporary German history, such as Antony Beevor,[32] Richard Evans,[33] or Ian Kershaw,[34] should sell many more copies of their books in Germany than they do on their home ground. It is almost unimaginable that a German academic historian would write a well researched book on, say, children's lives under the Nazis, as the Oxford historian Nicholas Stargardt has done (he also tells us how children witnessed the bombing war).[35] In that sense, Friedrich, a private scholar and writer, is the exception because he appeals to the general reader, a species often neglected by German academic historians who do not depend on royalties for their living. It will be interesting to see whether, now that Friedrich's book has been translated into English, it gets appreciated for its literary merits by its British readers, and whether it reignites an old controversy.

Several of Friedrich's critics have objected to his use of language. No doubt, in his effort to convey the unimaginable extent of suffering, he resorts to a provocative terminology. Although it is perfectly legitimate to mention the German response to the *Holocaust* film, comparing the bombing war with genocide as such is a transgression gone too far.[36] Attention has been drawn to certain terms that have hitherto been associated with the deliberate destruction of the Jewish people, such as *Vernichtungskrieg* (for the war on civilians), *Einsatzgruppe* (for Bomber Group 5) or *Krematorien* (for burning cellars).[37] Even the title *Der Brand (The Fire)*, I feel, alludes to the Holocaust, even though the author has to my knowledge refrained from explicitly making this comparison. Both the deliberate destruction of the German urban landscape and that of the Jewish people were unique historical events. But here the comparison stops because area bombing was after all perceived to be the only effective strategy at the time in a legitimate war against a tyrannical regime, in fact a kind of substitute for the second front demanded by Stalin.[38] Friedrich would have been well advised to explain that the Germans saw their fate as a kind of holocaust, in retrospect perhaps even in the sense of atonement. There is, after all, evidence to show that people believed that they were being punished for their government's treatment of the Jews. In a strange way, Goebbels' propaganda of an all-powerful Jewish conspiracy now rebounded on him and the Nazi regime. Nicholas Stargardt found that ten percent of letters addressed to Goebbels in 1943 took exception to the anti-Semitic campaign and some pointed out that the Germans now had to suffer for what they had done to the Jews. In September 1943, the *Stutt-*

garter NS-Kurier felt it necessary to rebut the argument that world Jewry would not have fought Germany had the latter not solved the Jewish question in such a radical manner.[39]

On the whole, the younger generation of German historians who have no idea of the postwar state of German cities tends to be more critical of Friedrich's tale of terror than their older colleagues who reviewed the book for the quality papers rather than for academic journals. They are appalled by the emotional, and in their view sensational, tone of the narrative, hitting the reader like an action movie, and by its focus on the fate of the victims.[40] However, their criticism is not always misguided. According to Dietmar Süß, Friedrich underrates both the strategic dimension of the bombing war and the impact it had on public morale at the time.[41] Horst Boog, one of the few leading experts on the subject, regrets that Friedrich gives the impression that area bombing had been a deliberate policy right from the beginning rather than a strategic necessity. He would have been happier with a subtitle such as "a drama" or "a tragedy:" "Then one could say: splendid!"[42] No doubt, the author takes sides in his story: it is history from below. But how could he otherwise reach the reader who is expected to identify with the *Angst*-ridden tenants in their cellars, and who would not know or want to know what could possibly justify their ordeal? For young German scholars, recognition by their peers is more important for their career than selling books and satisfying their publisher. Since they are more aware of what has been published in their field of research than the average reader, some experts dispute the assumption of most reviewers that, due to its repercussions, *Der Brand* broke a taboo.

There are two questions that seem to have informed almost all of the reviews. Should the Germans now be permitted to perceive themselves as victims as well? Did Friedrich break a taboo in the sense that hitherto scholarship had refrained from tackling this painful chapter of German history? These questions constitute the core of the debate and should now be addressed.

Has the psychological trauma of the wholesale destruction of German cities been repressed in postwar Germany, as Sebald and Friedrich would have it, or is this just another myth, as Volker Ulrich and some younger historians would argue?[43] In the context of Germany's debating society with its penchant for quasi-theological controversies (*Streitkultur*), a clear-cut answer is required. However, the reality is more complex than that, particularly inasmuch as we do not yet have a comprehensive history of the culture of memory of the bombing war. To be sure, there has been a continuous tradition of public memorials on the local level, ruins as monuments (like the *Gedächniskirche* in Berlin), exhibitions or commemorations in newspapers on the occasion of anniversaries. The catalogue of the Munich Institute of Contemporary History (*Institut für Zeitgeschichte*) comes up with more than 250 titles on the bombing war. On close inspection, most of these books turn out to deal with raids on specific cities and have not been published before the mid 1970s. Only a handful of books published since the late 1980s and based on comprehensive research have covered the air war as a whole. The first sentence of Friedrich's short editorial note at the end of his book reads: "A lot has been written about the air war, but for a long time that included nothing about the suffering on the ground."[44] And he goes on to give due credit to the research of the experts on this subject, notably Horst Boog and Olaf Groehler, an East-German historian. He also feels greatly indebted to Hartwig Beseler and Niels Gutschow, who have documented, though only for West Germany, what the war had done to Germany's architectural heritage.[45] These pictures convey the impression that no vandalism in the past, stretching back to antiquity, could have been more devastating. In previous books on the bombing war, the fate of the victims and that of unique monuments was only one aspect of a broad panorama, or was left out altogether. One local TV station produced a documentary on the bombing war that was subsequently published as a book.[46] It did not cause the same furor as Friedrich's narrative. Generally speaking, recollections of what really had happened have been consigned to family history or were meant to satisfy individual curiosity. Ruins such as those of the *Gedächniskirche* in Berlin or the *Frauenkirche* in Dresden were silent memorials left as a warning to future generations.

Thus, until the publication of Friedrich's book, there had been no public awareness of the sheer horror and magnitude of the destruction and its impact on the German collective psyche such as has existed in Britain. Sebald, who had spent most of his working life in Britain, was of course struck by the discrepancy of perception in both countries. If today remembrance of World War II is an integral part of British national consciousness, then perhaps the Blitz provides the most potent ingredient.[47] Every child in Britain has been fed on the "People's War," on what the people of London and other cities had to endure during the autumn of 1940 and the summer of 1944 (the flying bombs V1 and V2).[48] However, compared to Britain, the damage to housing in Germany has been immeasurably worse and the number of casualties ten times higher. Sebald could confidently write about Germany at the end of the century: "if those born after the war were to rely solely on the testimony of writers, they would scarcely be able to form any idea of the extent, nature and consequences of the catastrophe inflicted on Germany by the air-raids."[49] It is true that testimonies were collected and damage was registered (though more for the record and for the purpose of compensation). However, in comparative terms—and here one might even refer to September 11 in the US—the horrific reality of the air war has indeed been banned from the national discourse in postwar Germany. Peter Schneider, a representative of the 1968 generation, admits that to depict Germans not only as perpetrators of the war, but also as its victims would have been "a moral and aesthetic impossibility."[50] The reasons for this are many and they all point to the political and psychological situation in which the Germans found themselves after the war.

When the war was over, people in the Western zones of occupation were relieved not to have been conquered by the Red Army. For ordinary Germans, there was plenty of evidence at hand to reinforce the effects of anti-Bolshevik propaganda during the final phase of the Nazi regime, in particular the reports from refugees about widespread rape and plunder in the Soviet zone of occupation.[51] Anglo-American forces also entered Germany as conquerors and were issued anti-fraternization orders. But they were equally concerned with the well-being of a starving and bombed-out population of which they were now in charge.[52] The sight of German concentration camps was a shocking experience, but so was, if not in equal measure, witnessing the extent of destruction caused by indiscriminate bombing raids. After the war, Allied observers felt that Germany had been "overbombed."[53] Up to 50 percent of the fabric of most of the larger cities had been destroyed, while industrial capacity had not been damaged to anything like the same extent. Some of the 130 towns and cities affected by Allied carpet-bombing were virtually obliterated. Architectural gems such as Dresden and Würzburg were attacked as late as February and March 1945, only a few months before the end of the war, which had not been brought forward by these acts of vandalism. Strategically unimportant towns of character such as Donauwörth, Bayreuth, and Freudenstadt (in the Black Forest) were attacked as late as April 1945. Berlin had been particularly hard hit, both by the incessant bombing raids and the final assault on the city. Harry Hopkins, special advisor to President Roosevelt, was reminded of Carthage, and Averell Harriman remembered "a wasteland of crumbled brick and stone, whole blocks of apartment houses and factories having been toppled into the streets as if a sulky child had smashed a sandcastle in blind rage."[54] Up to 600,000 people had perished in the inferno of the burning cities, among them nearly 100,000 children. Moreover—as mentioned before—more than three times as many had died during the great exodus from the Eastern territories of the Reich in what Western terminology euphemistically labeled "population transfer."[55]

As a result of these ordeals, ordinary Germans saw themselves first and foremost as victims of the war. Allied observers noted a widespread feeling of what from their point of view would best be described as self-pity.[56] This to their mind could only be countered by a growing awareness of the overall political context, a war that had been unleashed by a popular Nazi government prepared to plunge the rest of Europe into immeasurable misery. It was the task of public opinion, mainly radio and press under Allied supervision, to set the record straight. The devastating effects of the bombing war were there for all to see, the real cause had to be made clear in no uncertain terms. Today, the situation is totally different and therefore in need of a new approach: the ruins of the war have vanished and the new generations are now fully briefed about the wartime record of the Nazi regime, but unaware of what their parents and grandparents had to endure and of the price they had to pay for the criminal follies of their own government. Rather than drawing a new balance sheet, it was a matter of driving home, as a permanent lesson, the maddening cost of waging war to both victors and the vanquished.

However, there were even more obvious reasons why the bombing war should be dutifully remembered and yet not granted the status of the great national catastrophe it really was. Germany became the battleground of the Cold War with the East Germans on the losing side and the West Germans on the winning side. In the perception of Germans, the Western Allies soon turned from victors into "protecting powers" (*Schutzmächte*), owing to a variety of experiences: the winding down of reparations (that had been exacted mainly by means of dismantling German industrial plants), genuine political participation, Marshall Plan aid, a new currency and an end to the black market, and, above all, the Berlin airlift.[57] The same planes that had showered German cities with explosives were now dropping food parcels, including sweets for children (*Rosinenbomber*). Against this background of growing dependency it would have been most inopportune to remind the Western powers that their war record had not been unblemished either. The order of the day was reconstruction, not recrimination.

Moreover, the Cold War produced its own dialectics as far as the politics of remembrance was concerned. No West German historian wished to play into the hands of Communist propaganda in the East, which depicted the destruction of Dresden as a barbarous act of the "Anglo-Americans" against children, women, and old men, meant to deprive the Russians of an intact German city. East Germans were invited to see themselves as the victims and look upon their "re-nazified" West German cousins as the old-new perpetrators. East German propaganda even employed some of the Nazi terminology in its denouncing of the "Anglo-American imperialists" as the modern vandals lacking respect for the architectural heritage of old Europe.[58]

The political agenda at work here can be easily summarized. No less important was the psychological fallout of the war, which is difficult to pinpoint. While Germany's unexpected collapse in 1918 and subsequent conclusion of the war brought about revolutionary turmoil, the long-awaited surrender in 1945 led to a completely different state of mind: general numbness coupled with individual eagerness to forget and to survive. The struggle for survival amidst chaos followed its own dictates, which make much more sense to the social psychologist than to the psychotherapist dealing with individual trauma: in 1945/46, coming to terms with the present and future was more helpful than working through the past. Sometimes repressing, if not denying, mind-shattering experiences is the only way to cope with life. We know from those who had survived the extermination camps that they felt shame to have been in hell and to have escaped alive: all too often, they were unwilling to unburden themselves after the war and had to wait some 30 or 40 years to be able to talk and be heard. The same psychological reflex prevailed in Germany after the war, whether it concerned soldiers as perpetrators on the Eastern front or survivors of the bombing war as victims. When young German soldiers taken prisoner after D-Day were interrogated about their views of the future, they revealed an astonishing degree of political immaturity rather than fanaticism: interest in their own private life and professional career, but no identification with the nation at large that was to be ruled by the Allies.[59] After May 1945, the much-propagated *Volksgemeinschaft* (national community) had been immobilized overnight and transformed into an atomized society of individuals craving to hold on to life.[60]

This state of mind manifested itself above all in two ways: cultural distraction and frantic reconstruction. Cultural historians often cultivate a distorted view of the past in order to educate the present: they emphasize the few Nazi films meant to indoctrinate the audience and the few serious postwar movies that were meant to stir the public conscience, and tend to forget that 95 percent of production during and after the war provided for light-hearted entertainment. Up to the early 1960s, German moviegoers flocked to folklorist *Heimatfilme* that helped them to escape into a sugar-coated world.[61] Recreating the hellish experience of bombing shelters would not have been a commercially viable proposition. Much criticism can be leveled against the bleak and functional Bauhaus architecture, which served as a blueprint for West Germany's reconstruction. But the speed with which German cities were rebuilt from scratch in order to accommodate the millions of bombed-out citizens and refugees was breathtaking, faster than the redevelopment of the GDR after 1990. This was a kind of unconscious exit strategy from the war propelled by human nature, not humanist ethics, which would have suggested more time for pausing and reflecting.⁶² Removing the ruins as fast as possible had almost a symbolic meaning, like burying the remains of an unsavory family secret. The general urge to forget was a necessary if perhaps unpleasant precondition for a new beginning. As always, the historian is not required either to judge or to sympathize, but to understand—in this case to understand the reaction of a traumatized society.

Let me sum up. It makes no sense to continue the debate as to whether the bombing war had been a taboo in postwar Germany, only to be put on the national agenda 50 years later. The first generation of adults was too traumatized to draw public attention to what everybody could see anyway. Nor was it politically opportune to do so during the Cold War. Remembering the dead in a ceremonial manner was a different matter. However, 50 years on, with the growing loss of first-hand testimonies, it seems to be fully justified to recall in vivid detail in what way previous generations had paid for the follies of their leaders. If history is to teach the living how to avoid mistakes made the last time, visual instruction should not go amiss. Today, the latter is being provided by the media, mainly television and books that appeal to the young reader.

As is well known, the destruction of Dresden on 13/14 February 1945 has gained a special place in the collective memory of the bombing war. The reasons for its elevated status are manifold: the questionable strategic importance of the city toward the end of the war; the attack being unexpected and Dresden, a city of singular architectural distinction, left undefended; the high death toll as a result of the influx of refugees from the East; the Western powers being blamed as the chief culprits for this act of "vandalism" during the Cold War. As a consequence, there is no shortage of literature on Dresden and its symbolic meaning for the bombing war as such—the most recent publication in German being the outcome of a conference organized by the Hannah Arendt Institute (Dresden) in 2005.⁶³ One of the key speakers at that conference was Frederick Taylor; he was given the chance to advertize the German publication of his book, which argues that the attack had been justified on military grounds.⁶⁴ What needs to be stressed here is the total absence of recrimination about the most devastating and controversial of the bombing raids. Few if any in the audience would have concurred with the indictment of Churchill as a "mass murderer."⁶⁵ Indeed, very few Germans today would accept a comparison of Churchill or Truman with Stalin or Hitler on the ground that they were all responsible for the death of innocent civilians. For the victims, the motives of the decision-makers may be irrelevant; for posterity, they are not.

The desire to be fair, to avoid anything which may be interpreted as revisionism, is most clearly, almost pathetically, demonstrated in the recent melodrama on Dresden, the most expensive German TV-production watched by a record number of viewers. The script had been checked by German and British historians, and British actors were being employed as commanders and pilots.[66] The terror of the Nazi regime, with its ruthless racism and summary executions, was shown as more abhorrent than the approaching planes and their deadly cargo. The message was one of peace and reconciliation symbolized by the love affair between a British pilot and a German nurse and the finale, the reopening of the *Frauenkirche*. The Dresden drama has already been sold to ten countries, including France, Italy, and Japan—but not to Britain, even though British correspondents had the benefit of an exclusive preview. While some German critics objected to the unlikely plot and the US-style trivialization of a serious event in German history,[67] British correspondents claimed that the film did not address the Holocaust (which it did, so that was a case of deliberate misinformation) and was thus confirming the "new trend" of the Germans now depicting themselves as victims of the war.[68] The lookout for any signs of revisionism is an obsession of the British media, not shared by Whitehall or the educational establishment. In this respect, as in others, it is not Germany but Britain that is out of tune with the rest of Europe. Considered as a war with a just cause that was also fought justly, World War II still constitutes an integral part of British national identity, more so than in other countries. One is reminded of what Donald C. Watt wrote at the end of his magisterial work *How War Came:* "For the British, old stereotypes die hard. The images formed *by* war and the images formed *in* war, to enable public morale to maintain itself *through* war, have a half-life of their own."[69]

What about the claim that, all of a sudden, the Germans tend to see themselves as victims of the war, tacitly insinuating that they wish to set the record straight? Here, I have evidence of a personal nature that sheds some light on how debates are sometimes manipulated for the sake of increased publicity. At the time when Daniel Goldhagen's controversial book *Hitler's Willing Executioners* hit the German market, a clever editor working for the publishing house Campus suggested bringing out the reviews in book form under the title "A People of Perpetrators?"[70] Several years later, now an employee of Rowohlt publishers, he came up with the same idea when Friedrich's book produced a similar furor in Germany and abroad. This time, he picked the title from my review in *Die Zeit*, "A People of Victims?"[71] The latter had not been my choice in the first place, nor did it make sense as a heading for my article, which dealt with the bombing war in the context of Anglo-Soviet relations.[72] In both cases, the question mark was of crucial importance in the sense that this was by no means a foregone conclusion. Subsequently, this debate developed a life of its own within the fertile field of a most sensitive memory culture, as though this were a serious, soul-searching dilemma. Common sense would suggest that the crime of aggressive warfare was to rebound on the perpetrators in retreat. It makes no sense to deny that the German population suffered, too. People at the time knew perfectly well that the misery their soldiers had brought to Europe would be visited upon them once the tables had turned. After all, this was one of the secrets of Goebbels' propaganda success.

Why should later generations feel that to mention the punishing ordeal of the bombing war would detract from Germany's overall responsibility? To take in the whole horror of the war, one must allow for an acknowledgment of the suffering on both sides. The end of the Cold War favored a climate of reassessment and national self-awareness. When German magazines such as *Der Spiegel* and authors such as Günter Grass felt it was time to mourn over German victims of the war, they were not trying to meddle with the long-established historical record. But they did not want to leave the story of a suffering people to the neo-Nazis, thus forestalling collective recrimination as a reaction to a pendulum swinging too far in the direction of one-sided condemnation. Churchill agreed with Burke when he told Morgenthau in 1944: "You cannot indict a whole nation."[73] After the war, the Allies wisely refrained from any official pronouncement of collective guilt. Instead of condemning the German nation, they tried and punished its unelected leaders.

Finally, what was the immediate impact of the bombing war on the German people and how did it affect their political culture in the long run? When it comes to social psychology, hypotheses are a safer bet than assertions that cannot be proven with certainty. It is safe and sensible to assume that the firestorm in all major cities has been perceived as a national catastrophe on a par with the Thirty Years' War, the worst calamity in German history up to World War II. The last twelve months of the war, when the Western Allies reigned supreme over German skies, were the most devastating: more than half of the civilian casualties and more than half of the buildings destroyed were lost in the flames within that period. After D-Day, the war was lost to all intents and purposes. Yet neither the *Wehrmacht* nor the Nazi regime was prepared to call for an armistice in order to stop the suffering. The Allies knew that the way the war was brought to an end would determine the future. They were therefore intent on unconditional surrender and total occupation, followed by a cooling-off period before a peace treaty could be contemplated. These were the lessons to be learnt from the mistakes made in 1918/19.

Versailles provided the terms of reference for postwar planning, not the reality of the Gestapo-state and the terror of nighttime bombing raids, which went beyond the comprehension of most policy planners. Unconditional surrender and military occupation were to drive home to every German in every corner of the country the lesson that this time the *Reich* had been defeated once and for all. It was supposed to be the crucial foundation on which to rebuild German democracy. However, at that time, the essential ingredients for a long-term "change of heart" were already in place: the relief of most Germans that they had survived the war against all odds. The stark reality of a country in ruins turned out to be a more convincing teacher than any orders or textbooks issued by military authorities.

After the war, US investigators came to the conclusion that the effects of bombing did more to discredit Nazism than military defeat. Friedrich tends to agree with this assessment.[74] I would go one step further. In the eyes of most Germans, their own experience coupled with the news of Hiroshima and Nagasaki condemned war as a legitimate means of politics. It was the impact of extensive fire and destruction that in the long run brought about the final catharsis, a total reassessment of what had gone wrong in German history since unification on the battlefield in 1871. One might even say that "morale bombing," though a disastrous failure at the time inasmuch as it was meant to break German morale and thus end the war, did make a most important contribution to the long-lasting reorientation of the German nation. With the growing awareness of the enormous crimes against humanity committed in Germany's name, the bombing war has been increasingly understood as a kind of punishment: not just or morally justified punishment, but punishment all the same. As a consequence, the idea that war does not pay, the chief goal of Allied re-education, has been internalized beyond all expectation. A nation on which war has inflicted so much damage, both physical and moral, is not likely to be persuaded that conflicts can be solved by force.

Notes

1. "German Reactions to Defeat," 10 January 1945; Public Record Office London (PRO): WP (45) 18, FO 371/46791/C150.
2. Richard J. Overy, *Goering: The "Iron Man"* (London: Routledge & Kegan Paul, 1984), 19.
3. BBC News, 8 February 2002: "Grass breaks German taboos"; also Tim Adams in *The Observer*, 10 February 2002.
4. Hans-Ulrich Wehler, *Deutsche Gesellschaftsgeschichte*, vol. 4 (München: C.H. Beck, 2003), 942–946.
5. Günter Grass, *Im Krebsgang* (München: dtv edition, 2004), 99. (English translation: *Crabwalk* (London: Faber & Faber, 2002), 103.)
6. *Frankfurter Allgemeine Zeitung*, 9 February 2002.

7. Cf. Theodor Schieder, ed., *Dokumentation der Vertreibung der Deutschen aus Ost-Mitteleuropa*, 5 vols. (München: Bundesministerium für Vertriebene, 1961).
8. Frank-Lothar Kroll, ed., *Flucht und Vertreibung in der Literatur nach 1945* (Berlin: Mann, 1997).
9. For this thorny issue during the unification process see Horst Teltschik, *329 Tage* (Berlin: Siedler, 1991), 147–210; Richard Kiessler and Frank Elbe, *Ein runder Tisch mit scharfen Ecken. Der diplomatische Weg zur deutschen Einheit* (Baden-Baden: Nomos, 1993), 113–118.
10. The first memoirs translated into English were Hans Graf von Lehndorff, *East Prussian Diary. A Journal of Faith 1945–1947* (London: Wolff, 1963). Others, like the memoirs of Marion Gräfin Dönhoff, followed; see her *Namen die keiner mehr nennt* (Düsseldorf: Diederichs, 1962).
11. One of the reasons was the need to enlist Poland's cooperation. But the Polish government still feels uneasy about the project. It has vetoed the nomination of Erika Steinbach, member of the federal parliament for the Christian Democratic Union, as a member of the governing board of the Center. Steinbach had initiated the campaign for the setting up of such a center. After being vilified by the Polish media, she resigned as the delegate of the Association of Expellees (*Bund der Vertriebenen*) on the board, in order not to imperil the entire project.
12. See Martin Broszat, "Plädoyer für eine Historisierung des Nationalsozialismus," *Merkur*, no. 5, 1985: 373–385.
13. "*2 plus 4*". *Die Verhandlungen über die äußeren Aspekte der deutschen Einheit. Eine Dokumentation* (Bonn: The German Foreign Office, 1991).
14. The GDR also paid the reparations demanded by the Soviet Union from Germany as a whole in 1945. See Alexander K. Cairncross, *The Price of Victory: British Policy on German Reparations 1941–1949* (Oxford: Blackwell, 1986).
15. Winfried Georg Sebald, *Luftkrieg und Literatur* (München: Carl Hanser, 1999). (English translation: *On the Natural History of Destruction* (London: Hamish Hamilton, 2003).)
16. Jörg Friedrich, *Der Brand. Deutschland im Bombenkrieg 1940–1945*, 10th reprint, München: Propyläen, 2002. (English translation: *The Fire: The Bombing of Germany 1940–1945*, New York: Columbia University Press, 2006.)
17. There were a few literary efforts to convey the sheer horror of the bombing war, like Gert Ledig, *Vergeltung* (Frankfurt/M.: S. Fischer, 1956) (English translation: *Payback* (London: Granta Books, 2003)); Hans Erich Nossak, *Der Untergang. Hamburg 1943* (Hamburg: Suhrkamp, 1948) (English translation: *The End: Hamburg 1943* (Chicago and London: The University of Chicago Press, 2004)); or Heinrich Böll, *Der Engel schwieg* (Köln: Kiepenheuer und Witsch, 1992) (written after the war, but not published until 1992; English translation: *The Silent Angel* (New York: St. Martin's Press, 1994)). But Sebald argues that they did not have an impact on the collective psyche of the Germans at the time.
18. Cf. Hans Mommsen, "Moralisch, strategisch, zerstörerisch," in *Ein Volk von Opfern? Die neue Debatte um den Bombenkrieg 1940–45*, ed. Lothar Kettenacker (Berlin: Rowohlt, 2003), (hereafter cited as *Ein Volk von Opfern?*), 145.
19. Heribert Seifert, "Rekonstruktion statt Richtspruch," in Kettenacker, *Ein Volk von Opfern?*
20. See Kettenacker, *Ein Volk von Opfern?* 171–187.

21. Sebald, *On the Natural History of Destruction*, 11.
22. Ibid., 10.
23. Ibid., 70.
24. Ibid.
25. Cf. Cora Stephan, "Wie man eine Stadt anzündet," and Martin Walser, "Bombenkrieg als Epos," both in *Ein Volk von Opfern?*
26. Willi Winkler, "Nun singen sie wieder," in *Ein Volk von Opfern?* 105.
27. Mentioned by Seifert, "Rekonstruktion statt Richtspruch," 154.
28. Mommsen, "Moralisch, strategisch, zerstörerisch," 148–150.
29. Friedrich, *The Fire*, 232–236.
30. Susanne Brandt, "'Wenig Anschauung'? Die Ausstrahlung des Films 'Holocaust' im westdeutschen Fernsehen (1978/79)," in *Erinnerungskulturen. Deutschland, Italien und Japan seit 1945*, eds. Christoph Cornleißen, Lutz Klinkhammer, and Wolfgang Schwendtker (Frankfurt/M.: Fischer Taschenbuch, 2003), 257–268.
31. Cf. Thomas Mann, *Betrachtungen eines Unpolitischen* (Berlin: S. Fischer, 1918).
32. Antony Beevor, *Stalingrad* (London: Viking, 1998), as well as *Berlin: The Downfall 1945* (London: Viking, 2002). Both have been translated into German and have had very good sales.
33. Richard Evans, *The Coming of the Third Reich* (London: Allen Lane, 2003); *The Third Reich in Power* (London: Allen Lane, 2005); both have been translated into German.
34. Ian Kershaw, *Hitler*, 2 vols. (London: Allen Lane, 1998–2000); translated into German and reviewed all over the country.
35. Nicholas Stargardt, *Witnesses of War: Children's Lives under the Nazis* (London: Jonathan Cape, 2005), 231–260.
36. For an argument that the bombing of German cities and towns *was* genocidal, see chapter 7 in this book [editor].
37. In particular Hans-Ulrich Wehler, "Wer Wind sät, wird Sturm ernten," and Ralph Giordano, "Ein Volk von Opfern?," both in *Ein Volk von Opfern?*
38. Cf. Lothar Kettenacker, "Churchills Dilemma," in *Ein Volk von Opfern?*
39. Stargardt, *Witnesses of War*, 254. On the relation between the bombing war and the "Jewish question" see also Peter Longerich, *"Davon haben wir nichts gewusst". Die Deutschen und die Judenverfolgung 1933–1945* (München: Siedler, 2006), 304–311.
40. Typical for the young and "academically correct" German scholars: Angelika Ebbinghaus, "Deutschland im Bombenkrieg. Ein missglücktes Buch über ein wichtiges Thema," *Sozialgeschichte*, New Series 18 (2003), no. 2: 101–122.
41. Dietmar Süss, "'Massaker und Mongolensturm'. Anmerkungen zu Jörg Friedrichs umstrittenem Buch 'Der Brand. Deutschland im Bombenkrieg 1940–1945'," *Historisches Jahrbuch* 124 (2004): 521–543. This is by far the most comprehensive examination of Friedrich's book.
42. Horst Boog, "Ein Kolossalgemälde des Schreckens," in *Ein Volk von Opfern?* 136. Boog is one of two experts singled out by Friedrich for special credit (*The Fire*, Editorial Remarks, 481). Boog's contributions on the strategic bombing war are part of Germany's official history of World War II, vols. 6 and 7, ed. by Militärgeschichtliches Forschungsamt, *Das Deutsche Reich und der Zweite Weltkrieg* (Stuttgart: Deutsche Verlagsanstalt, 1990–2001). The other author is the East

German historian Olaf Groehler, *Bombenkrieg gegen Deutschland* (Berlin: Akadamieverlag, 1990).
43. Volker Ulrich, "Ach, wie wir gelitten haben," *Die Zeit*, 18 December 2002; see also Malte Thießen, "Gedenken an 'Operation Gomorrha'. Zur Erinnerungskultur des Bombenkrieges von 1945 bis heute," *Zeitschrift für Geschichichtswisssenschaft* 53 (2005): 46–61.
44. Friedrich, *The Fire*, 481.
45. Hartwig Beseler and Niels Gutschow, *Kriegsschicksale deutscher Architektur* (Neumünster: Wachholtz, 1988).
46. Jochen von Lang, *Krieg der Bomber. Dokumentation einer deutschen Katastrophe* (Berlin: Ullstein, 1986).
47. Cf. Lothar Kettenacker, "Der Zweite Weltkrieg als Bestandteil des britischen Nationalbewusstseins," in *Sieger und Besiegte. Materielle und ideelle Neuorientierungen nach 1945*, eds. Holger Afflerbach and Christoph Cornelißen (Tübingen: Francke Verlag, 1997), 75–86.
48. See Angus Calder, *The People's War 1939–1945* (London: Jonathan Cape, 1969), and *The Myth of the Blitz* (London: Jonathan Cape, 1991).
49. Sebald, *On the Natural History of Destruction*, 69.
50. Peter Schneider, "Deutsche als Opfer? Über ein Tabu der Nachkriegsgeneration," in *Ein Volk von Opfern?* 159.
51. There is more on that in Antony Beevor's description of the conquest of Berlin by the Red Army (see note 32) than in any German book on that subject.
52. Cf. Victor Gollancz, *In Darkest Germany: The Record of a Visit* (London: Gollancz, 1947). See also the biography of the British Military Governor: David G. Williamson, *A Most Diplomatic Soldier: The Life of General Lord Robertson, 1896–1974* (London: Brassey's, 1996).
53. Stephan, "Wie man eine Stadt anzündeet," in *Ein Volk von Opfern?* 99.
54. W. Averell Harriman and Elie Abel, *Special Envoy to Churchill and Stalin, 1941–1946* (London: Hutchinson, 1976), 484.
55. Cf. Alfred M. de Zayas, *Nemesis at Potsdam: The Anglo-Americans and the Expulsion of the Germans* (London: Routledge & Kegan Paul, 1977).
56. In a report of 23 August 1945, the Political Intelligence Department of the Foreign Office referred to "a feeling of self-pity characteristic of many Germans when in distress" (FO 1049/267).
57. See the summary portrayal of postwar German society in Wehler, *Deutsche Gesellschaftsgeschichte*, vol. 4: 941–972.
58. See Thomas Widera, "Gefangene Erinnerung. Die politische Instrumentalisierung der Bombardierung Dresdens," in *Alliierter Bombenkrieg. Das Beispiel Dresden*, eds. Lothar Fritze and Thomas Widera (Göttingen: V&R Unipress, 2005).
59. The Mind of the German Army, 21 September 1944, FO 371/4066/U7549.
60. Cf. Peter Hüttenberger's excellent article, "Deutschland unter britischer Besatzungsherrschaft. Gesellschaftliche Prozesse," in *Britische Besatzung in Deutschland*, eds. Adolf M. Birke and Eva M. Mayring (London: The German Historical Instituite, 1992), 61–80.
61. Cf. Friedrich P. Kahlenberg, "Film," in *Geschichte der Bundesrepublik Deutschland*, ed. Wolfgang Benz, vol. 4 (Frankfurt /M.: Fischer Taschenbuch, 1989), 464–512.

62. See Alexander and Margarete Mitscherlich, *Die Unfähigkeit zu trauern. Grundlagen kollektiven Verhaltens* (München: R. Piper, 1968).
63. Fritze and Widera, *Alliierter Bombenkrieg. Das Beispiel Dresden*.
64. Frederick Taylor, *Dresden: Tuesday, February 13, 1945* (London: Harper Collins, 2004). German edition: *Dresden, Dienstag, 13. Februar 1945. Militärische Logik oder blanker Terror?* (München: C. Bertelsmann, 2004).
65. See Douglas P. Lackey, "Four types of mass murderer: Stalin, Hitler, Churchill, Truman," chapter 6 in this volume.
66. "Krieg und Frieden. Der ZDF-Zweiteiler 'Dresden'," *Süddeutsche Zeitung*, 4/5 March 2006.
67. See for instance Oliver Storz, "Ärzte, Flammen, Sensationen. Nachbetrachtungen zu 'Dresden'—oder: Die Modeerscheinung des Event-Fernsehens," *Süddeutsche Zeitung*, 7 March 2006.
68. Cf. Roger Boyes, *The Times*, 6 March 2006. A day later, Boyes took exception to the display of swastikas for a film setting in Berlin, which seems to prove what Donald C. Watt says: that British correspondents in Germany are briefed to look out for anything connected with the Nazi past (see note 69). For a summary of British press reactions to the Dresden TV film see *Frankfurter Allgemeine Zeitung*, 8 March 2006. Apparently the British ambassador, Sir Peter Torry, was deeply impressed by the film.
69. Donald C. Watt, *How War Came* (London: Heinemann, 1989), 623.
70. Julius H. Schoeps, ed., *Ein Volk von Mördern? Die Dokumentation zur Goldhagen-Kontroverse und die Rolle der Deutschen im Holocaust* (Hamburg: Hoffmann und Campe, 1996).
71. See note 18.
72. See note 38.
73. Lord Moran, *Churchill: The Struggle for Survival 1940–65* (London: Constable, 1966), 177 (13 September 1944).
74. Friedrich, *The Fire*, 353. He refers to *United States Strategic Bombing Survey*, vol. 4 (New York, 1976), 1.

Notes on Contributors

Earl R. Beck (1916–2002) was Professor of History at Florida State University at Tallahassee. He wrote *Death of the Prussian Republic*, *Verdict on Schacht: A Study in the Problem of Political "Guilt,"* and *Under the Bombs: The German Home Front, 1942–1945*.

Mark Connelly is Professor of Modern British History at the University of Kent at Canterbury. He is the author of *Reaching for the Stars: A New History of Bomber Command in World War II*, *We Can Take It! Britain and the Memory of the Second World War*, and *The Great War: Memory and Ritual*.

Stephen A. Garrett (1939–2011) was Professor at the Graduate School of International Policy Studies, Monterey Institute of International Studies (USA). He wrote *Ethics and Airpower in World War II: The British Bombing of German Cities*, *Conscience and Power: An Examination of Dirty Hands and Political Leadership*, and *Doing Good and Doing Well: An Examination of Humanitarian Intervention*.

Lothar Kettenacker has been Deputy Director of the German Historical Institute, London, and Adjunct Professor of Contemporary History, Johann Wolfgang Goethe University, Frankfurt/M. He is the author of *Germany since 1945*, *Krieg zur Friedenssicherung. Die Deutschlandplanung der britischen Regierung während des Zweiten Weltkrieges*, *Nationalsozialistische Volkstumspolitik in dem Elsaß*, and *The German Revolution and Its Aftermath*, and editor of *Ein Volk von Opfern? Die neue Debatte um den Bombenkrieg 1940–45*.

David Kopf is Professor Emeritus of History at the University of Minnesota. He is the author of *British Orientalism and the Bengal Renaissance*, *The Brahmo Samaj and the Shaping of the Modern Indian Mind*, and *The Holocaust and Strategic Bombing: Genocide and Total War in the Twentieth Century* (with Eric Markusen).

Douglas P. Lackey is Professor of Philosophy at Baruch College and the Graduate Center, City University of New York. He is the author of *God,

Immortality, Ethics: A Concise Introduction to Philosophy, Ethics and Strategic Defense: American Philosophers Debate Star Wars and the Future of Nuclear Deterrence, Moral Principles and the Nuclear Weapons, and *The Ethics of War and Peace.*

Eric Markusen (1946–2007) was Professor of Sociology at Southwestern Minnesota State University, Marshall, and Director of the Danish Center for Holocaust and Genocide Studies, Copenhagen. He wrote *The Genocidal Mentality: Nazi Holocaust and the Nuclear Threat* (with Robert Jay Lifton), and *The Holocaust and Strategic Bombing: Genocide and Total War in the Twentieth Century* (with David Kopf), and edited *Collective Violence: Harmful Behavior in Groups and Governments* (with Craig Summers), *Nuclear Weapons and the Threat of Nuclear War* (with John Harris), and *Genocide in Darfour: Investigating the Atrocities in Sudan* (with Samuel Totten).

Martin Middlebrook is a military historian, focusing on twentieth-century warfare. He is the author of numerous books, including *The First Day on the Somme: 1 July 1916, The Kaiser's Battle: 21 March 1918, The Battle of Hamburg: Allied Bomber Forces against a German City in 1943, The Berlin Raids: RAF Bomber Command, Winter 1943–44, The Nuremberg Raid: 30–31 March 1944, Bomber Command War Diaries: An Operational Reference Book, 1939–1945* (with Chris Everitt), *The Falklands War,* etc.

Igor Primoratz is Emeritus Professor of Philosophy at the Hebrew University, Jerusalem, and Adjunct Professor at the Centre for Applied Philosophy and Public Ethics, Charles Sturt University, Canberra. His publications include *Banquos Geist: Hegels Theorie der Strafe, Justifying Legal Punishment, Ethics and Sex,* and *Terrorism: A Philosophical Investigation,* as well as a number of edited books, including *Terrorism: The Philosophical Issues, Politics and Morality, Civilian Immunity in War,* and *Military Ethics* (with C.A.J. Coady).

Bibliography

"2 plus 4". *Die Verhandlungen über die äußeren Aspekte der deutschen Einheit. Eine Dokumentation.* Bonn: The German Foreign Office, 1991.
Aldgate, Anthony, and Jeffrey Richards. *Britain Can Take It! The British Cinema in the Second World War.* Oxford: Basil Blackwell, 1986.
Allen, H.R. *The Legacy of Lord Trenchard.* London: Cassell, 1972.
Alperowitz, Gar. *Atomic Diplomacy, Hiroshima and Potsdam.* New York: Simon and Schuster, 1965.
Anderson, Barbara, and Brian Silver. "Demographic Analysis and Population Catastrophes in the USSR." *Slavic Review,* vol. 44 (1985).
Andreas-Friedrich, Ruth. *Der Schattenmann. Tagebuchzeichnungen, 1939–1945.* Berlin: Suhrkamp, 1947.
Armstrong, K.G. "The Retributivist Hits Back." *Mind,* vol. 70 (1961).
Balfour, Michael. *Propaganda in War, 1939–1945.* London: Routledge & Kegan Paul, 1979.
Barnouw, Dagmar. *The War in the Empty Air: Victims, Perpetrators, and Postwar Germans.* Bloomington: Indiana University Press, 2005.
Beck, Earl R. *Under the Bombs: The German Home Front, 1942–45.* Lexington: The University Press of Kentucky, 1986.
Becker, Jasper. *Hungry Ghosts: Mao's Secret Famine.* New York: Free Press, 1966.
Bedau, Hugo Adam. "Genocide in Vietnam?" In *Philosophy, Morality, and International Affairs,* edited by Virginia Held, Sidney Morgenbesser, and Thomas Nagel. New York: Oxford University Press, 1974.
Bedford, Duke of. *Wholesale Bombing.* Glasgow: Strickland Press, 1944.
Beevor, Antony. *Berlin: The Downfall 1945.* London: Viking, 2002.
———. *Stalingrad.* London: Viking, 1998.
Bell, George. *The Church and Humanity.* London: Longmans, 1946.
Benn, Gottfried. *Briefe an F.E. Oelze, 1932–1945.* Frankfurt/M.: Fischer Taschenbuch, 1975.
Bernstein, Barton Jay, ed. *The Truman Administration.* New York: Harper and Row, 1966.
Beseler, Hartwig, and Niels Gutschow. *Kriegsschicksale deutscher Architektur.* Neumünster: Wachholtz, 1988.
Best, Geoffrey. *Humanity in Warfare.* New York: Columbia University Press, 1980.
Bialer, Uri. *The Shadow of the Bomber: The Fear of Air Bombardment and British Politics, 1932–1939.* London: Royal Historical Society, 1980.
Bielenberg, Christabel. *The Past Is Myself.* London: Chatto & Windus, 1970.

Blackett, P.M.S. *Military and Political Consequences of Atomic Energy.* London: Turnstile Press, 1948.
Boberach, Heinz, ed. *Meldungen aus dem Reich. Auswahl aus den geheimen Lageberichten des Sicherheitsdienstes der SS 1939–1944.* Neuwied and Berlin: Luchterhand, 1965.
Böll, Heinrich. *Der Engel schwieg.* Köln: Kiepenheuer und Witsch, 1992. Translated by Breon Mitchell as *The Silent Angel.* New York: St. Martin's Press, 1994.
Bond, Brian. *Liddell Hart: A Study of His Military Thought.* London: Gregg Revivals and King's College London, 1991.
Boog, Horst. "Ein Kolossalgemälde des Schreckens." In *Ein Volk von Opfern? Die neue Debatte um den Bombenkrieg 1940–45,* edited by Lothar Kettenacker. Berlin: Rowohlt, 2003.
———. "Der Strategische Bombenkrieg der Alliierten gegen Deutschland 1939–1945. Ein Überblick." In *Alliierter Bombenkrieg. Das Beispiel Dresden,* edited by Lothar Fritze and Thomas Widera. Göttingen: V&R Unipress, 2005.
Boyer, Paul. "The Cloud Over the Culture: How Americans Imagined the Bomb They Dropped." *The New Republic,* 12 August 1985.
Brandt, R.B. "Utilitarianism and the Rules of War." *Philosophy and Public Affairs,* vol. 1 (1971/72).
Brandt, Susanne. "'Wenig Anschauung?' Die Ausstrahlung des Films 'Holocaust' im westdeutschen Fernsehen (1978/79)." In *Erinnerungskulturen. Deutschland, Italien und Japan seit 1945,* edited by Christoph Cornließen, Lutz Klinkhammer, and Wolfgang Schwendtker. Frankfurt/M.: Fischer Taschenbuch, 2003.
Brittain, Vera. *Humiliation with Honour.* London: Andrew Dakers Ltd., 1942.
———. "Massacre by Bombing: The Facts behind the British-American Attack on Germany." *Fellowship,* March 1944.
———. *Seeds of Chaos: What Mass Bombing Really Means.* London: Committee for the Abolition of Night Bombing, 1944.
Broszat, Martin. "Plädoyer für eine Historisierung des Nationalsozialismus." *Merkur,* no. 5, 1985.
Broszat, Martin, Elke Fröhlich, and Anton Grossmann, eds. *Bayern in der NS-Zeit.* Volume 1. München: R. Oldenbourg, 1981.
Brown, Kenneth L. "'Supreme Emergency': A Critique of Michael Walzer's Moral Justification for Allied Obliteration Bombing in World War II." *Manchester College Bulletin of the Peace Studies Institute,* vol. 13 (1983).
Brunswig, Hans. *Feuersturm über Hamburg.* Stuttgart: Motorbuch Verlag, 1979.
Bullock, Alan. *Hitler: A Study in Tyranny.* New York: Harper & Row, 1952.
Caidin, Martin. *The Night Hamburg Died.* New York: Ballantine Books, 1960.
Cairncross, Alexander K. *The Price of Victory: British Policy on German Reparations 1941–1949.* Oxford: Blackwell, 1986.
Calder, Angus. *The Myth of the Blitz.* London: Jonathan Cape, 1991.
———. *The People's War 1939–1945.* London: Jonathan Cape, 1969.
Calvocoressi, Peter and Guy Wint. *Total War.* New York: Pantheon Books, 1972.
Chalk, Frank, and Kurt Jonassohn. *The History and Sociology of Genocide: Analyses and Case Studies.* New Haven: Yale University Press, 1990.
Charny, Israel W. "Genocide and Mass Destruction: Doing Harm to Others as a Missing Dimension in Psychopathology." *Psychiatry,* vol. 49 (1986).

Churchill, Winston S. *Complete Speeches.* Edited by Robert Rhodes James. Volume 3. London: Chelsea House Publishers, 1974.
———. *The Second World War.* 6 volumes. London: Cassell & Co., 1949–1954.
———. *The War Speeches.* Compiled by Charles Eade. Volume 2. London: Cassel & Co., 1952.
Clark, Alan. *Barbarossa: The Russian-German Conflict, 1941–1945.* New York: Morrow, 1965.
Clark, Ronald. *The Rise of the Boffins.* London: Phoenix House, 1962.
Clarke, I.F.C. *Voices Prophesying War 1763–1984.* Oxford: Oxford University Press, 1992.
Coady, C.A.J. *Morality and Political Violence.* Cambridge: Cambridge University Press, 2008.
Coffey, Thomas M. *Decision over Schweinfurt.* New York: David McKay, 1977.
Colville, John. *The Fringes of Power.* New York: W.W. Norton & Co., 1985.
Connelly, Mark. *Reaching for the Stars: A New History of RAF Bomber Command in World War II.* London: I.B. Tauris, 2000.
Conquest, Robert. *The Harvest of Sorrow.* New York: Oxford University Press, 1986.
Crane, Conrad C. *Bombs, Cities, and Civilians: American Airpower Strategy in World War II.* Lawrence, KS: University Press of Kansas, 1993.
Craven, Wesley Frank, and James Lea Cate. *The Army Air Forces in World War II.* 3 volumes. Chicago: University of Chicago Press, 1949–1950.
Cross, Robin. *The Bombers.* New York: Macmillan Publishing Company, 1987.
Dalrymple, Dana. "The Soviet Famine of 1932–34." *Soviet Studies,* vol. 15 (1964).
Davies, R.W. *The Socialist Offensive: The Collectivization of Soviet Agriculture 1929–1930.* Cambridge, MA: Harvard University Press, 1980.
Dawidowicz, Lucy S. *The Holocaust and the Historians.* Cambridge, MA: Harvard University Press, 1981.
———. *The War Against the Jews 1933–1945.* New York: Holt, Rinehart & Winston, 1975.
de Wijze, Stephen. "Dirty Hands: Doing Wrong to Do Right." In *Politics and Morality,* edited by Igor Primoratz. Basingstoke and New York: Palgrave Macmillan, 2007.
de Zayas, Alfred M. *Nemesis at Potsdam: Anglo-Americans and the Expulsion of the Germans.* London: Routledge & Kegal Paul, 1977.
Deak, Istvan. "Misjudgment at Nuremberg." *The New York Review of Books,* 7 October 1993.
Dicks, Henry V. *Licensed Mass Murder: A Socio-Psychological Study of Some SS Killers.* London: Heinemann, 1972.
Domarus, Wolfgang, ed. *Hitler. Reden und Proklamationen, 1932–1945.* München: Süddeutscher Verlag, 1965.
Dombrowski, Daniel A. "What Does 'War Is Hell' Mean?" *The International Journal of Applied Philosophy,* vol. 1 (1983).
Dönhoff, Marion Gräfin. *Namen die keiner mehr nennt.* Düsseldorf: Diederichs, 1962.
Douhet, Giulio. *The Command of the Air.* Translated by Dino Ferrari. New York: Coward-McCann, 1942.
Ebbinghaus, Angelika. "Deutschland im Bombenkrieg. Ein missglücktes Buch über ein wichtiges Thema." *Sozialgeschichte,* New Series 18 (2003).

Edoin, Hoito. *The Night Tokyo Burned*. New York: St. Martin's Press, 1987.
Ellison, Herbert. "The Decision to Collectivize Agriculture." In *Russian Economic Development from Peter the Great to Stalin*, edited by William Blackwell. New York: New Viewpoints, 1974.
Ellsberg, Daniel. "The Responsibility of Officials in a Criminal War." In *Papers on the War*. New York: Simon & Schuster, 1972.
Enzensberger, Hans Magnus. *Civil War*. Translated by Piers Spence and Martin Chalmers. London: Granta Books, 1994.
Evans, Richard. *The Coming of the Third Reich*. London: Allen Lane, 2003.
———. *The Third Reich in Power*. London: Allen Lane, 2005.
Farrar, Marjorie. "World War II as Total War." In *War: A Historical, Political, and Social Study*, edited by L.L. Farrar. Santa Barbara, CA: ABC-Clio, 1978.
Fein, Helen. "Discriminating Genocide from War Crimes: Vietnam and Afghanistan Reexamined." Paper prepared for the First Raphael Lemkin Symposium on Genocide, Yale University Law School, February 1991.
———. "Genocide, Terror, Life Integrity, and War Crimes: The Case for Discrimination." In *Genocide: Conceptual and Historical Dimensions*, edited by George I. Andreopolous. Philadelphia: University of Pennsylvania Press, 1994.
Feis, H. *The Atomic Bomb and the End of World War II*. Princeton: Princeton University Press, 1966.
Fest, Joachim. *Hitler: A Biography*. New York: Harcourt Brace Jovanovich, 1974.
Finnis, John. *Moral Absolutes: Tradition, Revision, and Truth*. Washington, DC: The Catholic University of America Press, 1991.
Fischer, Josef. *Köln '39–'45. Der Leidensweg einer Stadt*. Köln: J.P. Bachem, 1970.
Ford, John C., S.J. "The Morality of Obliteration Bombing." *Theological Studies*, vol. 5 (1944).
Frankland, Noble. *The Bombing Offensive against Germany*. London: Faber & Faber, 1965.
Friedrich, Jörg. *Der Brand. Deutschland im Bombenkrieg 1940–1945*. 10th reprint. München: Propyläen Verlag, 2002. Translated by Allison Brown as *The Fire: The Bombing of Germany 1940–1945*. New York: Columbia University Press, 2006.
Fritze, Lothar. *Die Moral des Bombenterrors. Alliierte Flächenbombardements im Zweiten Weltkrieg*. München: Olzog Verlag, 2007.
Garrett, Stephen A. *Ethics and Airpower in World War II: The British Bombing of German Cities*. New York: St. Martin's Press, 1993.
Gilbert, Martin. *Churchill: A Life*. New York: Henry Holt & Co., 1991.
Giordano, Ralf. "Ein Volk von Opfern?" In *Ein Volk von Opfern? Die neue Debatte um den Bombenkrieg 1940–45*, edited by Lothar Kettenacker. Berlin: Rowohlt, 2003.
Gollancz, Victor. *In Darkest Germany: The Record of a Visit*. London: Gollancz, 1947.
Grass, Günter. *Crabwalk*. Translated by Krishna Winston. London: Faber & Faber, 2002.
———. *Im Krebsgang*. München: dtv edition, 2004.
Grayling, A.C. *Among the Dead Cities: Was the Allied Bombing of Civilians in WWII a Necessity or a Crime?* London: Bloomsbury, 2006.
Groehler, Olaf. *Bombenkrieg gegen Deutschland*. Berlin: Akademie-Verlag, 1990.
Hamann, Brigitte. *Hitler's Vienna: A Dictator's Apprenticeship*. New York: Oxford University Press, 1999.

Hampe, Erich, ed. *Der zivile Luftschutz im Zweiten Weltkrieg*. Frankfurt/M.: Bernard & Graefe Verlag für Wehrwesen, 1963.
Hansell, Haywood, Jr. *The Air Plan that Defeated Hitler*. Atlanta: Higgins-McArthur/ Longino & Porter, 1972.
Harriman, W. Averell, and Elie Abel. *Special Envoy to Churchill and Stalin, 1941–1946*. London: Hutchinson, 1976.
Harris, Sir Arthur. *Bomber Offensive*. London: Collins, 1947.
Harrisson, Tom. *Living Through the Blitz*. Harmondsworth: Penguin Books, 1990.
Hastings, Max. *Bomber Command*. New York: Dial Press, 1979.
Herken, Gregg. *The Winning Weapon*. New York: Knopf, 1980.
Hewlett, Richard, and Oscar Anderson. *A History of the Atomic Energy Commission*. Volume 1: *A New World*. University Park, PA: State University of Pennsylvania Press, 1962.
Hilberg, Raul. *Perpetrators, Victims, Bystanders*. New York: Harper Perennial, 1993.
———. *The Destruction of the European Jews*. Chicago: Quadrangle Books, 1961.
Hillgruber, Andreas, and Gerhard Hümmelchen. *Chronik des Zweiten Weltkrieges*. Düsseldorf: Athenäum/Drosche, 1978.
Hitler, Adolf. *Mein Kampf*. Translated by Ralph Mannheim. Boston: Houghton Mifflin, 1943.
Hobsbawm, Eric. "Barbarism: A User's Guide." *On History*. London: Weidenfeld & Nicolson, 1997.
Hughes, Everett C. "Good People and Dirty Work." *Social Problems*, vol. 10 (1962).
Hüttenberger, Peter. "Deutschland unter britischer Besatzungsherrschaft. Gesellschaftliche Prozesse." In *Britische Besatzung in Deutschland*, edited by Adolf M. Birke and Eva M. Mayring. London: The German Historical Institute, 1992.
Irving, David. *The Destruction of Dresden*. New York: Holt, Rinehart and Winston, 1963.
———. *Hitler's War*. New York: Viking, 1977.
———. *The Rise and Fall of the Luftwaffe: The Life of Field Marshal Erhard Milch*. Boston: Little, Brown & Co., 1973.
Iwamatsu, Shigetoshi. "A Perspective on the War Crimes." *Bulletin of the Atomic Scientists*, February 1982.
James, Robert Rhodes, ed. *Winston Churchill: His Complete Speeches*. London: Chelsea House Publishers, 1974.
Kahlenberg, Friedrich P. "Film." In *Geschichte der Bundesrepublik Deutschland*, edited by Wolfgang Benz, volume 4. Frankfurt/M.: Fischer Taschenbuch, 1989.
Kaldor, Mary. *New and Old Wars: Organized Violence in a Global Era*. Cambridge: Polity Press, 1999.
Keegan, John. *The Second World War*. New York: Viking, 1989.
Kershaw, Ian. *Hitler*. 2 volumes. London: Allen Lane, 1998–2000.
Kettenacker, Lothar. "Churchills Dilemma." In *Ein Volk von Opfern? Die neue Debatte um den Bombenkrieg 1940-45*, edited by Lothar Kettenacker. Berlin: Rowohlt, 2003.
———. "Der Zweite Weltkrieg als Bestandteil des britischen Nationalbewusstseins." In *Sieger und Besiegte. Materielle und ideelle Neuorientierungen nach 1945*, edited by Holger Afflerbach and Christoph Cornelißen. Tübingen: Francke Verlag, 1997.
Khrushchev, Nikita. *Khrushchev Remembers*. Translated and edited by Strobe Talbott. Boston: Little Brown, 1970.

Kiernan, Ben. *Blood and Soil: A World History of Genocide and Extermination from Sparta to Darfour.* New Haven: Yale University Press, 2007.

Kiessler, Richard, and Frank Elbe. *Ein runder Tisch mit scharfen Ecken. Der diplomatische Weg zur deutschen Einheit.* Baden-Baden: Nomos, 1993.

Kroll, Frank-Lothar, ed. *Flucht und Vertreibung in der Literatur nach 1945.* Berlin: Mann, 1997.

Kruk, Zofia. *The Taste of Fear: A Polish Childhood in Germany, 1939–1946.* London: Hutchinson, 1973.

Kuby, Erich. *Mein Krieg.* München: Nymphenburger Verlag, 1975.

Kuper, Leo. *Genocide: Its Political Use in the Twentieth Century.* New Haven, CT: Yale University Press, 1981.

———. *The Prevention of Genocide.* New Haven, CT: Yale University Press, 1985.

———. "Theoretical Issues Relating to Genocide: Uses and Abuses." In *Genocide: Conceptual and Historical Dimensions,* edited by George L. Andreopolous. Philadelphia: University of Pennsylvania Press, 1994.

Lackey, Douglas. "The Evolution of the Modern Terrorist State: Area Bombing and Nuclear Deterrence." In *Terrorism: The Philosophical Issues,* edited by Igor Primoratz. Basingstoke and New York: Palgrave Macmillan, 2004.

Lammers, Stephen E. "Area Bombing in World War II: The Argument of Michael Walzer." *The Journal of Religious Ethics,* vol. 11 (1983).

Lange, Horst. *Tagebücher aus dem Zweiten Weltkrieg.* Mainz: Von Hase und Koehler, 1979.

Ledig, Gert. *Vergeltung.* Frankfurt/M.: S. Fischer, 1956. Translated by Michael Hofmann as *Payback.* London: Granta Books, 2003.

Lehndorff, Hans Graf von. *East Prussian Diary. A Journal of Faith 1945–1947.* London: Wolff, 1963.

Liddell Hart, B.H. *Paris or the Future of War.* London: Kegan Paul, Trench, Trubner & Co., 1925.

———. *History of the Second World War.* New York: G.P. Putnam's Sons, 1970.

Lieberman, Benjamin. *Terrible Fate: Ethnic Cleansing in the Making of Modern Europe.* Chicago: Ivan R. Dee, 2006.

Lifton, Robert Jay. *Death in Life: Survivors of Hiroshima.* New York: Random House, 1967.

Lindqvist, Sven. *A History of Bombing.* Translated by Linda Haverty Rugg. London: Granta Books, 2001.

Lipstadt, Deborah. *Denying the Holocaust: The Growing Assault on Truth and Memory.* New York: The Free Press, 1993.

Lochner, Louis L., ed. and trans. *The Goebbels Diaries, 1942–1943.* Garden City, NY: Doubleday, 1948.

Longerich, Peter. *"Davon haben wir nichts gewusst". Die Deutschen und die Judenverfolgung 1933–1945.* München: Siedler, 2006.

Longmate, Norman. *The Bombers.* London: Hutchinson, 1983.

MacDonogh, Giles. *After the Reich: The Brutal History of the Allied Occupation.* New York: Basic Books, 2007.

Mann, Thomas, *Betrachtungen eines Unpolitischen,* Berlin: S. Fischer, 1918.

Markusen, Eric, and David Kopf. *The Holocaust and Strategic Bombing: Genocide and Total War in the Twentieth Century.* Boulder: Westview Press.

McCullough, David. *Truman*. New York: Simon & Schuster, 1992.
McKee, Alexander. *Dresden 1945: The Devil's Tinderbox*. New York: E.P. Dutton, 1982.
McKeogh, Kolm. *Innocent Civilians: The Morality of Killing in War*. Basingstoke and New York: Palgrave, 2002.
McLaine, Ian. *Ministry of Morale, Home Front Morale and the Ministry of Information in World War II*. London: Allen & Unwin, 1979.
Michie, Allan A. *The Air Offensive Against Germany*. New York: Henry Holt, 1943.
Middlebrook, Martin. *The Battle of Hamburg: Allied Bomber Forces against a German City in 1943*. London: Cassell & Co., 2000.
———. *The Nuremberg Raid, 30–31 March 1944*. London: Allen Lane, 1973.
Middlebrook, Martin, and Chris Everitt. *The Bomber Command War Diaries*. London: Viking, 1985.
Miles, Rufus E. "The Strange Myth of a Million Lives Saved." *International Security*, vol. 10 (1985).
Militärgeschichtliches Forschungsamt. *Das Deutsche Reich und der Zweite Weltkrieg*. Volumes 6–7. Stuttgart: Deutsche Verlagsanstalt, 1990–2001.
Minear, Richard. *Victor's Justice: The Tokyo War Crimes Trial*. Princeton, NJ: Princeton University Press, 1971.
Mitscherlich, Alexander and Margarete. *Die Unfähigkeit zu trauern. Grundlagen kollektiven Verhaltens*. München: R. Piper, 1968.
Mommsen, Hans. "Moralisch, strategisch, zerstörerisch." In *Ein Volk von Opfern? Die neue Debatte um den Bombenkrieg 1940–45*, edited by Lothar Kettenacker. Berlin: Rowohlt, 2003.
———. "Wie die Bomben Hitler halfen." In *Als Feuer vom Himmel fiel. Der Bombenkrieg in Deutschland*, edited by Stephan Burgdorf and Christian Habbe. München: Deutsche Verlags-Anstalt, 2003.
Moran, Lord. *Churchill: The Struggle for Survival 1940–65*. London: Constable, 1966.
Mumford, Lewis. "The Morals of Extermination." *The Atlantic*, October 1959.
Musgrove, Gordon. *Operation Gomorrah: The Hamburg Firestorm Raids*. London: Jane's, 1981.
Nadler, Fritz, ed. *Eine Stadt im Schatten Streichers. Bisher unveröffentlichte Tagebuchblätter, Dokumente und Bilder vom Kriegsjahr 1943*. Nürnberg: Fränkische Verlagsanstalt, 1969.
Naimark, Norman M. *Fires of Hatred: Ethnic Cleansing in Twentieth-Century Europe*. Cambridge, MA: Harvard University Press, 2001.
Newby, Leroy W. *Target Ploesti*. Novato, CA: Presidio Press, 1983.
Nielsen, Kai. "There is No Dilemma of Dirty Hands." In *Politics and Morality*, edited by Igor Primoratz. Basingstoke and New York: Palgrave Macmillan, 2007.
Nossak, Hans Erich. *Der Untergang. Hamburg 1943*. Hamburg: Suhrkamp, 1948. Translated by Joel Agee as *The End: Hamburg 1943*. Chicago and London: The University of Chicago Press, 2004.
Orwell, Sonia, and Ian Angus, eds. *The Collected Essays, Journalism and Letters of George Orwell*. Volume 3. London: Secker & Warburg, 1968.
Overy, Richard. *Bomber Command, 1939–1945: Reaping the Whirlwind*. London: HarperCollins, 1996.
———. *Goering: The "Iron Man."* London: Routledge & Kegan Paul, 1984.

Paul, Wolfgang. *Der Heimatkrieg, 1939 bis 1945.* Esslingen am Neckar: Bechtle Verlag, 1980.
Pimlott, John. "The Theory and Practice of Strategic Bombing." In *Warfare in the Twentieth Century,* edited by Collin McInnes and G.D. Sheffield. London: Unwin Hyman, 1988.
Porter, Jack Nusan. "What Is Genocide? Notes Toward a Definition." In *Genocide and Human Rights: A Global Anthology,* edited by Jack Nusan Porter. Washington, DC: University Press of America, 1982.
Primoratz, Igor, ed. *Civilian Immunity in War.* Oxford: Oxford University Press, 2007.
———. "What Is Terrorism?" In *Terrorism: The Philosophical Issues,* edited by Igor Primoratz. Basingstoke and New York: Palgrave Macmillan, 2004.
Reck-Malleczewen, Friedrich Percyval. *Diary of a Man in Despair.* Translated by Paul Rubens. London: Macmillan, 1966.
Redlich, Fritz. *Hitler: Diagnosis of a Destructive Prophet.* New York: Oxford University Press, 1998.
Rhodes, Richard. *The Making of the Atomic Bomb.* New York: Simon & Schuster, 1986.
Richards, Denis, and Hilary St. George Saunders. *Royal Air Force, 1939–1945.* Volume 3. London: HMSO, 1954.
Richards, Jeffrey. *The Age of the Dream Palace: Cinema and Society in Britain 1930–1939.* London: Keegan Paul, 1984.
Rummel, R.J. "Power Kills; Absolute Power Kills Absolutely." *Internet on the Holocaust and Genocide,* no. 38, June 1992.
Rumpf, Hans. *The Bombing of Germany.* Translated by Edward Fitzgerald. London: Frederick Muller Ltd., 1963. US edition New York: Holt, Reinhart, Winston, 1965.
Russell, Bertrand. *Principles of Social Reconstruction.* London: Allen & Unwin, 1916.
Sabini, John P., and Maury Silver. "Destroying the Innocent with a Clear Conscience: A Sociopsychology of the Holocaust." In *Survivors, Victims, and Perpetrators,* edited by Joel E. Dimsdale. Washington, DC: Hemisphere, 1980.
Saunders, Hilary St. George. *Royal Air Force 1939–1945.* Volume 3. London: HMSO, 1954.
Schaffer, Ronald. *Wings of Judgment: American Bombing in World War II.* New York and Oxford: Oxford University Press, 1985.
Schieder, Theodor, ed. *Dokumentation der Vertreibung der Deutschen aus Ost-Mitteleuropa.* 5 volumes. München: Bundesministerium für Vertriebene, 1961.
Schmitz, Hubert. *Die Bewirtschaftung der Nahrungsmittel und Verbrauchsgüter, 1939–1950. Dargestellt an dem Beispiel der Stadt Essen.* Essen: Stadtverwaltung, 1956.
Schneider, Peter. "Deutsche als Opfer? Über ein Tabu der Nachkriegsgeneration." In *Ein Volk von Opfern? Die neue Debatte um den Bombenkrieg 1940–45,* edited by Lothar Kettenacker. Berlin: Rowohlt, 2003.
Schoeps, Julius H., ed. *Ein Volk von Mördern? Die Dokumentation zur Goldhagen-Kontroverse und die Rolle der Deutschen im Holocaust.* Hamburg: Hoffmann und Campe, 1996.
Schramm, Percy Ernst. *Neun Generationen. Dreihundert Jahre deutscher "Kulturgeschichte" im Lichte der Schicksale einer Hamburger Bürgerfamilie (1648–1948).* Göttingen: Vandenhoeck & Ruprecht, 1964.
Sebald, Winfried Georg. *Luftkrieg und Literatur.* München: Carl Hanser, 1999. Trans-

lated by Anthea Bell as *On the Natural History of Destruction*. London: Hamish Hamilton, 2003.

Seifert, Heribert. "Rekonstruktion statt Richtspruch." In *Ein Volk von Opfern? Die neue Debatte um den Bombenkrieg 1940–45*, edited by Lothar Kettenacker. Berlin: Rowohlt, 2003.

Sherman, William Tecumseh. *Memoirs*. New York: The Library of America, s.a.

Sherry, Michael. *The Rise of American Air Power: The Creation of Armageddon*. New York and London: Yale University Press, 1987.

Shirer, William L. *The Rise and Fall of the Third Reich*. London: Secker & Warburg, 1960.

Short, Ken. "RAF Bomber Command's Target for Tonight (1941)." *Historical Journal of Film, Radio and Television*, vol. 17 (1997).

Slessor, Sir John. *The Central Blue*. London: Cassell & Co., 1956.

Spaight, J.M. *Bombing Vindicated*. London: Geoffrey Bles, 1944.

Stargardt, Nicholas. *Witnesses of War: Children's Lives under the Nazis*. London: Jonathan Cape, 2005.

Stephan, Cora. "Wie man eine Stadt einzündet." In *Ein Volk von Opfern? Die neue Debatte um den Bombenkrieg 1940–45*, edited by Lothar Kettenacker. Berlin: Rowohlt, 2003.

Storz, Oliver. "Ärzte, Flammen, Sensationen. Nachbetrachtungen zu 'Dresden'—oder: Die Modeerscheinung des Event-Fernsehens." *Süddeutsche Zeitung*, 7 March 2006.

Süss, Dietmar. "'Massaker und Mongolensturm'. Anmerkungen zu Jörg Friedrichs umstrittenem Buch 'Der Brand. Deutschland im Bombenkrieg 1940–1945'." *Historisches Jahrbuch*, vol. 124 (2004).

Tal, Uriel. "On the Study of the Holocaust and Genocide." *Yad Vashem Studies*, vol. 13 (1979).

Taylor, Frederick. *Dresden: Tuesday, February 13, 1945*. London: Harper Collins, 2004. Translated in German as *Dresden, Dienstag, 13. Februar 1945. Militärische Logik oder blanker Terror?* München: C. Bertelsmann, 2004.

Taylor, Telford. *Nuremberg and Vietnam: An American Tragedy*. New York: Quadrangle Books, 1970.

Tedder, Sir Arthur. *With Prejudice*. Boston: Little Brown & Co., 1966.

Teltschik, Horst. *329 Tage*. Berlin: Siedler, 1991.

Thießen, Malte. "Gedenken an 'Operation Gomorrha'. Zur Erinnerungskultur des Bombenkrieges von 1945 bis heute." *Zeitschrift für Geschichichtswisssenschaft*, vol. 3 (2005).

Ulrich, Volker. "Ach, wie wir gelitten haben." *Die Zeit*, 18 December 2002.

United States Strategic Bombing Survey. Volume 4. New York, 1976.

Verrier, Anthony. *The Bomber Offensive*. New York: Macmillan, 1969.

von Kardoff, Ursula. *Diary of a Nightmare: Berlin 1942–1945*. Translated by Ewan Butler. London: Rupert Hart-Davis, 1965.

von Lang, Jochen. *Krieg der Bomber. Dokumentation einer deutschen Katastrophe*. Berlin: Ullstein, 1986.

Walser, Martin, "Bombenkrieg als Epos." In *Ein Volk von Opfern? Die neue Debatte um den Bombenkrieg 1940–45*, edited by Lothar Kettenacker. Berlin: Rowohlt, 2003.

Walzer, Michael. *Just and Unjust Wars: A Moral Argument with Historical Illustrations*. 3rd ed. New York: Basic Books, 2000.

---. "Political Action: The Problem of Dirty Hands." *Philosophy and Public Affairs*, vol. 2 (1972/73).

Wasserstrom, Richard A., ed. *War and Morality*. Belmont, CA: Wadsworth Publishing Co., 1970.

Watt, Donald C. *How War Came*. London: Heinemann, 1989.

Webster, Sir Charles, and Noble Frankland. *The Strategic Air Offensive Against Germany, 1939–1945*. 4 volumes. London: HMSO, 1961.

Wehler, Hans-Ulrich. *Deutsche Gesellschaftsgeschichte*. Volume 4. München: C.H. Beck, 2003.

---. "Wer Wind sät, wird Sturm ernten." In *Ein Volk von Opfern? Die neue Debatte um den Bombenkrieg 1940–45*, edited by Lothar Kettenacker. Berlin: Rowohlt, 2003.

Widera, Thomas. "Gefangene Erinnerung. Die politische Instrumentalisierung der Bombardierung Dresdens." In *Alliierter Bombenkrieg. Das Beispiel Dresden*, edited by Lothar Fritze and Thomas Widera. Göttingen: V&R Unipress, 2005.

Williamson, David G. *A Most Diplomatic Soldier: The Life of General Lord Robertson, 1896–1974*. London: Brassey's, 1996.

Winkler, Willi. "Nun singen sie wieder." In *Ein Volk von Opfern? Die neue Debatte um den Bombenkrieg 1940–45*, edited by Lothar Kettenacker. Berlin: Rowohlt, 2003.

Wolff-Mönckeberg, Mathilde. *On the Other Side: To My Children, from Germany, 1940–1945*. Tranlsated and edited by Ruth Evans. London: Peter Owen, 1979.

Index

Afghanistan, Soviet war in, 173
Africa Corps, 60
air power, 20–25, 29
 in strategic role, 21–25
 in tactical role, 20
air warfare, 126–27
Alexander II, Tsar, 3
Alster Lake, 91, 93
Amin, Idi, 12, 174
anti-nazis, 80, 145
anti-semitism, 140, 141, 142
area bombing, 21, 22, 24, 26, 27, 28, 31, 33, 34, 39–45, 49, 50–51, 57, 87, 145, 155 n.14 (*see also* strategic bombing)
Aryans. 141–42
Atlanta, 117
atomic bombing, 149, 150, 151, 152, 159, 160, 161, 164, 165, 167, 168, 169, 170, 172, 173, 199 (*see also* nuclear weapons)
Attlee, Clement, 199
Auschwitz, 161
AWPD1, 41–45, 47, 48, 54, 57, 58 n.6

Barmbek, 72, 88
Barnouw, Dagmar, 13
Bataan, 149
Battle of Berlin, 31–32
Battle of Britain, 123, 195
Battle of the Bulge, 34, 145
Bayreuth, 212
BBC, 194, 195
Beck, Earl R., 9, 223
Bedau, Hugo Adam, 173
Bedford, Duke of, 190

Belgrade, 51, 192
Bell, George, 155 n.14, 186–87, 188–89
Benn, Gottfried, 65–66, 79, 80
Bergdorf, 108
Berlin, 31, 32, 34, 39, 49, 51, 67, 68, 69, 73, 80, 108, 146, 149, 183, 184, 188, 192, 194, 195, 196, 210, 211, 213
Bielenberg, Christobel, 75
Billwarder Ausschlag, 86, 87, 88
Blitz, 27, 45, 145, 146, 147, 185, 190, 191, 195, 197, 207, 211
Blockade of Germany in World War I, 4, 130
Bolsheviks, 135, 137, 140, 141, 142, 212
Bomber Command, 2, 7–8, 9, 19, 24, 26–37, 86, 87, 109, 123, 127, 144, 146, 181–190, 194–200
Bombing Restriction Committee, 190
Bochum, 61
Boog, Horst, 210, 211
Borgfelde, 87, 92, 95, 102
Boyer, Paul, 164
Braidwood, G.L., 192
Brandt, Richard B., 125–26
Brecht, Herbert, 98–99, 103
Bremen, 185
British Bombing Survey Unit, 35
Brittain, Vera, 52, 58 n.22, 114, 189
Broszat, Martin, 204
Brunswig, Hans, 92
Bucharest, 51
Bulgaria, 51
bureaucracy, 158–59
Burmeister, Johann, 98
Butt, D.M., 28

235

Casablanca Conference, 30, 45
Catchpool, T. Corder, 189
Chalk, Frank, 161
Chamberlain, Neville, 19, 20, 26, 183
Charny, Israel W., 159, 161, 173
Chemnitz, 146
Cherwell, Lord, 28, 129, 144, 146, 149, 155 n.16
Churchill, Winston, 7, 10, 11, 26, 30, 34, 45–46, 119, 120, 122, 123, 129, 132 n.29, 134–35, 142, 144, 146–49, 153, 155 n.17, 156 n.18, 187, 194, 196, 199, 197, 200, 203, 206, 215, 217
civilian immunity, principle of, 2–7, 10, 53, 113–130
civilians, deliberate attack on, 2–14, 19, 20, 113, 118, 121, 124, 126, 129, 170, 171, 173, 188
Clausewitz, Carl von, 187
Coffey, Thomas, 47
Cold War, 4–5, 213, 215, 217
collateral damage, 5, 40, 55
collective responsibility, 119–120
collectivism, 148, 153, 203
Cologne, 29, 30, 49, 61–68, 73, 76–80, 191, 195, 197
combatant immunity, 5
Combined Bombing Offensive, 30
Committee for the Abolition of Night Bombing, 188
Committee of Operations Analysis, 47
concentration camps, 74, 160, 212, 214
Connelly, Mark, 12, 223
consequentialism, 125–26 (*see also* utilitarianism)
Corradini, Claudia, 51
Coventry, 26, 147, 167, 192
crimes against humanity, 164, 166, 167, 218

Daily Express, 185, 191, 194, 195, 196
Daily Mail, 184, 196
Daily Mirror, 184, 195, 196
Daily Sketch, 196
Daily Telegraph, 184, 186, 189, 192, 196
Darmstadt, 128

daylight bombing, 74, 85, 144, 183
D-Day, 32, 57, 214, 217
Dehler, Herr, 99
dehumanization, 127, 128, 159, 164–65
demoralization, *see* morale
dirty hands problem, 121–22
Donauworth, 212
Dortmund, 61, 62
double effect, doctrine of, 53, 176 n.38
Douhet, Giulio, 22–23, 126
Dresden, 7, 11, 19, 20, 39, 41, 45, 56, 57, 82 n.41, 117, 135, 144–49, 160, 163, 170, 196–97, 199, 211, 212, 213, 215, 216
Duisburg, 61, 73, 76
Dunkirk, 26, 123, 190
Düsseldorf, 49, 61, 62, 73, 77

Eaker, Ira, 45–46
Eckhardt, William, 158
Eichmann, Adolf, 166
Eilbek, 88, 107
Einstein, Albert, 137
Eisenhower, Dwight David, 41
El Alamein, 124
Elbe, 68, 86, 87, 91, 93, 107
Elliot, Gil, 158
Ellsberg, Daniel, 177 n.41
Emden, 51
Engels, Frederick, 3
Enoch, C.D.L., 192
Enzensberger, Hans Magnus, 115–116
Ervine, St. John, 187
Esher, Lord, 187
Essen, 61, 73, 76
ethics of war, 3
extermination camps, *see* concentration camps

Fein, Helen, 161, 168, 169, 170, 171, 172, 173, 175 n.12
Fest, Joachim, 206
Fischer, Josef, 61–65, 79, 80
flak, 85, 86, 89
Florence, 51
Ford, John, 52–53

Fortnightly Review, 186
France, 6, 24, 42, 41, 42, 44, 46, 49, 56, 123, 183, 208, 216
Frankfurt, 51
Freudenstadt, 212
Friedrich, Jörg, 2, 13, 205, 206, 207, 208, 209, 210, 211

Garbett, Cyril, 188
Garrett, Stephen A., 7, 10, 120, 176 n.38, 223
Gelsenkirchen, 73
genocide, 11, 158–77
German economy/industry, 29, 35–37, 43, 46–48, 57, 181, 182, 186, 188
Gestapo, 80, 129, 145, 186
Goebbels, Joseph, 41, 49, 62, 65, 77, 209, 217
Goldhagen, Daniel J., 216
Gordon, John, 119
Göring, Hermann, 67, 77, 203
Grass, Günter, 2, 203–04, 217
Great War, The, *see* World War I
Groehler, Olaf, 128, 211
Guernica, 182
Gutschaw, Niels, 211

Hague Conventions, 3, 45, 182
Hamburg, 9, 14, 19, 31, 32, 44, 47, 49, 50, 55–56, 61, 66–73, 76, 78, 80, 82 n.41, 83 n.51, 85–109, 145, 147, 160, 163, 191
Hamm, 86, 87, 94, 102, 105
Hammer Landstrasse, 87, 88, 103
Hammerbrook, 86, 87, 89, 90, 91, 92, 96, 98, 100, 103, 104
Hannah Arendt Institute, 215
Hansell, General, 54, 58 n.6
Harris, Arthur, 2, 4, 13, 27, 29, 30, 32, 33, 34, 37, 66, 67, 117, 119, 120, 145, 146, 166, 183, 194, 195, 198–99, 190, 191, 198–200, 206, 208
Harrison, Tom, 197
Hart, Basil H. Liddel, 126, 131 n.13, 133 n.33
Himmler, Heinrich, 142

Hiroshima, 7, 11, 135, 149–52, 160, 161, 164, 168, 218
Hitler, Adolf, 11, 12, 13, 36, 56, 61, 72, 76, 77, 88, 124, 127, 134–35, 140–44, 145, 153, 174, 184, 187, 191, 203, 205, 215
Hobbes, Thomas, 187
Hobsbawm, Eric, 3
Hoffmeister, Kate, 96–7
Holocaust, 135, 140–44, 161–67, 168, 169, 171–72, 173, 216, 208, 209
Holz, Gauleiter Karl, 73
Hopkins, Harry, 42, 212
Hopper, Bruce, 160
Horn, 87, 93
Horowitz, Irving Louis, 161
House of Commons, 27, 148, 156 n.26

Italy, 51, 66, 216
Iwamatsu, Shigetoshi, 160
Iwo Jima, 149, 150

Jameson, Storm, 187
Japan, 4, 6, 8, 42, 45, 130, 146, 149–52, 160, 164, 168
Jews, 140–44, 162, 164, 165, 209–210 (*see also* anti-semitism)
Jonassohn, Kurt, 161
just war theory, 113, 120, 121, 125
jus ad bellum, 3, 117
jus in bello, 3, 113, 117, 118, 120, 121, 125, 130

Kardorff, Ursula von, 78, 80
Kaufmann, Gauleiter, 86, 91, 109
Keegan, John, 38 n.33
Kettenacker, Lothar, 13, 223
Kiel, 51, 61, 69
Kluge, Alexander, 207
Koch, Traute, 94–95, 102
Kopf, David, 11–12, 223
Korda, Alexander, 182
Kosova, 5
Kroger, Hermann, 90, 91, 102
Khrushchev, Nikita, 139
Kuby, Erich, 75
kulaks, 136–38, 140

238 *Index*

Kuper, Leo, 160, 161, 170, 172
Kuter, Lawrence, 54
Kyoto, 146

Lackey, Douglas P., 6, 8, 10–11, 223–24
Lancaster plane, 30, 34, 191
Lange, Horst, 65
League of Nations, 182
Leahy, William, 167
LeMay, Curtis, 7, 164, 166, 175 n.15
Lenin, V.I., 135, 137
Leverkusen, 73
Ley, Robert, 77
Lifton, Robert Jay, 168
Lindqvist, Sven, 13–14
London, 2, 13, 14, 48, 55, 93, 114, 119, 147, 148, 149, 154, 156 n.26 167, 183, 184, 185, 192, 193, 194, 196, 197
Lübeck, 29, 44, 69, 191
Luftwaffe, 33, 47, 51, 52, 66, 203

Machiavelli, Niccolo, 122
Manchester, 147
Mann, Thomas, 209
Mannheim, 26, 43, 196
Markusen, Eric, 11–12, 224
Marshall Plan, 213
mass murder, 10, 11, 134, 152, 153, 215
Matthies, Hermann, 106
Maynard, B.M., 192
McCullough, David, 152
McKee, Alexander, 146
media, 5, 12, 41, 53, 141, 163, 181, 183, 184, 190, 192, 196, 203, 204, 215, 216
Mein Kampf, 141, 142
Meurthe, Boulaye de la, 37
Michie, Allan A., 49–50, 54
Middlebrook, Martin, 9, 224
Milan, 51
Milch, Erhard, 76
Milne, G.F., 24
Ministry of Information, 183, 190
Mommsen, Hans, 128, 205, 207
Mönchen-Gladbach, 89

morale, 1, 6, 8, 20, 22, 23, 24, 27, 35–37, 43–45, 66, 70, 121, 125–29, 145, 170, 172, 182, 184, 187, 207, 210, 218
Morgenthau, Hans J., 54
Mosley, Oswald, 190
Mumford, Lewis, 160
Munich, 75, 192
Munich Institute of Contemporary History, 211
Mussolini, Benito, 70

Nagasaki, 7, 150, 161, 164, 218
National Review, 193
National Socialism, 203
Nazis, 1, 2, 6, 35, 36, 41, 45, 49, 55, 62, 72, 88, 113, 115, 116, 119, 122, 123, 127, 128, 129, 140–44, 151, 162, 163, 167, 169, 181, 183, 189, 191, 192, 195, 203, 204, 207, 208, 209, 212, 213, 216, 217
neo-Nazis, 204, 217
Nevinson, Henry, 187
New Statesman, 197
new wars, 5
New York Times, 41, 49, 52, 55, 56
Newby, Leroy, 47
News Chronicle, 197
Nietzsche, Friedrich, 158
non-combatant immunity, *see* civilian immunity, principle of
Norden, 44, 51
Normandy, 54
nuclear weapons, 4, 5, 7, 130, 152, 164, 172, 199 (*see also* atomic bombing)
Nuremberg, 32, 72, 76, 154, 167, 203

O'Neill, Con, 203
obliteration bombing, 50, 52–53
Okinawa, 149, 150
Operation Chastise, 195
Operation Citadel, 61
Operation Gomorrah, 31, 66, 73
Oppenheimer, Robert J., 150, 151
Orwell, George, 114–15, 116

pacifism, 52, 114

Padua, 51
Passchendaele, 193
Paulus, Field Marshal, 60
payback, 10, 11, 15 n.13, 27, 118–21, 191, 195–98, 207
Peace Pledge Union, 182, 193
Pearl Harbor, 41, 124, 149
Ploesti, 47, 48, 74
Pointblank, *see* Combined Bombing Offensive
Pol Pot, 12, 174
Poland, 2, 15, 19, 42, 143, 219 n.11
Portal, Charles, 33–34, 127, 146
Porter, Jack Nusan, 161
Potsdam, 34
precision bombing, 21, 22, 24, 33, 39–41, 43, 48, 49–51, 57
Primoratz, Igor, 224
propaganda, 77–78, 136, 163, 207, 213, 216
punishment, 116, 141, 147, 148, 190, 193, 218 (*see also* payback)

Queensborough, Lord, 186

RAF, 1, 7–8, 9, 12, 23, 26–37, 39, 44, 45, 46, 49, 50, 55, 85, 86, 87, 88, 91, 93, 106, 109, 118, 123, 124, 127, 130 n.1, 145, 181, 183, 184, 186, 187, 188, 191, 192, 194, 196, 197
Rauschning, Hermann, 187
Red Army, 56, 61, 145, 148, 149, 203, 212
Regensburg, 47, 48, 73
Reifkogel, Fräulein, 106
Remscheid, 73
reprisal, 10, 120, 130, 197
retaliation, *see* payback
retribution, *see* payback
revenge, *see* payback
River Bille, 93
Rohrbach, 75
Romania, 51
Rome, 51
Rommel, Erwin, 60
Roosevelt, Franklin D., 26, 41–42, 59 n.32, 53–54, 212

Rostock, 29
Rothenburgsort, 87, 89
Rotterdam, 27, 41, 147, 167, 192, 194, 195
Ruhr, 21, 28, 31, 61–62, 73, 77, 195
Rumpf, Hans, 128, 147
Russell, Bertrand, 137
Russell, Richard, 150

Sankey, Viscount, 187
Sankt, Georg, 87, 88
Sartre, Jean Paul, 122
Saundby, Sir Robert, 117, 118
Sayers, Dorothy L., 187
Schaffer, Ronald, 54
Schmidt, Anne-Lies, 104
Schramm, Percy Ernst, 78
Schulz, Margot, 108
Schweinfurt, 47–48
Sebald, Winfried Georg, 48–50, 205, 206, 210, 211
Seifarth, Frau Anne-Kaete, 107, 109 n.9
Seifert, Heribert, 206
self-defense, 42, 134, 141, 181, 183, 185
Serbia, 51
Shaw, Gorge Bernard, 186, 188
Sherman, General, 117–18
Shirer, William L., 116
Siberia, 136
Sicily, 60
Sinclair, Archibald, 146, 188
Social Democrats, 67
socialism, 139–140
Soviet Union, 2, 15 n.19, 124, 137, 219 n.14
Spaight, J.M., 192
Spectator, 186, 192
Speer, Albert, 48, 76
Spiegel, Hubert, 204
SS, 9, 70, 81, 127, 142, 162
Stalin, Joseph, 11, 12, 33, 134–140, 142, 149, 153, 154 n.2, 174, 194, 209, 215
Stalingrad, 60, 61, 124
Stargardt, Nicholas, 209
state terrorism, 5, 6, 7, 130 (*see also* terrorism; terror bombing)

Stephan, Cora, 205
Stokes, Richard, 187–88, 193
strategic bombing, 7, 11, 23, 25, 26, 28, 29, 30, 38 n.10, 41, 44, 45, 53, 158, 160–174, 190, 192, 220 n.42 (*see also* area bombing)
Stuttgarter NS-Kurier, 209–10
Süddeutsche Zeitung, 206
Sunday Dispatch, 193
supreme emergency, 121–25, 130, 132 n.26, 155 n.15
Süß, Dietmar, 210

Tal, Uriel, 169
Taylor, Frederick, 215, 216
Taylor, Telford, 167
Tedder, Arthur, 36
Temple, William, 188
terror bombing, 8, 41, 44, 45, 48–54, 124, 128, 130 n.1 (*see also* area bombing; strategic bombing; state terrorism; terrorism)
  American protests against, 52–57
terrorism, 5–11, 19 (*see also* state terrorism, terror bombing)
Thirty Years War, 217
Thomas, Wynford Vaughan, 194
Times (London), 186, 188, 195
Tizard, Henry, 146
Tokyo, 149, 163, 167
total war, 4, 11, 27, 67, 159–60, 163
totalitarianism, 6, 128, 203
Trenchard, Hugh, 23–25, 181–82
Tribune, 114
Truman, Harry, 11, 134–35, 146, 149–52, 153, 164, 167–168, 215

U.S. Strategic Bombing Survey, 30–31
Ukraine, 61
Ukrainian Famine, 135–140, 142, 154 n.1

Ulrich, Volker, 210
UN Convention on Genocide, 11–12, 160, 161, 168, 169
USAAF, 8, 9, 39–57, 127, 130 n.1
utilitarianism, 152 (*see also* consequentialism)

Vansittart, Robert, 192, 193
vengeance, *see* payback
Vergangenheitsbewältigung, 13–14
Versailles Peace Treaty, 4, 217
Vietnam War, 173, 199

Walser, Martin, 206
Walzer, Michael, 120, 121–24, 129, 139 n.26, 155 n.15, 167, 175 n.19
Wandsbek, 87, 88, 93, 102
"war is hell" doctrine, 10, 117–18, 130
war on terror, 5
Warsaw, 27, 192
Washington Conference, 30
Watt, Donald, 216, 222 n.68
Watt, Harry, 194, 216, 222 n.68
Weber, Max, 122
Wells, H.G., 182
Wendenstrasse, 90, 95, 102
Wilken, Herr, 97–98
Wimsey, Peter, 187
Winkler, Willi, 206
Witt, Rolf, 95–96
Wolff-Mönckeberg, Mathilde, 74
Woodward, Clifford, 186, 189, 193
World War I, 4, 6, 20, 24, 35, 115, 130, 160, 187, 193
Wuppertal, 31, 61, 62, 73
Würzburg, 34, 212

Yalta Conference, 147–48

Zuckerman, Solly, 146

www.ingramcontent.com/pod-product-compliance
Lightning Source LLC
Chambersburg PA
CBHW072151100526
44589CB00015B/2174